ASSESSING LANGUAGE AND LITERACY WITH BILINGUAL STUDENTS

Also from Lori Helman

Literacy Development with English Learners, Second Edition:
Research-Based Instruction in Grades K–6
Edited by Lori Helman

ASSESSING LANGUAGE AND LITERACY WITH BILINGUAL STUDENTS

Practices to Support English Learners

Lori Helman
Anne C. Ittner
Kristen L. McMaster

THE GUILFORD PRESS
New York   London

Copyright © 2020 The Guilford Press
A Division of Guilford Publications, Inc.
370 Seventh Avenue, Suite 1200, New York, NY 10001
www.guilford.com

Printed in the United States of America

This book is printed on acid-free paper.

Last digit is print number: 9   8   7   6   5   4   3   2

Library of Congress Cataloging-in-Publication Data is available from the publisher.

ISBN 978-1-4625-4088-4 (paperback)
ISBN 978-1-4625-4089-1 (hardcover)

*To the students who share their abundant language and cultural resources,
knowledge, personalities, and experiences in the classroom,
and to the teachers who learn about and support them*

About the Authors

Lori Helman, PhD, is Professor in the Department of Curriculum and Instruction at the University of Minnesota, where she is also Director of the Minnesota Center for Reading Research. Her research interests include literacy development, assessment, and instruction in English and Spanish; word study and vocabulary learning and teaching; and ways to support literacy professionals to implement schoolwide systems of support in literacy. She is the author or editor of a number of books, including *Literacy Development with English Learners, Second Edition: Research-Based Instruction in Grades K–6* and *Words Their Way with English Learners.*

Anne C. Ittner, PhD, is Assistant Professor of Literacy Education in the Division of Education and Leadership at Western Oregon University. Her research interests include literacy education for emergent bilinguals in elementary schools, specifically in the areas of assessment, intervention, and multi-tiered systems of support, and literacy professional development and teacher education.

Kristen L. McMaster, PhD, is Professor of Special Education in the Department of Educational Psychology at the University of Minnesota. Her work addresses creating conditions for successful response to intervention for students at risk and students with disabilities. Her specific research interests include promoting teachers' use of data-based decision making and evidence-based instruction, and developing intensive, individualized interventions for students for whom generally effective instruction is not sufficient.

Introduction

Welcome to *Assessing Language and Literacy with Bilingual Students*. We, the authors of this book, are enthusiastic about sharing information and ideas with you about language and literacy assessments for students learning in a new language at school. The three of us have served as classroom teachers in bilingual and monolingual settings; special education teachers; English learner specialists; university researchers in literacy, educational psychology, and second-language acquisition; teacher educators; and school and district leaders. The goal of this book is to achieve a better understanding of the big picture of the interconnections among oral language, reading, and writing and how they are assessed. We also hope that you will learn about the details of formal and informal assessments and how these assessments can guide the day-to-day classroom instruction that is so critical for student success. Our intent is to be helpful to educators by distilling complex topics into hands-on practices using clear and accessible language.

We believe that the time is right for a book focused not on literacy assessment in general, but on highlighting students who speak one language at home and learn to read and write in a different language at school. Students who interact in more than one language throughout their daily activities are described in many ways, and we want to take a minute to clarify how we use these various descriptors throughout the book.

- **English learners (ELs)** or **English language learners (ELLs)**: Most texts, policy documents, and educational discussions use these terms to describe students who come to school with a home language other than English and need support at school to learn in English. We believe that these labels position students in a way that highlights what they lack, rather than what they possess. Whenever possible, we have attempted to use the term *emergent bilingual* to describe a student who possesses a home language and learns a new language at school. When we use the terms *English learner* or *EL student,* we do so because the citation we are sharing uses that descriptor.

- **Emergent bilinguals:** Students who speak one language at home and learn a new language at school. Emergent bilinguals are on the path to becoming bilingual. As they learn the language of schooling, they increase their bilingual capabilities.

- **Multilingual students:** Students who operate in more than one language or a variety of languages throughout their in- and out-of-school lives. Multilingual students may be bilingual (or trilingual, etc.) already, or they may be emergent bilinguals who are on the path to bilingualism.

- **Linguistically diverse students:** Students whose home language differs from the dominant academic English used in schooling. These students may speak languages other than English or varieties of English, such as African American English or Spanish-influenced English.

This book is geared toward current and future teachers, specialized literacy professionals, EL specialists, school psychologists, school and district leaders, and policymakers. We see it as an important text for initial licensure courses focusing on linguistically diverse populations and also as an important component of assessment classes in both curriculum and instruction and educational psychology. We believe that the content would be helpful for educators to use in book–study groups as they implement inclusive and responsive systems of support for their students.

A quick review of the table of contents highlights the material we cover in the book. We begin by setting up a framework for understanding assessment with multilingual students in Chapter 1, including presenting foundational theories of language and literacy development. Next, in Chapter 2, we provide background information on educational assessment, and define and explain key terms and processes. In Chapter 3, we ground the assessment in sociocultural theory and invite readers to bring a culturally and linguistically specific lens to understanding the assets that students possess. The next four chapters span the language arts—from oral language to beginning reading, to language-based literacy skills, and finally to writing. In each of these chapters, we highlight theories and foundational concepts that undergird the topic. We also share information on both the formal, standardized assessments that are used in each strand and the informal, classroom-based formative assessments that guide daily instruction. We describe follow-up instructional practices that can be implemented to support growth in each language or literacy area. We conclude, in Chapter 8, by addressing how to systematically establish responsive and ongoing assessment practices in a school setting.

Following the content chapters, we have included an Appendix with forms and tools that have been featured in the book. Throughout the book we use **bold** font to indicate key concepts and terms. We also provide a Glossary of these important key concepts and terms and References for the academic citations we have included.

Before heading into the content of this book, we want to share an insight that we had while writing it. As each chapter came together, we found that we were constantly connecting back to language development theory, sometimes wondering, "Haven't we already talked about that enough?" After more reflection, it became clear that language development cannot be neatly contained in separate chapters in a book about literacy development with emergent bilinguals. Language is a part of every literacy assessment and every literacy interaction. The entwined nature of language and literacy means that we write about language in every chapter. We hope that as you encounter recurring themes about language and literacy development throughout the book that you come to the same realization we did: these topics cannot and should not be in separate silos. Only their integration will support educators' success in working with emergent bilingual students.

Contents

Purchasers of this book can download and print enlarged versions of Appendices A–F at *www.guilford.com/helman2-forms* for personal use or use with students (see copyright page for details).

CHAPTER 1

Understanding Assessment with Multilingual Students

Assessment is an essential part of the planning–teaching–reflection cycle for educators. Without assessment, teaching is a disconnected activity that misses its key purpose: to facilitate the acquisition of new knowledge, skills, and abilities for students. Done well, assessment helps educators understand what students already know, how much progress they have made, and what academic tasks they may be ready to tackle next. It is only with this information in hand that educators will be able to tailor their instruction to help all students meet academic goals.

In this first chapter, we present information that provides a foundation for the rest of the book: demographic data on multilingual students in the United States and the educational settings they participate in, a summary of the process of literacy development and how the process might look different for students learning to read and write in a new language, a description of the intertwined relationship between language and literacy development, and an overview of the unique capabilities of multilingual learners. These foundational understandings are key to the detailed and varied discussions of assessment with multilingual students—particularly emergent bilinguals—that follow in later chapters. We conclude the chapter with a set of principles for understanding assessment with multilingual students that frame every chapter in the book and will help educators not only understand *how* particular literacy assessments work and *what* they measure, but also help educators to *set aspirations* for using assessments that create equitable and enriched learning environments for all students.

LANGUAGE LEARNERS AND THEIR SCHOOL SETTINGS

In the Introduction, we provided information about the audience for this book as well as the descriptors we use to identify the students we highlight. Before moving ahead,

1

we'd like to talk more specifically about the demographics of emergent bilingual students in the United States and share characteristics about the instructional programs in which they participate. We close this section by making the case that tailoring assessment for emergent bilinguals and students developing literate multilingual proficiencies is an essential knowledge base for every educator.

Students We Highlight in This Book

Many students operate in multilingual worlds. That is, they use various languages to engage with others and accomplish daily tasks both in and out of school. For example, some students speak with their families using a home language and learn English as a new language at school. Others live in bilingual (or multilingual) households, and their schooling is conducted in one of their already known languages. Some students attend dual immersion classroom settings where they follow a structured process for learning content in a new language, while ultimately also developing academic skills in a home language. Students may live in communities where they hear a variety of languages and see a range of scripts in stores, churches, and community centers. Students who speak English with their families and communities use many varieties of the language; these variations can influence the pronunciation, vocabulary, and even the grammar used. Some variations are more or less similar to the language of schooling (academic English); however, all of the variations that communities use are powerful and purposeful.

For many educators, students' rich linguistic background knowledge has been invisible at school. Students are often judged by what they *don't* possess—fluency in oral or written academic English—as opposed to what they *do* bring to the school setting. Instead of digging deeper into students' multilingual capacities, educators lament what they perceive as missing. In this book, we work to provide educators with tools to gain a more comprehensive picture of students' linguistic resources that may be built upon to lead students to **literate bilingualism** (Moll, 2014). The goals of literate bilingualism include becoming proficient orally and in reading and writing for both the language of school and of home.

English learners (ELs) represent approximately 10% of the students in public schools in the United States (U.S. Department of Education, 2017). Table 1.1 highlights 2016 data showing the top-9 student home languages other than English of the approximately 4.95 million K–12 EL students in the United States. Spanish is by far the most predominant home language for multilingual students, but this list shines a light on the amazing language resources that many U.S. students can potentially contribute to the greater society. These emergent bilinguals are already on the path to literate bilingualism because they possess oral skills (and perhaps more) in their home languages.

Many states have implemented policies that encourage their students to achieve biliteracy (cf. *sealofbiliteracy.org*). Steps that have been identified to actively support this outcome include recognizing and honoring biliteracy skills; preparing students for a diverse and multilingual world; and using educational approaches that are responsive to students' needs, set high expectations, and are aligned across grade levels and

TABLE 1.1. Top-9 Home Languages Other Than English of K–12 EL Students, 2016

Language	% distribution
Spanish	76.6
Arabic	2.6
Chinese	2.1
Vietnamese	1.6
Somali	0.8
Hmong	0.7
Russian	0.7
Haitian/Haitian Creole	0.6
Portuguese	0.6

Note. Data from *https://nces.ed.gov/programs/digest/d18/tables/dt18_204.27.asp.*

settings (see the California Department of Education Roadmap Policy at *www.cde.ca.gov/sp/el/rm/elroadmappolicy.asp*). If educators expand on the linguistic resources students already possess, students come to see their assets as valuable at school and are motivated to cultivate their literate bilingualism.

Emergent bilinguals are not a monolithic or homogeneous group. Their diversity is marked by a range of language backgrounds; amount of time in the United States; academic experiences; economic resources; culture, race, and ethnicity; religion; and more. Figure 1.1 provides a graphic representation of some of the ways that emergent bilinguals possess unique capabilities and background experiences even as compared to others considered part of the same group.

As Figure 1.1 elucidates, emergent bilinguals bring unique experiences and aspirations to their language learning at school. Some students have already developed literacy in a home language, which will facilitate learning a new language at school. If their home language and the new language use similar writing systems and sound–spelling correspondences, the learning will be more seamless. Students vary in the amount of time they have spent learning a new language at school; some are newcomers to listening to and speaking the new language, while others have a great familiarity and experience with it. Students vary in their opportunities to practice the new language outside of school and in their real-world purposes for becoming bilingual, such as communicating with friends and family members. All language learners grow when they are motivated and encouraged to become bilingual. When individual emergent bilingual students enter the classroom, educators have much to learn about their capabilities and experiences. Consider the following example that highlights one way in which educators can learn about students.

Kevin immigrated to the upper Midwest with his mother 2 weeks before beginning first grade. He had not had many prior experiences hearing or using English. The classroom

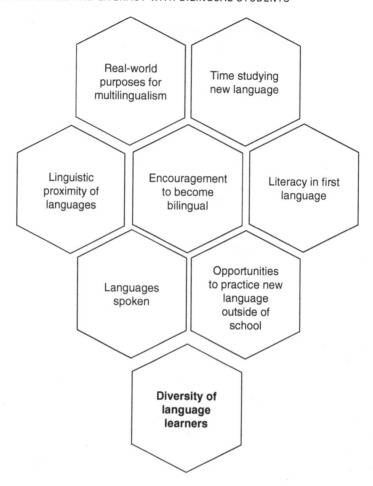

FIGURE 1.1. Diversity of language learners.

he entered provided extra support for newcomer emergent bilinguals, but it would still be difficult for him to follow much of what was going on in class for quite a while. With a little support from the community liaison at school, his teacher was able to learn that Kevin had attended kindergarten in Mexico and knew some letter–sound correspondences in Spanish, a language that shares many phonetic commonalities with English. In discussions with Kevin's mother, the teacher also learned that there was strong encouragement in the home to develop bilingual skills that could be used with the family and in the new English-speaking community. This beginning understanding of Kevin's background helped his teacher to connect and build on previous learning and motivate him to use all of his linguistic resources at school.

School Settings and Instructional Programs

Just as emergent bilinguals vary in the linguistic backgrounds they bring to school, so too do the types of instructional programs they participate in once they get there.

Prior to the 1980s, most students in the United States who spoke a language other than English at home were tacitly or explicitly asked to shroud that language while at school, where all instruction would take place in English. The effect of such programs over time was to erase the student's home language skills, and is often referred to as a **subtractive approach** (Valenzuela, 2010). As the population of emergent bilinguals in many schools grew over time, specialist teachers were sometimes hired to work with students learning English. Typically, these **English as a second language (ESL)** or **English language development (ELD)** educators brought students new to English into separate language classes to fortify their linguistic skills at some point in their school day.

Over the past 40 years, demographic shifts in the national school population have compelled educators and school systems to more formally address the ways they serve emergent bilingual students. Policy guidelines and accountability systems seek to ensure that all students progress in their acquisition of statewide academic standards and experience success on exit measures. Currently, a range of instructional programs operate across the country that support students' English acquisition or literate bilingualism, thus engaging in an **additive approach** to schooling. In this section, we share a brief description of some of these programs that are referred to throughout the book.

Newcomer Programs

Students such as Kevin, described in the last section, are new to the United States and the English-speaking environment. Newcomers have a variety of previous experiences with languages, literacies, schooling, and cultural interactions. Some newcomers to the U.S. school system have had quite similar experiences outside of the country, while others may have been a part of school systems that were very different or may not have had the opportunity to attend school at all. Newcomer programs are specially designed to ease the transition to American schools for newly arrived students, especially those who are just beginning to learn English or who may have limited or interrupted formal schooling. The programs typically focus on learning essential English for communication, becoming familiar with local schooling procedures, backfilling academic content that is necessary for academic success, and potentially bolstering students' native language literacy skills. They are intended to be a short-term experience for students, may serve students across the K–12 spectrum, and can vary in scope or size, depending on the needs of a district or geographical area.

Dual Immersion Programs

An increasingly common structure for developing students' bilingual capacities are dual immersion programs, also known as *bilingual* or *two-way immersion programs*. In these instructional settings, students follow a proscribed pathway of learning in two languages over many years. For example, students in Spanish–English dual immersion programs may begin school by experiencing 90% of their instruction in Spanish and 10% in English. With each consecutive grade level, the balance moves closer to

50% for each language, so that when students exit from the program they are literate bilinguals who also have mastered grade level expectations. In a 50/50 dual immersion program, both languages are used equally throughout the program from the start. Students who speak English at home and enter a dual immersion program in Spanish, for example, are also emergent bilinguals, because they are learning a new language and bring capabilities in their home language to school.

Primary-Language Literacy Instruction

In some educational settings, students who start school speaking languages other than English enroll in programs that develop their home language literacy skills prior to studying in English. This process allows students to connect their reading and writing skills more directly to the oral language resources they already have. Becoming literate in a language that one already speaks is much easier than learning to read in a language that is new (Genesee, Lindholm-Leary, Saunders, & Christian, 2005). In addition, once literacy has been achieved in any language, many skills are transferable to literacy skills in a second or third language (Genesee et al., 2005). For example, students who can track print, understand spaces between words, and use a phonics decoding system in their home language can apply these skills to the new language with minor adjustments. Thus, primary-language literacy instruction reduces some of the linguistic challenges that face students who are immediately enrolled in academic programs that are delivered in a language they don't yet understand.

General Education with English Language Support

Many schools do not have specialized programs for supporting bilingualism but do provide assistance for students as they learn English. These programs may include pullout English classes for emergent bilinguals; push-in services, such as English lessons delivered in class; EL assistant educators or coteachers embedded within classrooms; opportunities for English language development in before-school or after-school programs; or volunteer tutoring programs. In some states, teachers have received professional development to assist them in tailoring instruction for emergent bilinguals through specially designed instructional approaches or, at a minimum, are provided with curriculum materials that describe how to adapt their teaching for students learning English.

No Support—"Sink or Swim"

Unfortunately, many emergent bilingual students do not receive any extra support when they enter classrooms where English is the only language spoken. Students are expected to "pick up" the language by simply being surrounded by it. Referred to as the "sink-or-swim" method, this model is often de facto and unexamined; it ignores research showing that the language needed for school success requires intentional instructional focus and does not develop by osmosis or simply having seat time in a classroom (Saunders & Goldenberg, 2010).

A Pervasive Need

According to current achievement data, ELs perform significantly below students who speak English fluently (National Assessment of Educational Progress [NAEP], 2018). In 2017, NAEP data revealed that reading scores for EL students at the fourth-grade level were 37 points below non-EL students and 43 points lower for eighth-grade students (NAEP, 2018). In the 2013–2014 academic year, the national average high school graduation rate was 82.3%, but for EL students the figure was 62.6% (Office of English Language Acquisition [OELA], 2018). These figures indicate that students do not receive adequate or appropriate instruction to ensure that they succeed. Using assessments that are asset oriented, that identify student learning needs, and that inform instruction is key to improving educational opportunities for all students, but it is especially critical for emergent bilinguals. Throughout this book, we shine a light on assessments that (1) seek to identify what students bring to school and what they are already able to do, (2) help educators to identify the important next steps in literacy development for each student, and (3) make direct connections between what is assessed and what needs to be taught in the language arts. At the same time, we consider how assessment can best capture the strengths and needs of students who have yet to become fluent in the language of the assessment and support both monolingual and multilingual educators to best guide their students' progress.

Now that we have shared some background information about the contexts of schooling for emergent bilinguals, we turn to two other pieces of important foundational information: models of literacy and language development. First, we provide a cohesive summary of how learners move from being emergent readers and writers to developing proficiency and strength. Following this discussion, we take a similar look at language acquisition, and review the intertwined relationship of language and literacy.

LITERACY DEVELOPMENT

Becoming a capable reader and writer occurs when a variety of components work together in unison. Some of these capabilities emerge from within individuals, and others are related to factors in the social and physical world. Watching a student pick up a book and become engrossed in the content or observing the student transcribe thoughts in a personal writing journal may seem effortless and almost magical. In reality, many factors are involved in becoming what an observer would call a proficient "reader" or "writer." To call upon a simple metaphor, reading may be thought of as an operational automobile: it seems to turn on automatically, but there is a lot going on "under the hood." Readers use their knowledge of a language, including words and what they mean, the sounds that go into producing words, and the ways that words and phrases are structured into sentences and larger chunks of meaningful utterances. Readers also bring problem-solving skills to the task; they know how to decode printed text using the sounds, patterns, and the word parts of the written language. Finally, readers bring purpose or motivation to a reading task. If there is no reason to read, it doesn't happen.

In the simplest of terms, becoming literate involves the ability to decode text and use linguistic and background knowledge to understand it (Gough & Tunmer, 1986; Scarborough, 2001). For emergent bilinguals, this process is more complex for several reasons. First, although emergent bilinguals have language knowledge, it is typically not in the language of instruction. Thus, students are required to learn *what* the words mean at the same time they learn *how* to read them. In addition, because their home language may use sounds that are distinct from English, language learners may have difficulty perceiving phonetic variations that come more easily to a native speaker. For example, distinguishing the short vowel sounds in words such as *pan, pin,* and *pen* could be difficult for students whose home language uses only open vowel sounds, such as in the words *saw, see,* and *so.* Native speakers are immersed in a sea of words that provide a foundation for developing sound–symbol correspondence in the written language. Students learning to read in a new language, however, are unlikely to be able to call upon dozens of examples of "words that begin with . . ." or "words that have the ____ sound" in the same way that native speakers can. Finally, research has shown that, with systematic instruction, emergent bilinguals can learn the decoding skills required to develop reading proficiency in a relatively straightforward manner (Lesaux & Siegel, 2003); however, there is a danger that when language-based skills are not addressed, reading comprehension does not flourish (Mancilla-Martinez & Lesaux, 2011). For these reasons, literacy educators need to be able to identify and address the unique capabilities and challenges that emergent bilinguals bring to the literacy-learning process. To connect back to our previous metaphor, to start the car and help it move down the road, educators will need to know which aspects of students' literacy development systems are connecting, and which need focused attention. This book is designed to help educators identify these components and provide guidance on how to support students as they move forward.

Students do not develop their literacy "engines" overnight; it is a step-by-step process. Throughout this book, we will refer to a developmental model of literacy learning that highlights students' growing insight over time about the complexity of the writing system and how to make meaning from it (Bear, Invernizzi, Templeton, & Johnston, 2020; Ehri, 1995; Templeton & Gehsmann, 2014). We use terms such as *emergent, beginning,* and *transitional* to describe developing readers who call upon particular understandings as they engage with text in predictable ways. In the next few sections, we highlight the reading behaviors of students as they progress from novice to more advanced.

Emergent Readers

Prior to being able to accurately recognize words, yet-to-be readers learn about text by observing others read and write. At first, these **emergent readers** listen to stories; watch people in their world get information or enjoyment from paper or electronic texts; and notice how people use writing to jot down messages to others, make lists for themselves, and much more. Emergent literacy begins from children's first moments in the world; it is the conscious and unconscious learning about print that happens in their social interactions within their environment.

EMERGENT READERS

- ◆ Begin to notice features of print.
- ◆ "Pretend" read and write.
- ◆ Learn the alphabet.
- ◆ Play with the sounds of language.

With experience and guidance, emergent readers develop an awareness of the unique features of print. If they have opportunities to listen to books read aloud, they come to understand that print has permanence. In other words, every time they listen to the same story, it remains consistent. Emergent readers "pretend read" a familiar story, making up their own version of the script and changing pages based on the pictures. Emergent readers begin to distinguish text and, in particular, letters, from other visual information. At this point, young children are often introduced to the alphabet, which opens the door to new learning about the shapes of capital and lower-case letters, and the sounds represented by each one. Early literacy learning happens in formal and informal ways. At home, family members often interact with books, magazines, or digital texts and share these experiences with young ones, answering questions and pointing out relevant information such as "Look, there is an 'M' like in your name, Maya!" At preschool or day care, adults often share books, write messages together, facilitate children's story writing, practice the alphabet, and attend to the sounds in oral language, such as rhymes and **alliteration.** Emergent literacy blossoms when children have opportunities to engage in sound play (**phonological awareness**), learn about letters (alphabet knowledge), notice aspects of the writing system (**concepts about print**), and express themselves on paper (developmental writing) (Johnston, Invernizzi, Helman, Bear, & Templeton, 2015).

With focused attention on the types of learning activities just described, emergent readers discover that letters and sounds are not arbitrary; rather, letters represent particular sounds in predictable ways in the English writing system. This insight, called the **alphabetic principle,** is profound. It enables emergent readers to move from a phase of thinking that reading and writing are "magical' processes in which they pretend read and write or simply memorize a few words, to an understanding that they need to learn the sounds that the letters of the alphabet represent in order to actually decode the message written down. As they learn a growing number of words by sight and begin to use their knowledge of letter sounds to decipher words in text, emergent readers move into the beginning reading stage.

Are all emergent learners in the birth to 5 age range? Definitely not. Emergent literacy is a foundational phase that is strengthened by experiences with print—whether they be opportunities to engage with printed materials or to see oral language in a written form. Preschool and kindergarten settings consistently expose children to print experiences, but not every child has the opportunity to attend these classes. Furthermore, students may start school at later grade levels with limited or interrupted formal schooling, or the quality of instruction in classes they attended may have been inadequate or the classrooms may have been overcrowded. Emergent bilinguals may bring literate experiences with home languages in which sounds are not used to represent written words. In these cases, it will be important to identify whether students have an understanding of the alphabetic principle, a key to becoming a beginning reader in English. Assessments are outlined in future chapters of this book to guide educators in identifying students' understanding of the sound-based nature of written English.

Beginning Readers

The beginning stage of reading is characterized by a growing understanding of the alphabetic nature of written language and by students' application of sound–symbol relationships in decoding and producing text. **Beginning readers** have typically developed sight recognition of a number of frequently used words and reread familiar memorized texts, although not yet with full one-to-one tracking. With new material, beginning readers attempt to use their **phonics** knowledge to access unknown words. Early on, this process is slow and full of effort—novice readers use their knowledge of phonics to sound out individual letters in words and blend them together with varying degrees of success. All students need instruction in how phonics works (e.g., letter–sound correspondences and blending sounds to make words), and some students will need more **explicit instruction** and intensive guided practice. Beginning readers also need numerous opportunities to read material that is not too difficult, so that they can begin to more automatically decode common words and become more expert at applying their spelling–sound knowledge. Soon they are recognizing word families and using analogies to more efficiently decode unknown words. For example, whereas an early beginning reader might expend a lot of effort to decode the word *pet* by vocalizing and blending each individual sound, a progressing beginning reader will notice that *pet* is part of the *-et* word family and will apply this knowledge to new words, such as *set, met, bet,* or *wet,* by simply substituting a different beginning sound. This knowledge makes reading much more streamlined.

BEGINNING READERS

- ◆ Understand the alphabetic principle.
- ◆ Have phonemic awareness.
- ◆ Develop comprehensive knowledge of sound–symbol relationships.
- ◆ Begin to use analogy to decode words.
- ◆ Generally read in a word-by-word manner.

To revert to the automobile analogy, beginning readers are like drivers of cars that are operating only in low gear. Reading is happening, but it takes a while to get where they are going, and it is not a very smooth process. Beginning readers need many opportunities to read texts that stretch but do not overtax their decoding capacity. Every reading experience provides practice in using important word recognition skills and gaining familiarity and automaticity for a growing number of words. With consistent practice, most beginning readers start to read individual words faster and thereby hold the meaning of phrases and sentences together more cohesively. They are moving into second gear!

How is the beginning reading stage the same or different for emergent bilinguals? First off, it should be noted that learning to decode words alphabetically in English can be a relatively straightforward process, especially if the student's home oral language shares many of the same sounds. Being able to pull apart the individual sounds in words, or **phonemic awareness,** is needed in order to profit from phonics instruction, and it is a skill that transfers across alphabetic languages (Branum-Martin, Tao, & Garnaat, 2014; Durgunoglu, Nagy, & Hancin-Bhatt, 1993). Thus, teaching students to distinguish the sounds within English words and attaching graphemes to these sounds can be effective if it is done clearly and systematically, and is based on the home language sounds students already know. Complications in early phonics instruction may arise when students meet a sound in English that does not exist in their home language. For example, some of the short vowels in English are not present in many other languages. Students attempting to match sounds to letters will find it difficult when they can't distinguish the difference between ĕ and ĭ, as in the words *pen* and *pin.* In future chapters of this book we provide informal assessments and guidance on how to identify letter sounds that may be difficult for students with particular home language backgrounds.

Another challenge for emergent bilinguals at the beginning reading stage is understanding the words they are now able to decode. Word recognition is obviously an important aspect of reading, but both students and their teachers may assume that when they can decode, they have "read" a text. It is critical that even beginning readers seek meaning in what they read, self-monitor to identify when they do not understand, and enact strategies for extracting meaning. Regular comprehension checks are essential to confirm that students are understanding, not simply decoding, the texts they read.

Transitional Readers

As decoding becomes more automatic, students move beyond the word-by-word reading that is characteristic of beginning readers. They process text more quickly and efficiently and become **transitional readers** who are now moving along in a higher gear—no longer fledglings, but not yet completely proficient either (Bear et al., 2020). Transitional readers have the phonics skills to decode most single-syllable words in a straightforward way, testing out a word's pronunciation by using their knowledge of spelling patterns and matching it to a real word that they think would fit in the text. At this level, students apply what they know about decoding to longer multisyllable words, which sometimes trip them up. Reading longer words also presents the challenge that this vocabulary is typically more complex and less known to developing readers.

TRANSITIONAL READERS

- ◆ Are becoming more fluent in their reading.
- ◆ Read and write words with more complex spelling patterns.
- ◆ Will likely need to focus on phrasing and expression and attending to cues from punctuation.

A key reading skill that transitional readers need to work on is the development of **fluency.** Samuels defined fluency as the ability to decode and understand text at the same time (Samuels, 2006). Fluent reading grows as students see words over and over in the texts they read and can read them quickly. Returning to the automobile analogy, transitional readers are like novice drivers who can put their foot on the gas pedal but the ride doesn't yet feel smooth. These readers may read quickly one moment and then slowly during a patch containing difficult words. They may "run through" punctuation marks and not yet chunk the text into meaningful phrases. Transitional readers profit from being guided to read in phrasal units, a task that is helped by paying attention to punctuation marks. Students are also helped by repeated readings of the same material and from encouragement to use expression as they read.

When emergent bilinguals get to the transitional stage of reading they likely are good decoders, but it is possible that their vocabulary and language comprehension hasn't progressed at the same pace as their word recognition abilities. Students may be able to produce what sounds like fluent reading, but may not have a full understanding of the meaning of a text. For this reason, it is critical to check for understanding with readers at the transitional level and not assume that quick reading equates to comprehending the material. In future chapters we discuss the use of fluency measures for assessing reading progress and how educators can ensure that these assessments are tailored for students learning a new language. It is critical that students never doubt that real reading is more than pronouncing the words, but involves taking in meaningful content and engaging with it in a personal way.

Advancing Readers

Intermediate readers have developed good fluency in materials at the upper elementary level and, because of their speed in processing text, generally prefer reading silently. Intermediate readers can grasp online and print materials that have robust amounts of text, although these materials may still be oriented to children and young adults. For example, early intermediate readers may take on R. L. Stine's *Goosebumps* books, while more established intermediate readers can devour larger volumes such as J. K. Rowling's *Harry Potter* series. On the nonfiction side, intermediate readers seek out information from encyclopedias and websites geared toward youth, how-to books, biographies, and books and websites that help them learn about topics they are studying or interested in. In the analogy we have been using, intermediate readers handle the car well, and they now have plenty of preferences about what make and model they are driving. The ride is pretty smooth when the topic is familiar, and the reader has a high interest level. Reading can get challenging when complex or unknown language enters the scene, such as in driving in an unknown city.

INTERMEDIATE READERS

- ◆ Read grade-level materials with fluency.
- ◆ Prefer to read silently.
- ◆ Become lifelong readers when they are engaged with particular topics, genres, or purposes for reading.
- ◆ Continue to be challenged by unfamiliar and complex academic vocabulary and language structures.

During the intermediate stage of reading, students get pulled into becoming life-long readers (or not) and begin to identify themselves as "readers" (or not). It is an important growth period in literacy that can be enhanced by educators who share engaging texts, connect materials to students' interests, and scaffold difficult language and concepts so that reading materials make sense and help students to take on more challenges. When instruction is motivating and students have plentiful opportunities to engage in reading for purposeful activities and enjoyment, intermediate readers evolve into **advanced readers**—the level of efficient adult readers.

Emergent bilinguals who reach the level of intermediate readers have the same challenges as native language speakers, including understanding complex and highly technical texts, especially when readers have limited background experiences in the topic. However, emergent bilinguals' language proficiency at this point should be quite good in social settings, so gaps in academic vocabulary may go unnoticed in the classroom. In a longitudinal study of seven emergent bilinguals from first through sixth grades, Helman and colleagues found that although several of the students reached advanced proficiency in reading, they demonstrated significant gaps in their **academic language** skills—the words and phrases encountered in schooling and in written texts—as compared to national norms for their age group (Helman, Rogers, Frederick, & Struck, 2016).

LEARNING AN ADDITIONAL LANGUAGE

Humans are hardwired to learn language right from the start. Beginning in the third trimester, unborn babies react differently to native and non-native vowel sounds, recognize their mothers' voices, and have been shown to learn pseudowords that they were exposed to in utero (Partanen et al., 2013). Language development in one's home language is a natural process that unfolds through engagement with family members and others as the newest members of society attempt to engage with their community. Language learning is multifaceted and may be classified into five key areas (see Figure 1.2): **phonology** (the sounds of the language); **semantics** (the meanings of words and concepts and the schemas that hold them together); **syntax** (how meaningful

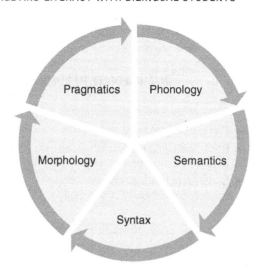

FIGURE 1.2. Key areas of language learning.

phrases and sentences are put together); **morphology** (how words are put together and changed with meaningful parts such as *kind–kinder–kindness*); and **pragmatics** (how language is used in particular contexts) (Otto, 2017).

During the first 2 years of life, babies play with sounds and refine their speech to more closely match the language(s) they hear in their environment. Their **receptive language** (what they understand) develops more quickly than their **expressive language** (what they are able to produce). Infants and toddlers develop purposeful communication strategies and advance in their ability to interact with others (Hoff, 2013). As they approach the age of 2 years, children typically experience a spurt in their expressive word vocabulary, begin to combine words into phrases, and start adding morphemes to words, such as *go-ing*. During the next 2 years of life (ages 2–4 years), children typically experience a surge of language learning: they develop narrative and conversational skills, create longer phrases and use negatives and questions, complete learning the phonemes of their language(s) and begin to acquire phonological awareness, exponentially expand their vocabulary, and create sentences with more complex grammatical structures (e.g., *We're playing*) (Brown, 1973; Hoff, 2013).

Learning an additional language at school does not occur in precisely the same way as initial language development, and it is harder to talk about "typical" development because of the variety of potential contexts that exist for this learning. Additional language learning depends on the age of the learner, the context of the language environment and instruction, the purposes for the new language use, what literacy skills the learner possesses, and the similarities or differences between the new language and other languages in students' repertoires (Collier, 1987; McLaughlin, 1985). School-age learners, for example, will not start at the beginning of language learning as if they were infants. They bring with them a knowledge of all of the systems of language—phonology, semantics, syntax, morphology, and pragmatics—from their home language. As they learn a new language, emergent bilinguals call upon oral communication in their home language and apply it to English. Figure 1.3 presents some of the skills within the five areas of language learning that emergent bilinguals need to acquire to become proficient speakers.

Without being overly technical, Figure 1.3 highlights some of the many aspects of a new language that speakers acquire from within or outside of the classroom setting using more or less formal instruction. For students who enter school at a young age as emergent bilinguals, development will tend to progress along a continuum from basic survival language, to the highly contextualized language of social interactions, to learning the decontextualized language of academic contexts found in texts, lectures, and procedural directions. Hakuta, Butler, and Witt (2000) found that for students learning English at school it typically took 3 to 5 years to develop oral

Language area	What needs to be learned in a new language?
Phonology	• Sounds used in the new language need to be matched to sounds already known. • Sounds that do not exist in the home language need to be perceived and approximated. • The sound qualities of words in the new language, including stress patterns, need to become familiar. • The speaker needs to produce words that don't follow the structure of words in the home language (e.g., ending a word with a consonant blend such as *west*).
Semantics	• Words in students' vocabularies need to be learned in the new language and matched to already known meanings and conceptual understandings. • Unknown words and concepts used in the classroom (including academic language) need to be learned for the first time.
Syntax	• Differences in grammatical rules between the home language and new language need to be applied (e.g., word order such as *red car* vs. *carro rojo*). • Differences in sentence structure between the home language and new language need to be applied (e.g., subject–verb–object vs. subject–object–verb). • The speaker needs to learn how questions and negative statements are formed.
Morphology	• Verb conjugation needs to be learned. • Differences in affixation between the home language and new language need to be applied (e.g., *longer* vs. *más largo*). • An understanding of cognates and how they can support word learning should be developed (e.g., *art/arte*).
Pragmatics	• What is seen as "appropriate" interpersonal spacing, eye contact, and gesturing in the new language needs to be figured out. • The tone of speech, amount of self-disclosure, use of apology, and much more will vary with cultural norms. • How children speak to adults or the respect that is used in dialogue with elders varies across cultures and is noted during conversations.

FIGURE 1.3. Examples of skills needed in a new oral language.

proficiency, and they found that developing academic English proficiency can take 4 to 7 years. We discuss the differences between **basic interpersonal communicative skills** (BICs; Cummins, 1979) and more abstract academic language, or the language of schooling and other decontextualized and technical settings, in depth in Chapters 4 and 6.

Students who start school having already developed literacy in their home language often are able to bootstrap their academic knowledge from their first language to English. In a study of the age and rate of academic language learning, Collier (1987) found that 8- to 11-year-old emergent bilinguals progressed the most quickly in academic development, reaching the 50th percentile on national academic norms in 2–5 years. Cummins was the first to describe a theory of interdependence that explains why students who have more advanced language proficiency in their home language may develop academically demanding language skills in a new language more readily than younger students: their academic knowledge is able to be transferred across languages (1981).

Collier's (1987) study of academic language learning had another interesting finding: English learners who began schooling in the United States between the ages of 12 and 15 years took the longest to achieve academic proficiency. She postulated that perhaps because of the rapid increase of academic content in the secondary grades, students who begin schooling in a new language at age 12 or later cannot afford the loss of a year of more of content that they cannot adequately comprehend while they develop advanced language proficiency (Collier, 1987).

Acquiring an additional language for success at school is a multifaceted and context-based process that is influenced by linguistic, psychological, sociocultural, and educational factors (Helman, 2016). Each student brings his or her background experiences, communicative capabilities, feelings of comfort or temerity in trying out a new language, and purposes for using the home and new languages. The relationship or distance between the linguistic characteristics and pragmatic usage of the two languages will also influence how easy or hard it might be for a student to acquire a new language. The more that educators learn about the language and literacy histories and goals of their students and families, the more likely this multifaceted acquisition process can be explored for each individual, and students can be provided the support they need to boost their learning. In this book, we highlight the role that assessment has in informing educators' understanding of language and literacy learning in relation to all of these important areas.

THE SYMBIOTIC RELATIONSHIP BETWEEN LANGUAGE AND LITERACY

As must be clear by this point in the chapter, when discussing literacy learning with emergent bilinguals it is impossible to separate the role of language development from the holistic processes of reading and writing. Students cannot read or write in a non-linguistic space; literate acts are always infused with language. A written word *means something* in an oral language. A letter or symbol represents *a sound, syllable, or meaning* in a given oral language. In the automobile analogy we have referenced throughout the chapter, language is the fuel that powers the vehicle. Without language, the literacy engine simply cannot run.

Language permeates all literate behaviors. Yet, for many educators, this simple idea has gone uninvestigated in their work with students. In other words, even as their students became more linguistically diverse, educators may have looked past the need to be knowledgeable about language development as the foundation for helping learners develop and use literacy for meaningful purposes in the world. Our goal in this book is to consistently shine a light on the symbiotic relationship between language and literacy and to remind educators that there is never a time in assessment or instruction when language can be taken for granted.

THE UNIQUE CAPABILITIES OF MULTILINGUALS

People who speak more than one language have access to more ideas than monolinguals. Flora Lewis, a longtime foreign correspondent, wrote, "Learning another language is not only learning different words for the same things, but learning another way to think about things." As multilinguals attach words from one language to concepts known in another, they gain a deeper sense of the meaning of the concept and how it takes shape in the world. For example, the word *spark* in English can be both a noun and a verb, meaning a fiery particle or the act of emitting such a particle; the act of ignition, including in a figurative sense; or a small quantity. The word can be translated into Spanish as *chispa,* which holds the same meanings, but may also be used to represent anger (*echar chispas*) or vivaciousness. As emergent bilinguals make connections across their two languages, they potentially develop a deeper understanding of vocabulary, conceptual meanings, diverse cultural perspectives, and an increased cognitive flexibility (Bialystok, Craik, & Luk, 2012). The cross-linguistic connections that emergent bilinguals make also assist them in developing **metalinguistic awareness,** the ability to think *about* language in a general way, beyond the concreteness of words used in a specific language. For example, certain aspects of grammar, such as subject–verb agreement, come quite naturally in one's home language (the child plays/ the children play), and it may only be through learning a new language that the concept of subject–verb agreement as a linguistic category becomes conscious knowledge in a speaker's mind.

Multilinguals have a repertoire of two or more languages to engage with as they communicate with others. A multilingual person will probably interact in only one language with a monolingual interlocutor, because they know what words that person is likely to understand. However, when speaking with someone with whom the speaker shares more than one language in common, especially in informal settings, the multilingual speaker may call upon more of his or her linguistic resources. García and Kleifgen (2010) describe the process wherein emergent bilinguals create structures for using interdependent language systems as developing "complex multicompetence" (p. 45). Multilinguals who use hybrid language practices (code switching, code meshing, translation, etc.) to enhance meaning and communication are **translanguaging**—enacting features of more than one language within the cohesive and interdependent language systems under their control (García, 2009). This multilingual capacity is becoming more widely recognized in classrooms and is currently leading to informal assessment and instruction practices that have the potential to more fully highlight the complex multicompetence of students who bring more than one language to schooling (García, Johnson, & Seltzer, 2017; Lee & Handsfield, 2018). Figure 1.4 highlights the idea that the languages students know contribute to an interdependent system and build metalinguistic knowledge. Additional languages learned in the future join this complex and interdependent system and further support the speaker's metalinguistic awareness.

Throughout the book, we suggest many ways for educators to assess students who speak more than one language, for example, by exploring their home language and literacy skills, their new language and literacy skills, and also their multilingual capabilities. The goal is to understand in a more comprehensive way how emergent bilinguals use their interdependent language systems to communicate, make meaning, learn skills, and problem solve.

PRINCIPLES FOR UNDERSTANDING ASSESSMENT WITH EMERGENT BILINGUAL STUDENTS

As we continue with the more specific, content-based chapters that follow, it is important to acknowledge the problematic situation that currently exists in many educational settings, where emergent bilingual students are assessed using measures that may be unreliable for language learners and are often not validated for use with their populations. Current assessments underestimate what emergent bilinguals can do, because the level of language or background knowledge needed to demonstrate success may only be available to those students in their home languages. The following guiding principles, culled from professional organizations and researchers who study students who are linguistically diverse, serve as touchstones for reducing bias and perceiving emergent bilinguals in more holistic ways.

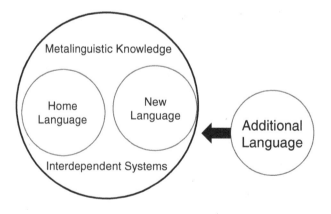

FIGURE 1.4. Interdependence of language systems for bilinguals.

Assessment with emergent bilinguals:

• Should be asset focused. Students bring resources and capabilities to school that may or may not be recognized institutionally, such as linguistic knowledge, and ways of being in the world and interacting with others based on their cultural frameworks, interests, goals, and on family **funds of knowledge** (Gee, 2015; Moll, Amanti, Neff, & González, 1992; Vygotsky, 1978).

• Should fairly assess the construct being examined and not be clouded by other factors, such as linguistic or cultural characteristics. Also, when tests are constructed, assessment should take into account validity with varied groups of students, including emergent bilinguals (Abedi, 2002; American Educational Research Association [AERA], 2014).

• Should acknowledge that it does not reflect a student's "ability." Ability is dynamic, not fixed, and varies based upon many things, including context (Cohen & Ball, 1999).

• Should not limit students' access to high-quality learning settings or opportunities (García & Kleifgen, 2010).

• When possible, should tap into the complexity of students' bilingual knowledge and the ways they use language in the school and community (Escamilla et al., 2013; Valdés & Figueroa, 1994).

• Should make it possible for students to demonstrate what they know and can do, not simply what they have yet to develop (Gottlieb, 2012). In order to make use of assessment data, students must have information about how their performance relates to expected or desired accomplishment in class. This information is key feedback for learning (Hattie, 2008).

• Should use multiple measures. No single assessment is foolproof or comprehensive in and of itself. To gain confidence in the results of a given assessment, and especially when high-stakes decisions are being made, it is important to triangulate results with multiple sources (NWEA & Grunwald Associates, 2012). In particular, culturally and linguistically diverse students may experience confusion if they do not understand the procedural language of the assessment with which they are engaging. For example, a student who is able to summarize her reading in class with a partner may not be able to demonstrate this behavior when asked to respond to a standardized prompt in a testing situation. In addition, the test may ask students to think or respond in culturally unfamiliar ways, such as presupposing that families participate in the same activities regardless of cultural background.

• Should ensure that a balanced assessment framework is in place that provides the appropriate information to the varied stakeholders who need it, including students and families, classroom educators, school and district leaders responsible for program improvement, and policymakers (Stiggins, 2017). Each form of assessment is used for the purpose it was designed.

Stiggins (2017) outlines a "Student's Bill of Assessment Rights" that sets guidelines for transparency and ethics in using assessments. This set of aspirational guidelines recommends transparency in explaining the purposes of an assessment and how its results will be used, in understanding the learning targets and scoring rubrics, in describing good and poor performance and how to self-assess, in using quality assessments that are dependable, and in effectively communicating the assessment results to students and/or their families (Stiggins, 2017). For many emergent bilingual students and families, clarity in understanding what classroom and school assessments mean and how students can work to improve their learning will only come about if educators share the information in child- or parent-friendly ways, including by using the family's home language.

SUMMARY

In this first chapter, we presented foundational knowledge that showcases the interconnectedness between language and literacy learning and how they must be assessed in tandem for emergent bilingual students. Emergent bilinguals are diverse in so many ways, including their language backgrounds, length of time in the United States, academic experiences, economic resources, race and ethnicity, religion, and more. Assessments should provide useful information on what students are able to do and on what they have learned or have yet to learn, and should provide guidance for instruction. Because language constraints may affect students' abilities to show what they know and cultural norms vary across groups, educators must take into account cultural and linguistic perspectives as they consider the assessments they use with emergent bilinguals.

We dedicated a substantial section of this chapter to describing the development of literacy from the emergent stage, to the characteristics of beginning readers and writers, to outlining a period of transition to proficiency, along with the behaviors of more advanced readers. At each stage, we described reading and writing tasks that may prove especially challenging for emergent bilinguals. Similarly, we provided background information on language development in a home or an additional language. Many factors influence learning a new language at school, including students' ages, the educational context, the goals for the new language use, prior literacy skills, and the relationship between the new language and other languages in students' repertoires.

Multilinguals use information from all of their linguistic resources to interact socially and garner information from the world. Because emergent bilinguals are in the process of learning a new language at school, assessments that are administered must take into account the inherent limitations on gathering accurate data on this population. We shared a set of helpful ethical principles gleaned from the research to guide the work of educators as they use assessments with emergent bilinguals. These guidelines aim to generate assessments that focus on students' assets, that show what students *can* do, that do not limit students' opportunities, and that examine the complexity of students' multilingual knowledge. In the next chapter we share the different types of and purposes for literacy assessments that are used for instructional decision making in schools and connect them to effective practices for emergent bilinguals.

CHAPTER 2

Using Assessment to Support Instruction

The teachers at Riverview Elementary are excited to begin a new school year with their students. Riverview Elementary is a midsized school located in a large urban district. Over the last two decades, the demographic makeup of Riverview students has shifted, because of an influx of refugees from Somalia. Now, Riverview is at the center of a Somali community, with families who have been in the United States for more than 20 years, as well as newcomers to the country in the last few months. The educators at Riverview have been challenged to meet the wide range of learning needs of their students, and they are committed to excellence. Over the last few years they have seen great strides in the academic progress of their students, particularly in science and math. Literacy scores, however, have remained significantly and steadily below state-level averages. The new principal, Dr. Shire, is determined to change this trajectory.

This year, Riverview Elementary has prioritized literacy, with a goal for all students to be on track to reach grade-level literacy standards by year's end. The school will be using a recently adopted districtwide assessment system, in which all students will complete brief screening assessments in fall, winter, and spring. Data from these assessments will be used to determine which students are at risk of not meeting end-of-year proficiency levels in literacy. These students' progress will be monitored on a more frequent basis to determine whether core instruction is sufficient, or whether they need additional intervention and support to be successful.

Riverview teachers and staff are attending a professional development week to learn about the new literacy assessment system before school starts. At breakfast on the first day, the teachers and staff are chatting about the new system. Ms. Carl, a second-grade teacher, notes how much she tries to ensure that her literacy instruction is of the highest quality, such that all students in her classroom have the opportunity to succeed. She wonders, "Will the assessments show that my teaching is effective for my students?"

Mr. Reed, the literacy specialist, adds, "That's important, but there's always at least a few kids who need more support. Will the assessments identify those kids soon enough so we can help them catch up?"

"Right," Ms. Kelly, the special education teacher, says. "And we'll also need to know if the additional support is working, or if something different is needed. Will the assessments tell us how to individualize instruction?"

Ms. Farhan, one of the EL specialists, chimes in: "Don't forget, we need to make sure these assessments are appropriate for our students. I wonder if the test developers actually included Somali students when they validated their assessments?"

"All of this testing is going to take a lot of time. When are we going to actually teach our students?" Ms. Carl worries.

Ms. Carl is not alone in her concerns. In fact, many educators express concern that time spent gathering assessment data is time that cuts into valuable instruction. Yet, although this concern has merit, time spent collecting assessment data can actually *improve* the efficiency and efficacy of instructional time. Educators' key to using assessment data to support efficient and effective instruction is knowing the *types* and *purposes* of various assessments, knowing which assessments will provide reliable and valid data for the intended purpose, and knowing when and how to use assessments. In the context of working with multilingual students from diverse cultural backgrounds, it is especially critical to ensure that assessments are appropriate for the specific population of students with whom they are being used.

Thus, the purpose of this chapter is (1) to describe and define the different types of literacy assessments that are used in schools, highlighting their strengths and limitations in the context of use with multilingual students and (2) to introduce a framework that provides guidance for when and how to use assessment data to guide literacy instruction for emergent bilinguals. We begin with an overview of assessment "basics" to lay the foundation for this content.

FOUNDATIONAL IDEAS

Literacy is multifaceted and multidimensional, comprising many layers of skills that must work in concert for learners to experience success. Literacy assessment must reflect these multiple dimensions if it is to inform instruction in a meaningful way. For all learners, but perhaps especially for emergent bilinguals, additional issues must be considered, such as the cultural and linguistic appropriateness of particular assessments, as well as bias that might be associated with particular test features. To evaluate whether particular literacy assessments are appropriate for instructional use, it is critical to understand the broad types of assessments as well as the basic **psychometric** properties (i.e., reliability and validity) of assessments and how they apply to different assessment purposes.

Broad Types of Assessments

A variety of terms are used to describe types of assessments, including **formative** versus **summative, formal** versus **informal,** and **norm-referenced** versus **criterion-referenced.** We first briefly define these terms, and then describe specific types of school-based assessments.

Formative versus Summative

Two broad types of assessments are used for educational decision making: formative and summative. Formative assessments are used to monitor student progress within a curriculum or instructional program to determine whether the instruction is effective, whether students are learning, and to identify students' specific strengths and needs. Formative assessment is used as part of a feedback loop: it can be used to provide educators with information about whether their instruction is meeting student needs and to provide students with feedback about their performance and progress. Formative assessment is ongoing, and serves as an indicator of whether the educator should continue delivering instruction as planned or make instructional changes for whole groups or individual students. For example, many schools use **curriculum-based measurement (CBM)** to monitor student progress in reading. CBM includes brief reading tasks, such as having a student read a grade-level text aloud for 1 minute, then counting the number of words read correctly (Deno, 1985). CBM is administered on a frequent basis (e.g., monthly or even weekly) to determine whether a student is making expected progress toward grade-level standards or whether an instructional change is needed. More examples of formative assessments are provided later in this chapter.

Summative assessments are used to evaluate whether and what a student has learned, often as the culmination of an instructional unit or end of an academic term. With summative assessments, student performance is typically evaluated against a specific benchmark or standard, and assessment data are often used to report student academic standing at a particular point in time (e.g., as a final grade). Summative assessments can be used for educational decision making for an individual student (e.g., whether an individual student met the minimum grade-level standards to advance to the next grade) or for groups of students (e.g., whether a school is in good standing based on passing rates on a state test). However, summative assessments, by definition, do not typically have immediate implications for ongoing instruction.

Formal versus Informal

Formal assessments typically involve administration of **standardized tests** (tests that are administered and scored according to a specific, predetermined procedure) for the purpose of assessing overall student achievement, either to compare students to normative peer groups or to identify an individual student's specific strengths and weaknesses in a particular subject area. Formal assessments might include district tests used for screening and benchmarking purposes, state tests used for accountability purposes, or standardized achievement tests used to assess an individual student's relative strengths and weaknesses—for example, across specific reading skills such as phonemic awareness, decoding and word recognition, fluency, vocabulary, and comprehension. Decisions based on formal assessments might include whether a school is on target to meet district or state literacy standards, whether a student will receive supplementary intervention in addition to core instruction, whether a student needs special education or other special services, or whether a specific skill should be addressed in a child's individualized education plan (IEP) as part of special education.

Educators often use **informal assessments** to assess their students' performance and progress toward daily learning targets that are the focus of instruction. Informal assessments are typically nonstandardized assessments that help educators gauge whether students are learning specific content, and can include educator-made quizzes and tests, portfolio assignments and other work samples, and even observations and interviews. Informal assessments typically occur in the context of the regular classroom environment and are often used for formative purposes (to provide feedback to students and gauge the effectiveness of instruction). They may also be used for summative purposes, such as determining end-of-term grades, but are not typically used for comparing students to others or for high-stakes decisions, such as educational placement.

Specific to literacy assessment, informal assessments might include running records and miscue analysis, comprehension questions asked during or after a read-aloud, spelling tests, prompted writing samples, or projects such as book reviews. Decisions based on informal assessments might include whether an individual student (or group of students) mastered specific content or can perform a specific skill (and often, whether additional instruction is needed), or what grade a student will earn at the end of a term.

Norm- versus Criterion-Referenced

Assessments can also be either **norm-referenced,** meaning the assessment provides information about student performance in relation to "typical" peers, or **criterion-referenced,** meaning the assessment provides information about student performance in relation to some criterion, such as a benchmark or grade-level standard. Norm-referenced scores (such as those obtained from standardized achievement tests) indicate the extent to which a student performs better or worse than others within a population; for example, a student performing at the 85th percentile achieved a score that was greater than 85% of the scores of others taking the test.

Educators should take necessary precautions in using norm-referenced tests with emergent bilinguals, because the population on which these assessments are normed may or may not include a representative sample of students with the same cultural and linguistic backgrounds as the specific students being assessed. Thus, emergent bilinguals' scores might reflect how they compare to students very unlike themselves, making those scores difficult to interpret. We strongly recommend using norm-referenced information cautiously and in tandem with other sources of information about student performance, including multiple literacy assessments, as well as information about students that goes beyond their academic skills. Chapter 3 delves into additional types of information that can help contextualize an emergent bilingual student's performance on traditional academic assessments.

Criterion-referenced scores, on the other hand, indicate a student's level of mastery or accuracy with respect to specific knowledge or skills. For example, a student who achieved 85% on a spelling test spelled 85% of the items correctly. Criterion-referenced scores can be used to determine how much progress is needed to meet a specific standard or goal. Unlike norm-referenced tests, criterion-referenced tests can show a student's progress over time, such that the student's current performance can be compared to his or her own past performance. Commonly used criterion-referenced tests include teacher-made quizzes and tests that show a student's mastery of specific content or universal screeners that have established benchmarks that show a student's current performance compared to past performance as well as in relation to specific standards.

Basic Psychometric Properties

In addition to understanding different types of tests, it's also important to understand their basic psychometric properties in order to select an assessment that is appropriate for the intended purpose. Basic psychometric properties include **reliability** and **validity**; in this section, we also discuss **bias** in assessment.

Reliability

When using assessments for instructional decision making and other educational purposes, the results of these assessments should be trustworthy. Thus, it is critical for educators to select assessments that will produce accurate results that reflect the knowledge and skills that they intend to measure. Any published assessment should include information about the accuracy or reliability of the measure (for those assessments that do not, we recommend using them with caution). Essentially, reliability refers to "the extent to which it is possible to generalize from an observation or test score made at a specific time by a specific person to a similar performance at a different time, or by a different person)" (Salvia, Ysseldyke, & Witmer, 2017, p. 65). Examples of random error might include fluctuations in how the measure is administered (e.g., the examiner varies in his or her administration of the test from one time to the next) or variations in other testing conditions (e.g., the presence of external distractions, a student's fatigue level). Reliability is typically reported as a correlation coefficient r, with 1.00 indicating perfect reliability. Although there are no hard-and-fast standards for reliability coefficients, we present some guidelines (based on Salvia et al.'s 2017 recommendations) in Table 2.1.

There are different types of reliability that might be reported for a given measure, including item reliability (consistency among different samples of test items), stability (consistency of test scores over time), and interobserver agreement (consistency among test scorers) (Salvia et al., 2017). For item reliability, a test publisher might

TABLE 2.1. Guidance for Minimum Standards for Reliability for Different Assessment Purposes

Assessment purposes	Minimum reliability	Rationale
Accountability (test scores reported and used at the group level)	$r = .60$	Relatively low but acceptable, as group means are not affected by a test's reliability.
Monitoring student progress on a frequent basis (e.g., weekly)	$r = .70$	Relatively low but acceptable, because random fluctuation in data is accounted for somewhat by frequent measurement.
Screening decisions (e.g., identifying students in need of intervention)	$r = .80$	Higher because screening can lead to decisions that affect an individual student's educational programming.
High-stakes decisions, such as special education eligibility	$r = .90$	High because such decisions can have significant long-term consequences on a student's educational outcomes.

report **alternate-form reliability,** which is calculated as the correlation between scores for the same students on two different forms of the same test. For example, a group of students might be given Form A and Form B of the same assessment. If the correlation between their scores on the two forms is strong, then the two forms can be used interchangeably. Another type of item reliability that is often published is **internal consistency,** which is calculated as the correlation between scores on individual test items. Essentially, if a test has evidence of strong internal consistency, the educator can expect that student performance will be consistent across test items.

Note that reliability is not an inherent quality of an assessment—there is no such thing as a "reliable assessment." Rather, evidence that an assessment produces reliable data is dependent on the sample to whom it is administered. Thus, it is important for educators to know the demographic characteristics of the student sample on which reliability data are based, particularly for learners who might have very different ethnic and language backgrounds, socioeconomic status, and other characteristics compared to that sample.

WHERE CAN I FIND DEMOGRAPHIC INFORMATION ABOUT AND OTHER FEATURES OF ASSESSMENTS?

- ◆ Published assessments typically include manuals that report information about sample demographics, reliability, validity, and other technical features.
- ◆ Test developers often conduct research on their assessments and report this research in journal articles that can be found through search engines and online databases, such as Google Scholar or the Education Resources Information Center (ERIC).
- ◆ Online clearinghouses that disseminate information about assessments include:
  - ❖ National Center on Response to Intervention (*www.rti4success.org*).
  - ❖ National Center on Intensive Intervention (*https://intensiveintervention.org*).

Validity

Reliability is a necessary, but not sufficient, piece of information to consider in selecting educational assessments. It is also important to consider the validity of an assessment, or the extent to which it assesses the content or construct of interest. Like reliability, validity is not an inherent characteristic of an assessment measure, but is specific to the individual student who is being tested (Salvia et al., 2017). For example, a test that is considered "valid" for "typical" U.S. students who have been systematically immersed in mainstream American culture, customs, language, and so on, may not be valid for—or lead to appropriate inferences about—a student who recently immigrated to the United States.

Test developers typically report on one or more of the following types of evidence that support the appropriateness of inferences that can be drawn from test results: evidence based on test content, internal structure, relations to other similar assessments, response processes, and consequences of using the test (Salvia et al., 2017). This information is typically included in testing manuals as well as in published journal articles and websites (see the box on p. 27). Confirming that test content is appropriate might be based on evidence that the items on the test really do represent the domain or construct of interest, that no important content was left out, and that the way content is measured parallels the way it is instructed. Confirming that the internal structure of a test is appropriate might be based on evidence that items and subtests represent the components and total score of a test. For example, reading is a multidimensional construct that includes phonemic awareness, decoding skills, fluency, vocabulary, and comprehension, so there should be evidence that the test items designed to measure these components are consistent with the theoretical basis of those components.

Evidence that scores from the test relate well to scores from other similar assessments is typically reported as a validity coefficient, which indicates the correlation between scores from two assessments. **Concurrent validity** is the extent to which an assessment correlates with another similar assessment given around the same time, whereas **predictive validity** is the extent to which an assessment correlates with another similar assessment given at a later time. Concurrent validity is useful for knowing whether an assessment will provide information similar to another assessment (that is perhaps more expensive or time-consuming to administer). Predictive validity is useful when one assessment is given to predict whether a student is likely to pass or fail a later assessment (such as giving a screening measure in the fall to identify students who might be at risk of failing a district or state literacy test in the spring).

Evidence related to **response processes** has to do with the way students respond to test questions as well as how their responses are scored. In some cases, educators might be more (or at least as) interested in the processes in which the student engaged to arrive at an answer as in whether it was answered correctly or not. For example, a teacher might wish to know what strategies a student uses to identify an unknown word or to answer a comprehension question. In these cases, a "valid" assessment approach might include scoring words based on whether a student sounded out and blended the letters or read them as sight words or having students think aloud or complete interview questions about how they arrived at their answers.

Finally, evidence regarding the consequences of using a test has to do with whether taking that test actually leads to some desired benefit. For example, if a specific assessment is used to monitor student progress for the purpose of individualizing instruction, it might be "validated" for this purpose by showing that, when teachers use progress monitoring data from such an assessment to individualize instruction, student outcomes really do improve. Educators might wish to carefully consider the consequences of selecting and using an assessment. Ultimately, if using a test does not lead to some benefit related to the purpose for which it is being used, it might not be worth administering.

Bias

No assessment is flawless; all tests are subject to some degree of error. While some measurement error is random (i.e., it doesn't systematically affect scores in one direction or the other), some error may be due to **bias** in that it is "systematic and predictable" (Salvia et al., 2017, p. 65). Systematic bias in measurement can either inflate or deflate students' scores, leading to misinterpretations or misjudgments of what they know and can do. Bias in measurement is a particular concern for emergent bilinguals. For example, many assessments given in schools require students to follow oral directions and to read and write in English, regardless of their level of English fluency. Items on tests might assume particular background knowledge and experiences that might be shared by students who have experienced a specific curriculum or share a similar cultural background, but not among students whose cultures are not represented or who have recently moved to the United States. In Chapter 3 we present a classroom vignette that highlights an example of this type of bias. Bias might also occur if the test administrator does not follow the standardized procedures of a test, or if scores are based on a normative sample that does not represent the demographics of a particular group of students.

In any of these examples, emergent bilingual students' performance might not reflect their actual knowledge or skills, which could result in instructional decisions that are not beneficial and may even be harmful. Thus, it is critical for educators to

---

WHAT SHOULD I CONSIDER IN DETERMINING THE POTENTIAL BIAS OF AN ASSESSMENT?

- What was the purpose of this assessment? Is that purpose relevant for my student(s)?
- How will the information be used? Is it possible it could lead to an inappropriate educational decision for my student(s)?
- What was the content in the assessment? Do my students have the relevant cultural and linguistic background knowledge to be able to respond to test items?
- How was the test administered to the student(s)? Were there any language barriers? What were the assumptions about the students' knowledge and experience related to test taking?

be aware of potential sources of bias in assessing emergent bilingual students' literacy and use caution in interpreting results. Using caution might include knowing the purpose, content, and conditions under which the test was administered to the student. It also includes understanding that the test score is just one piece of information about the student's performance and may or may not be an accurate reflection of that student's skills. Considering this test score in the context of multiple assessments and other information is critical. In Chapter 3 we provide suggestions on how to look beyond the skills that are measured by traditional assessment approaches.

TYPES AND PURPOSES OF SCHOOL-BASED LITERACY ASSESSMENTS

A wide range of literacy assessments are used in classrooms and schools, with purposes ranging from screening students to identify those at risk of not meeting proficiency goals; monitoring progress; identifying specific areas of strengths and needs; identifying students as eligible for EL support, special education, or other services; and making accountability decisions at the school or district level. In this section, we provide an overview of various types of assessments, highlighting those that are used primarily for instructional decision making. Table 2.2 summarizes the different types of assessments and their purposes, and whether they are for the most part formal or informal, formative or summative, and norm- or criterion-referenced. In using these different types of assessments, we strongly advocate for a collaborative data-based decision-making approach, in which educators work together to examine student data from multiple sources, and take into consideration issues of cultural and linguistic appropriateness and bias as well as other technical features of assessment (e.g., reliability, validity), as they make instructional decisions for emergent bilinguals.

Screening

Screening tools are used to identify students at risk and to determine the need for supplemental literacy intervention, such as those provided within **multi-tiered systems of supports (MTSS).** Universal (school- or districtwide) screening tools are typically given early in the school year and often also in winter and spring to identify students who might require supplemental support. Screening tools often have preidentified cut points that are used to determine students' likelihood for not meeting grade-level benchmarks, which are then used to determine instructional supports that might be put into place. These preidentified cut points might be based on national data gathered and summarized by the test publisher or based on local data collected within a particular school or district. For example, a school might administer a district literacy test, and all students performing below the 40th percentile based on district-level norms might be identified as needing more frequent progress monitoring. Those falling below the 25th percentile might receive supplemental intervention. Or, on a curriculum-based oral reading test, students scoring below a grade-level benchmark might be identified as needing additional supports.

TABLE 2.2. Types of Literacy Assessments

Type	Purpose	Formal or informal?	Formative or summative?	Norm- or criterion-referenced?	Example
Screening	Identify students at risk; identify baseline reading level	Formal	Formative	Norm or criterion	Measures of Academic Progress (MAP; NWEA, 2013); curriculum-based measures (CBM)
Progress monitoring	Determine responsiveness to instruction and need for instructional changes	Informal	Formative	Criterion	CBM, teacher-made quizzes and tests
Learning-needs assessments	Determine focus and content of instruction	Formal or informal	Formative	Criterion	Miscue analysis, informal reading inventories, skill checklists
Eligibility	Determine need for special services	Formal	Summative	Norm or criterion	Multiple assessments, including standardized achievement and/or language proficiency measures
Accountability	Make decisions about whether schools are meeting targets; resources allocation	Formal	Summative	Norm or criterion	Standardized district or state tests

An important consideration for screening assessments is how accurately they identify students who are truly in need of additional instruction, so that they are given needed supports in a timely fashion. It is also important that screening assessments accurately identify students who are *not* in need of additional instruction, so that resources are not unnecessarily directed to them. Test developers should report evidence of the accuracy of their screening measures for identifying "true positives" (those who are truly at risk for not meeting grade-level benchmarks) and "true negatives" (those who are truly likely to meet the benchmarks); however, finding the right balance can be challenging. Some schools and districts rely on more than one assessment or on "gated" screening processes (administering a universal assessment to all students, followed by additional assessments to confirm the risk status of those performing below established benchmarks on the first assessment) to increase the likelihood that the "right" students are identified and to make the best use of limited resources (Johnson, Jenkins, Petscher, & Catts, 2009).

Progress Monitoring

Progress monitoring assessments are used to track students' performance over time in order to evaluate the effectiveness of instruction and to determine the need for further intervention. Progress monitoring assessments might be given relatively infrequently, such as in fall, winter, and spring (as mentioned earlier) or once per grading quarter or term; or they may be given more frequently, such as monthly or even weekly. The frequency of progress monitoring is typically related to how much extra help a student will need to meet benchmarks (e.g., those identified as at moderate risk for not meeting goals might be monitored monthly, whereas those identified as at more significant risk might be monitored weekly or biweekly).

There are several important considerations for progress monitoring assessments, which were well articulated by Deno (1985), who developed CBM, one of the most frequently (and well-validated) progress monitoring approaches used in schools (Vaughn & Fuchs, 2003). Deno (1985) proposed that such assessments should have evidence of reliability, validity, and sensitivity to growth over short periods of time; and should be inexpensive, as well as relatively quick and easy to administer and interpret. A unique feature of CBM is that it serves as a **general outcome measure**; that is, it entails measurement of a brief behavior (e.g., reading aloud for 1 minute) that correlates strongly with overall reading proficiency. It is akin to a temperature check in that it provides a good indicator of a student's general performance and progress over time, but does *not* assess mastery of specific subskills. Decades of research have indicated that CBM has utility for progress monitoring in reading (Wayman, Wallace, Wiley, Tichá, & Espin, 2007) and in writing (McMaster & Espin, 2007), including some evidence of its utility for emergent bilingual students (Sandberg & Reschly, 2011).

To be most useful, it is critical that educators have a system for summarizing and interpreting progress monitoring data on a regular basis. Many schools have scheduled times for teachers, administrators, school psychologists, and other staff to look at student data together to make ongoing instructional decisions (e.g., during time designated for professional learning communities [PLCs] or data team meetings). It is helpful if the data are presented visually, so that potential problems can be identified relatively quickly. For example, data can be presented in a graph that shows both desired progress (e.g., the trajectory a student would need to meet to achieve an end-of-year benchmark) and actual progress (e.g., the student's trend based on collected data), so that it is clear when actual progress is not on track to meet academic expectations. It is also helpful to have specific rules for making decisions, so that educators can act on student data in a timely and consistent manner. For example, in comparing a student's current trend to desired progress, educators might proceed as follows (cf. Stecker, Fuchs, & Fuchs, 2005):

- If the overall trend is in line with desired progress, continue instruction as is.
- If the overall trend is above desired progress, consider raising end-of-year expectations or discontinuing intervention for the student.
- If the overall trend is below desired progress, make an instructional change.

Learning Needs Assessments

Learning needs assessments are used to identify students' specific strengths and needs in order to develop appropriate instructional plans or to make instructional changes when student progress monitoring data indicate this need. Learning needs assessments can take many forms, and could include a teacher's observations, interviews with a student, use of a checklist or rubric to analyze work samples, use of a spelling inventory or an error analysis of a student's oral or written work, and so on. A type of learning needs assessment commonly used in schools is the **Informal Reading Inventory (IRI)**, which can provide insight into students' reading comprehension skills, including recall and inference-making skills. However, note that there are few learning needs assessments, including IRIs, that have a strong research base to support their use with emergent bilingual students, and so they should be used with care (see Chapter 6 for more details). Also, whereas such assessments can help identify areas of strength and need, they have limited utility for detecting risk or showing growth over time (Klingbeil, McComas, Burns, & Helman, 2015), and thus we recommend that they *not* be used for screening or progress monitoring.

It is critically important that an assessment enable an educator or team of educators to reliably and accurately determine what knowledge or skills a student has yet to develop, is in the process of developing, or has mastered. Such information can then inform the *focus* of instruction (e.g., whether a student needs code- or meaning-based instruction), the *content* of instruction (e.g., specific letter sounds that the student needs to acquire), and the *format* of instruction (e.g., how that instruction might be delivered). For example, explicit instruction with modeling and guided practice might be needed for a student who is just beginning to acquire a skill, whereas more extended opportunities for practice might be more appropriate for a student who has acquired the skill but needs to build fluency.

Assessments for Eligibility and Other "High-Stakes" Decisions

Although this book primarily focuses on assessments that support instruction, we briefly touch on assessments used for "high-stakes" decisions, which include decisions about individual students' eligibility for specialized services (e.g., EL services, special education), as well as about the performance of groups (e.g., students at a given grade level) or subgroups (e.g., receiving EL services) for accountability purposes (e.g., whether a school is meeting target passing rates).

Individual-Level Eligibility Decisions

To determine a student's need for EL services, as well as proficiency levels for grouping and placement decisions, a variety of standardized language assessments are used. We provide an in-depth look at the assessments that states use to make decisions about the language development of their students in Chapter 4.

With respect to special education eligibility decisions, schools and districts vary in the types of assessments used as well as the way that data from these assessments are interpreted, depending largely on state definitions and criteria for different disabilities. Often, assessments used for this purpose include standardized, norm-referenced achievement and intelligence tests with specific cut points that are used to indicate eligibility. Unfortunately, this approach is fraught with problems. For example, the use of cut points is inherently arbitrary and unreliable, because it assumes that there is a "true" score, with students performing below that score having a "true" disability and students performing above that score not having a disability. However, no such true score exists, and because students' scores always contain some measurement error, it is impossible to know for sure that a student scoring below the cut point really has a disability or that a student scoring above the cut point does not (Fletcher, Steubing, Morris, & Lyon, 2013). Also, whether established cut points apply to emergent bilingual students, who may not be represented in normative samples and for whom the assessment may not have been validated, remains an important question. Related to this issue, it is often very difficult to disentangle emergent bilingual students' performance on standardized literacy tests from their English language proficiency. Misinterpretation of assessment performance has often led to both over- and underidentification of emergent bilingual students for special education services (Artiles, Rueda, Salazar, & Higareda, 2005; Klingner, Artiles, & Barletta, 2006; Sullivan, 2011).

An alternative approach that does not rely on standardized assessments for eligibility determination is a **response-to-intervention (RTI)** approach, in which children's responsiveness to research-based interventions implemented prior to the special education referral process is considered (Klingner & Edwards, 2006; Vaughn & Fuchs, 2003). This approach was included in the 2004 reauthorization of the Individuals with Disabilities Education Act, 20 U.S.C. § 1400 (2004) as an alternative to traditional IQ-achievement discrepancy approaches to identifying learning disabilities. In RTI, students identified as at-risk of academic failure receive increasingly intensive and individualized "tiers" of intervention while their progress is monitored. **Tier 1** consists (ideally) of research-based core instruction delivered with fidelity in their regular classroom. Students for whom Tier 1 is not sufficient to reach grade-level standards receive **Tier 2** supplemental intervention, which (again, ideally) consists of small-group research-based instruction that targets specific skills needed to succeed in Tier 1. If Tier 2 intervention is not sufficient, students receive even more intensive, individualized instruction in **Tier 3.** Tier 3 often either precedes special education referral or is delivered within special education. Typically, when special education eligibility decisions are made, multiple assessments are used (including progress monitoring data, standardized assessments, classroom observations, and parent and teacher interviews; Fletcher et al., 2013).

For emergent bilingual students who may also have reading-related disabilities, an RTI approach has some advantages, including that it does not rely solely on standardized assessments that may be culturally and linguistically inappropriate, but rather takes into account students' responsiveness to generally effective instruction and intervention that is matched to their specific learning needs. However, there are still some important issues to consider in using an RTI approach with emergent bilingual students, including whether the progress monitoring assessments and tiered instruction and interventions have been validated for use with students learning

English, and whether instruction and intervention delivered within the tiers make use of culturally and linguistically sustaining pedagogies (Brown & Doolittle, 2008; Klingner et al., 2006)—a point to which we return throughout this book.

Group-Level Accountability Decisions

Finally, some school-based literacy assessments are used primarily for group-level accountability decisions, such as whether schools are meeting district- or state-established proficiency rates on standards-based tests, or whether additional resources are needed to increase overall student performance. Such tests might include state-designed assessments or published tests (e.g., the Smarter-Balanced or PARCC assessments used to assess students' proficiency on the Common Core State Standards [CCSS]; National Governors Association Center for Best Practices & Council of Chief State School Officers, 2010). Often, school- and district-level data are disaggregated by subgroups of students (including emergent bilingual students) to ensure that subgroups are meeting standards and to identify discrepancies in achievement that need to be addressed. Because such assessments have limited implications for day-to-day instructional decision making, we devote less attention to them in this book. Still, it is important to keep in mind that the same considerations (e.g., reliability, validity, bias) in selecting and interpreting such assessments for use with emergent bilingual students apply to these assessments in the same manner as other types of school-based tests.

Focus of This Book

Throughout this book, we focus on "instructionally relevant" assessments, or those assessments that are used primarily to inform instruction. Although we touch on formal and informal literacy assessments that are part of school-based decision-making frameworks, we highlight formative assessments used for progress monitoring and assessing students' learning needs, such that educators can make timely and appropriate instructional decisions that will support emergent bilingual students' ongoing literacy development.

A FRAMEWORK FOR DATA-BASED INSTRUCTIONAL DECISION MAKING FOR EMERGENT BILINGUALS

The different types of literacy assessments described in this chapter are likely to be most effective if they are used within a systematic framework of instructional decision making. Here, we describe such a framework, with a primary focus on how educators can use individual student data to inform instruction. This framework is likely to be most useful in a collaborative data-based decision-making context in which classroom teachers, administrators, and other school personnel (e.g., school psychologists, EL specialists, special education teachers) work together to examine student data on a regular basis to ensure that students are receiving appropriate instruction that meets their needs. We describe this framework in the context of RTI—part of an MTSS that includes screening, progress monitoring, and increasingly intensive instructional supports—because such models are increasingly prevalent in schools today. Figure 2.1 provides an overall view of this framework and illustrates the types of assessments that inform instruction in each tier. Educators may also wonder how to adjust assessment and instruction to be more culturally relevant in the various tiers. We present a range of ideas on this topic in Chapter 3.

Universal Screening

Our framework begins with universal screening, in which all students within a classroom, grade level, or entire school building are administered brief literacy assessments that have good evidence of reliability and validity for the area(s) of interest (e.g., reading or writing proficiency). Students who fall below a prespecified benchmark (either according to published information or local norms) are identified for additional progress monitoring during Tier 1 (core) instruction and possibly even immediately provided with Tier 2 (supplemental) intervention.

Progress Monitoring and Instructional Decision Making within Tier 1

Within Tier 1, the classroom teacher delivers high-quality, research-based, and culturally relevant instruction that addresses core academic standards, and students' improvement from that instruction is monitored regularly (e.g., at least monthly). If many students are making little or no progress, the teacher should ask the following questions:

- "Am I implementing research-based instructional methods that have been validated for students like mine?"
- "Is the instructional focus and content aligned with core academic standards?"
- "Is the instructional focus and content culturally relevant and appropriate for my specific students?"
- "Am I implementing instruction with high quality and fidelity?"

If the answer to any of these questions is "no," then the educator should first adjust instruction such that it is aligned with research-based practices and core standards, that it is culturally relevant, and that it is implemented with high quality and fidelity. If the answer is "yes," then a validated classwide intervention that reinforces the specific foundational literacy skills needed to succeed within the curriculum might be required to accelerate progress for all students.

When the majority of students within the class *are* making expected progress toward midyear or end-of-year benchmarks, instruction can be assumed to be generally effective and additional classwide intervention is not necessary. In this case, if a subset of students is making insufficient progress, then it is likely that they require supplemental Tier 2 intervention. It is helpful to collaboratively examine progress monitoring data to determine the need for Tier 2 intervention, for example, among

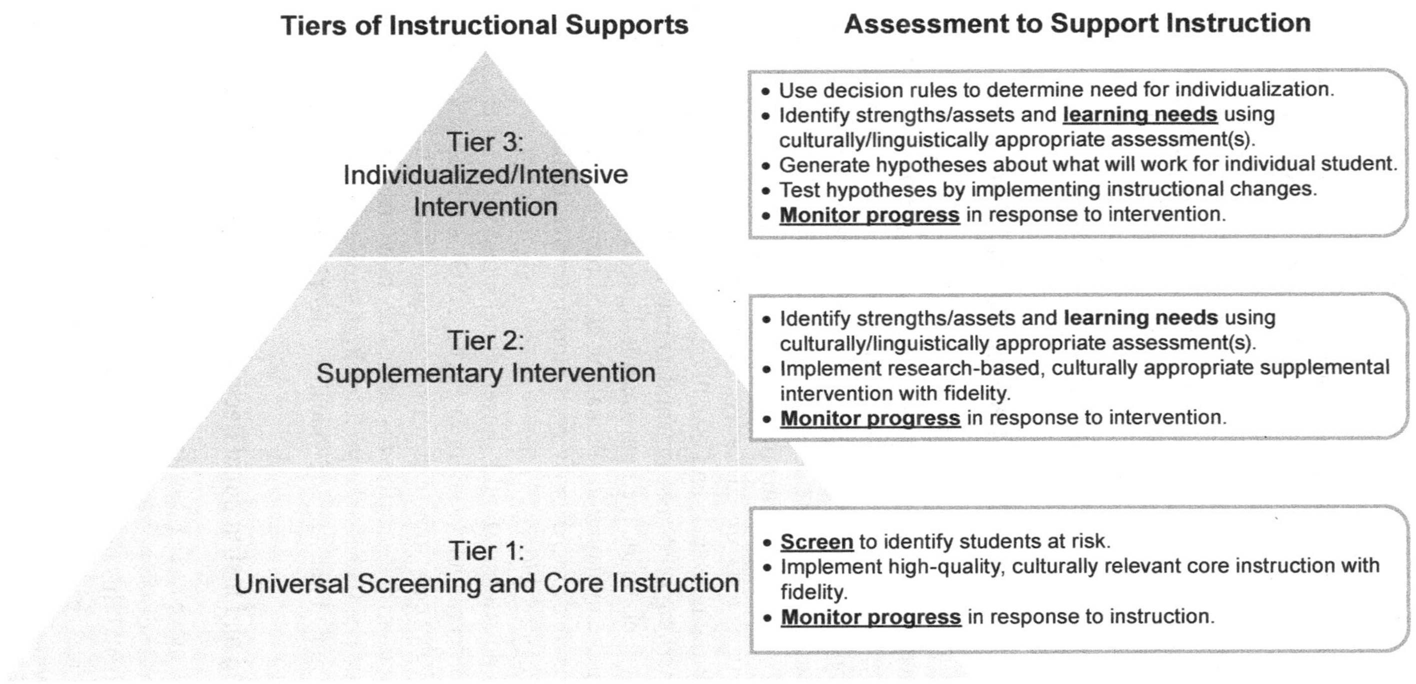

Tiers of Instructional Supports

Assessment to Support Instruction

Tier 3:
Individualized/Intensive
Intervention

- Use decision rules to determine need for individualization.
- Identify strengths/assets and **learning needs** using culturally/linguistically appropriate assessment(s).
- Generate hypotheses about what will work for individual student.
- Test hypotheses by implementing instructional changes.
- **Monitor progress** in response to intervention.

Tier 2:
Supplementary Intervention

- Identify strengths/assets and **learning needs** using culturally/linguistically appropriate assessment(s).
- Implement research-based, culturally appropriate supplemental intervention with fidelity.
- **Monitor progress** in response to intervention.

Tier 1:
Universal Screening and Core Instruction

- **Screen** to identify students at risk.
- Implement high-quality, culturally relevant core instruction with fidelity.
- **Monitor progress** in response to instruction.

FIGURE 2.1. A framework for assessment for instructional decision making within multitiered systems of support and types of assessments used at each tier. Adapted from Brown and Doolittle (2008).

grade-level staff and building administrators. The decision might be guided both by student performance levels (e.g., the student is performing significantly below grade-level peers) and growth rate (e.g., the student is making little or no progress). Students who are "dually discrepant" (whose performance and progress is below that of grade-level peers; Fuchs, Fuchs, & Speece, 2002) are most likely in need of Tier 2 intervention. At this point, brief learning-needs assessments should be administered to determine the focus and content of Tier 2 intervention. For example, many students who experience difficulty in a classroom instructional program might have relative weaknesses related to the foundational skills (e.g., decoding) needed to engage in higher-order literacy activities (e.g., reading comprehension). Identifying these specific needs can lead to efficient identification of appropriate instructional supports.

Progress Monitoring and Instructional Decision Making within Tier 2

Once students are identified as in need of Tier 2 intervention and appropriate targeted supplemental instruction is under way, student progress should be monitored on a regular basis (e.g., weekly or biweekly) to determine how students respond to the intervention. Cumulative progress monitoring data should be examined after about 8 weeks (e.g., Vaughn & Fuchs, 2003) and used for additional decision making. Again, if many students receiving the intervention are not making expected progress, then it's important to ask questions regarding instructional features such as fidelity, alignment, cultural relevance, and overall quality. If the overall quality is high, then reexamining learning needs assessment data may be warranted, because perhaps the focus and content of the intervention was misaligned with student needs. If most students receiving the intervention are making good progress, then those few students who are not making progress may need more intensive, individualized instruction, such as that provided within Tier 3.

Note that no student should "linger" indefinitely within Tier 2. After 8 weeks (2 months) of intervention (Vaughn & Fuchs, 2003), students who have made clear progress are likely ready to be exited from the intervention; however, it is critical to continue to monitor their progress to ensure they now thrive within core instruction. Students who do not appear to be profiting from supplemental intervention should be considered for more intensive, individualized instruction.

Progress Monitoring and Instructional Decision Making within Tier 3

When students move to Tier 3 instruction, the assumption is that they require something qualitatively different from the instruction provided in Tiers 1 and 2. The question is, what should this instruction look like? At this level, assessment data become even more critical, because the educator will need to rely heavily on information about the individual student to make timely and appropriate instructional decisions. In Tier 3, we recommend a "data-based individualization" (DBI) approach, in which the educator (1) establishes the student's present level of performance, (2) sets a long-term goal, (3) implements high-quality instruction with fidelity, (4) monitors student progress toward the goal, (5) uses decision rules to determine when instructional changes are needed, (6) develops data-based hypotheses about the types of changes needed, (7) implements changes in a systematic way, and (8) continues this process until the student reaches or exceeds the goal. As mentioned earlier, CBM is well suited for this process given its utility as a general outcome measure, its efficiency, and its sensitivity to growth over short time periods. Also, researchers have provided evidence of the reliability and validity of CBM for assessing emergent bilingual students' overall proficiency in reading (Sandberg & Reschly, 2011). Each step of the DBI process is described in further detail below.

1. *Establish the student's present level of performance.* To establish the student's present level of performance, screening assessments or the most recent progress monitoring assessment data can be used. These data are plotted as "baseline" data on a progress monitoring graph (see Figure 2.2).

2. *Set a long-term goal.* To set a long-term goal, the educator should first determine the end date of the monitoring period. This date could reflect the end of an instructional period (e.g., quarter) or the end of the school year. Then, the educator should identify the desired student performance level to be reached by that end date. This performance level could be based on grade-level benchmarks or on a more individualized goal that is determined to be appropriate for the student. Either way, the long-term goal should be reasonable and ambitious, such that expectations are high enough to close the gap between the student and grade-level peers, but not out of range of what could be expected within the time available. Once the goal is set, it is plotted on the graph, and a "goal line" is drawn from baseline to the goal. This goal line represents the rate of progress that the student will need to make over time in order to meet the long-term goal.

3. *Implement high-quality instruction with fidelity.* The next step is to implement high-quality, research-based instruction with fidelity. Ideally, research-based instruction is instruction that has empirical evidence of efficacy for students similar to those whose specific needs are being addressed; for emergent bilingual students, this instruction should support both language and literacy development. Although there is limited research on literacy instruction specifically for emergent bilingual students, it does exist (see Richards-Tutor, Baker, Gersten, Baker, & Smith, 2016, for a synthesis of this research). In the tiered model described thus far, such instruction might already have occurred in Tier 2, in which case it would be appropriate to skip to Step 6, because it is already clear that an instructional change is needed. The first attempt(s) at delivering high-quality instruction is typically denoted on the students' graph by inserting a vertical line after the baseline data and by labeling the first intervention (e.g., "Tier 1" and "Tier 2," as noted on the graph in Figure 2.2).

4. *Monitor student progress toward the goal.* As described in Tier 2, student progress should be monitored frequently to determine whether he or she is on track to meet the long-term goal or whether instructional changes are needed. Progress monitoring data are added to the graph on a regular basis, to allow for ease of interpretation

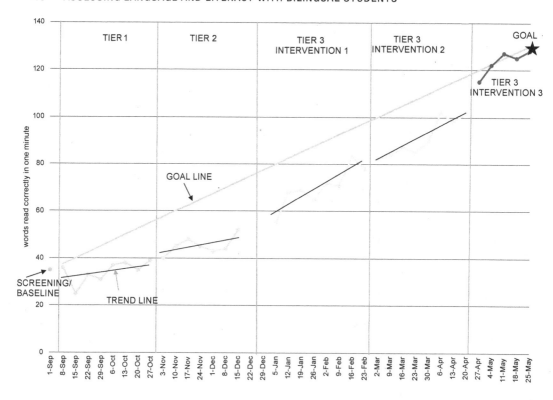

FIGURE 2.2. Graph of a student's progress from screening through Tiers 1, 2, and 3.

and timely decision making. It is helpful to add a trend line to get a better sense of the student's actual rate of progress in comparison to the desired rate of progress (goal line).

   5. *Use decision rules to determine when instructional changes are needed.* To determine whether an instructional change is needed, the educator should inspect the student's graph and consider the following options:

   a. Is the student's rate of progress (trend line) above the goal line? If so, this is great news! The goal could be adjusted to be even higher, or, if the student is on track to meet grade-level benchmarks, he or she could be exited from intervention. However, progress should be monitored continuously to make sure that regression does not occur.

   b. Is the student's trend line in line with the goal line? This is also good news! It means the instruction is effective and should continue as is.

   c. Is the student's trend line below the goal line? If so, it means that the instruction is not as beneficial as expected, and some kind of modification is needed.

   Sometimes there is a lot of **variability** in the data—in other words, the student's progress might appear to be moving up and down erratically. In this case, the educator might decide to collect a few more data points, until the data are more stable and interpretable.

6. *Develop data-based hypotheses about the types of changes needed.* Once the decision is made to change instruction, the million-dollar question is, *what type of change is needed?* Now, the educator becomes investigator by generating hypotheses about why the student is not make expected progress. Here is where learning-needs assessment data become particularly useful. By identifying the individual student's strengths and needs, the educator can start to predict what types of changes might be beneficial. The following questions can guide the educator's use of learning-needs assessment data.

  a. Does the student need a change in instructional *focus*? Perhaps the student has been receiving a decoding/phonics intervention, but a brief early reading assessment indicates that the student does not yet possess sufficient phonemic or alphabetic awareness to benefit from this instruction. The hypothesis might be, "The student needs instruction focused on phonemic awareness and the alphabetic principle."

  b. Does the student need a change in instructional *content*? Perhaps a focus on decoding is appropriate, but a decoding/spelling inventory reveals that, although instruction has been targeting multisyllabic words, the student has not yet mastered spelling patterns for single-syllable words. The hypothesis might be, "The student needs to work on CVC [consonant–vowel–consonant] words."

  c. Does the student need a change in instructional *delivery*? It might be that the focus and content of instruction is appropriate, but the way that it is being presented is not helping the student. The student may need more time, instruction in a smaller group, more explicit instruction, a behavioral plan, or other delivery modifications. The hypothesis might be, "The student needs more explicit instruction with modeling and guided practice," or "The student needs more opportunities to respond," or "The student needs a motivational plan."

Note that none of the changes we discussed necessarily requires stopping the original intervention and starting fresh with a new one. In some cases, such a drastic change is needed, but in many cases, relatively minor modifications will be sufficient to address the student's needs.

7. *Implement changes in a systematic way.* When one (or preferably more) hypotheses have been generated, it's time to put the most likely hypothesis to the test. It is useful to test one hypothesis at a time, systematically, in order to hone in on what will work best for the individual student. To test the hypothesis, the educator inserts another vertical line on the student's graph, labels the new intervention (see Figure 2.2), and implements the instructional change with fidelity (i.e., staying true to the change as it was initially conceptualized).

8. *Continue this process until the student reaches or exceeds the goal.* With the new intervention in place, the educator continues to monitor progress (as in Step 4), use decision rules to determine if and when further changes are needed (Step 5), generate new hypotheses when progress is insufficient (Step 6), and systematically

implement changes based on those hypotheses (Step 7). In this way, the process is ongoing and cyclical until the educator (turned investigator!) discovers the optimal instructional conditions to help the student reach the long-term goal.

SUMMARY

In this chapter, we described and defined the different types of literacy assessments that are used in schools, highlighting their strengths and limitations in the context of use with emergent bilingual students. Then, we introduced a framework that provides guidance for when and how to use assessment data to guide literacy instruction for emergent bilingual students. Key takeaways from this chapter are that (1) literacy is complex and multidimensional, and no single assessment is likely to be sufficient for gaining a comprehensive understanding of a student's current literacy performance and progress; (2) understanding the purpose of different types of assessments, along with their limitations, is critical; (3) data from literacy assessments should be considered with caution, and consider sources of potential systematic bias that might inflate or deflate scores for emergent bilingual students and whether the assessments are culturally and linguistically appropriate; and (4) a system of multitiered supports is a promising approach to using multiple assessments to inform instruction of emergent bilingual students. In the next chapter, we delve more deeply into additional information that educators can gather and consider to ensure that their assessment and instruction align seamlessly with emergent bilingual students' needs in culturally and linguistically sustaining ways.

CHAPTER 3

Going Beyond Skills
Learning about Students' Cultural and Affective Resources

The students in Ms. Carl's second-grade classroom vary in their English language proficiency: some are newcomers to the country, while others were born in the large urban area where the school was located. All 28 students speak Somali as their first language. Each day, Mr. Abdirahman, one of the Somali American educational assistants, came into the classroom during the literacy block to support the students. He led small groups to reinforce instruction, worked individually with students, or clarified concepts in Somali when the newcomer students needed help. At the end of the literacy block when the students went to recess, he and Ms. Carl worked together to plan instruction for the next day and talk about students' progress.

One day, Ms. Carl and Mr. Abdirahman were finishing up a series of lessons that focused on letter writing. While the students were gathered on the classroom rug, Ms. Carl introduced the final assessment of the letter writing unit.

"Today we will finish our letter writing unit by writing a thank-you letter for a birthday party. To start thinking about letters, let's get some ideas out: When is the last time that you wrote a thank-you letter to someone? Think for a moment and turn to your partner and tell him or her the last time that you wrote a thank-you letter to someone."

Students took the opportunity to talk to their partners for the time allotted, and the teacher called the students back together to share: "Ok, who can tell me the last time they wrote a thank-you letter?"

No response.

Ms. Carl waited.

Then, Ms. Carl wondered out loud to the class, "You mean no one here has ever written a thank-you letter? What about for your birthday? OK. Usually, at a birthday party you get lots of gifts. It's polite to thank the people who came to your birthday party and tell them you appreciate the gifts they brought you."

She continued her lesson by allowing the students to talk. "So, let me give you some think time. Think of a time you had a birthday party and people brought you gifts. What did they bring you? Who came to your party? Let's do a Turn and Talk. I'd like you to turn to your partner and tell your partner about the last time you had a birthday party."

As before, students took the time to talk to each other, but no one talked about a birthday party.

With a surprised look, Ms. Carl decided to use an example of her own. "All right, let's just pretend that you got a favorite toy from your aunt and uncle. I'll show you how to write a thank-you letter to your aunt and uncle who came to your birthday party and gave you a toy."

After the students left for recess that day, Mr. Abdirahman and Ms. Carl talked about the writing lesson. Ms. Carl shared with Mr. Abdirahman, "I was so surprised I didn't hear any examples about birthday parties in the writing lesson today. Are the students in our classroom accustomed to having birthday parties?"

"No, celebrating a birthday is not part of our culture." We celebrate other important events with giving gifts, but we generally don't celebrate birthdays. I would guess that none of our students have had a birthday party."

Learning about who students are is one of the most powerful tools that educators can employ to truly improve instruction and assessment for students. If Ms. Carl had known more about the culture and practices of her Somali students, she may have been able to tap into a topic of writing that more fully engaged them.

What is important for educators to know about their students? How does knowing about them help educators better plan language and literacy assessments? Why is it that knowing about students and connecting with them is so crucial to their well-being and academic progress? The title of this chapter, "Going Beyond Skills," refers to the important work that educators can do that will extend their understanding of students' language and literacy capacities beyond the reading and writing skills that are traditional indicators of progress. As described in Chapter 1, students bring diverse experiences, cultural backgrounds, and linguistic resources to school. Increasingly, students are bilingual or multilingual or have skills in varying their language use, depending on the setting or company. This reality offers educators a great opportunity to enhance their teaching practices so that they represent the diversity of all of their students. In this chapter, we describe ways that educators can gather information about students' cultural, linguistic, and affective resources, and use these resources to inform their assessment practices.

In the first part of the chapter we describe teaching frameworks that encourage teachers to support and sustain students' culture and language. We discuss how to get to know students, the resources that students bring, and the ways in which their resources might show up in everyday classroom moments. Then we discuss how the affective domain of motivation may influence students' language and literacy assessment. Finally, we suggest ideas for getting to know students through their families and communities.

FOUNDATIONAL IDEAS

The myriad languages and cultures that are part of students' backgrounds are strengths for developing a positive identity. Students' languages and cultures hold the potential for new learning in the classroom. Regardless of their cultural backgrounds and whether they speak one or more languages, all students have perspectives and experiences that are assets to learning. **Asset-based pedagogies** seek to use the languages and cultures of students as avenues for learning. There are several important asset-based pedagogies that educators use in their curriculum and instruction to draw on students' cultural and linguistic knowledge.

Asset-Based Pedagogies and Assessment

In order to fully understand what multilingual students are able to do, language and literacy assessment practices for emergent bilinguals should align with the asset-based approach of **culturally sustaining pedagogies** (**CSP**; Paris & Alim, 2017). The goal of CSP is to support practices that "perpetuate and foster—to sustain" students' multilingualism and multiculturalism (Paris & Alim, 2014, p. 88). This means that students are encouraged to use, develop, and hold onto their home languages and cultural practices even as they learn new ways of being at school.

As they pertain to assessment, fostering and sustaining multilingualism may include utilizing types of assessments that show educators the diversity of knowledge that students have. For example, Gottlieb (2016) suggests engaging in assessments that use real-life tasks that connect to students' experiences and interests.

Two other prominent asset-based pedagogies are *culturally relevant* and *culturally responsive* teaching. Ladson-Billings (1995) uses three criteria to define culturally relevant pedagogy: "a) students must experience academic success, b) students must develop and/or maintain cultural competence, and c) students must develop a critical consciousness through which they challenge the status quo of the current social order" (p. 160). Gay (2010) defines culturally responsive teaching as "using the cultural knowledge, prior experiences, frames of reference, and performance styles of diverse students to make learning encounters more relevant to and effective for them" (p. 31). Educators who engage in culturally responsive teaching work to eliminate a deficit perspective of students and communities and seek ways to analyze curriculum so that deficit perspectives do not persist (Gay, 2013). Gottlieb (2016) suggests that to create culturally and linguistically responsive assessment practices, educators can draw on diverse perspectives when planning instruction, administering assessments, and interpreting data.

One asset-based pedagogy that sets forth specific ways to build on multilingualism is *linguistically responsive teaching*. Lucas, Villegas, and Freedson-Gonzalez (2008, p. 366) define linguistically responsive teaching as an approach that encourages educators to become knowledgeable about linguistically diverse students in three ways.

1. Become familiar with students' linguistic and academic backgrounds.
2. Understand the language demands inherent in the learning tasks that students are expected to carry out in class.
3. Develop skills for using appropriate scaffolding so that EL students can participate successfully in those tasks.

The first component of this definition, that educators become familiar with students' linguistic and academic backgrounds, suggests that educators get to know their students' first language and, depending on the age of the student, obtain information about his or her previous education (see Figure 3.1 for ideas for learning about students' language backgrounds).

Linguistically responsive teaching also includes having a deeper understanding of the role that language plays in student identity (Lucas & Villegas, 2013). The languages that students speak are a part of who they are and how they see themselves.

Finding out about a student's language background

- **Review the home-language survey.** When students enroll in schools, family members fill out a home-language survey that prompts them to provide information about languages spoken in the home. This survey is used as a screening tool to begin to determine if a student may qualify for ELL services. Most home-language surveys ask questions such as: What language(s) is (are) spoken in your home? Which language did your child learn first? Which language does your child use most frequently at home? In which language do you most frequently speak to your child? In what language would you prefer to get information from the school? (*www2.ed.gov/about/offices/list/oela/english-learner-toolkit/chap1.pdf*)
- **Review English language proficiency levels.** Once educators (usually EL specialists) identify that students may benefit from EL services based on the answers of the home-language survey, they administer an assessment that determines a student's English proficiency level in the following areas: reading, writing, speaking, and listening. An assessment is given on a yearly basis to determine English language proficiencies. All educators (i.e., general education, special education, reading specialists) who teach multilingual students can benefit from reviewing students' English language and literacy proficiency levels. Chapter 4 features more information about proficiency levels.

Learning about languages spoken in the classroom and school

- **Learn about language through taking a class or reviewing online resources.** If students speak a language that educators are unfamiliar with, it is a worthwhile endeavor to learn about the language. Educators can take classes online. There are free online learning websites that teach languages. There are also online resources that provide information about various languages. For example, Omniglot (*www.omniglot.com/index.htm*) is an online encyclopedia of writing systems and languages.
- **Learn about the language from someone who speaks the language.** Some schools or districts hire *community liaisons* who serve as a bridge between the community and the school. Community liaisons may translate for school conferences or provide learning opportunities for teachers and families. Other educators in the school may also speak the same languages as students in the school.

FIGURE 3.1. Learning about students' languages.

Linguistically responsive educators who have an understanding that language is foundational to identity have a sociolinguistic consciousness, "an understanding that language, culture, and identity are deeply connected and understand that language diversity is worthy of cultivating" (Lucas & Villegas, 2013, p. 101). These belief systems are necessary if educators are to develop the expertise and practices that draw on and support students' rich cultural and linguistic knowledge.

One example of linguistically responsive teaching that is also considered a culturally sustaining practice (Valdés, 2017) is the practice of translanguaging (García, 2009). We introduced translanguaging in Chapter 1 as the purposeful practice of using two or more languages and linguistic resources to accomplish literacy events or tasks. Students who engage in translanguaging are using their linguistic knowledge in all the languages they have at their command. When considering translanguaging and assessment, educators should understand that translanguaging is an asset to the overall understanding and execution of a literacy task or event. García and Kleifgen (2018) point out, "Leveraging translanguaging in assessment is the only way to level the playing field between bilingual and monolingual students, giving bilingual students the opportunity that monolingual children have—to be able to show what they know and can do using all their linguistic resources" (p. 158).

In order to find out what students can do with their linguistic resources, educators should become familiar with the linguistic features of students' languages. Knowledge about students' languages can help educators as they create, administer, and analyze language and literacy assessments. For example, it may be beneficial to know the unique sounds of languages that are different from English when reviewing students' writing and spelling (Helman, 2004). While assessing students' reading using **running records,** a commonly used formative reading assessment (see Chapter 5), educators who are familiar with their students' academic and linguistic backgrounds may be able to notice how students use their first language to read and sound out words in English (Briceño & Klein, 2018; deJong & Harper, 2005).

Funds of Knowledge and Assessment

One of the most foundational understandings in asset-based pedagogies is that students have funds of knowledge (Moll et al., 1992). *Funds of knowledge* "refer to the historically accumulated and culturally developed bodies of knowledge and skills essential for household or individual functioning and well-being" (p. 133). Moll and colleagues (1992) found that students have an important knowledge repertoire and skills from their home and out-of-school experiences, and that they do not arrive in classrooms as blank slates. Examples *may* include knowledge about cultural events, plants and animals, local events and people, family occupations, or caregiving and child care. Educators can use students' funds of knowledge to connect home experiences with the classroom curriculum and instruction. It is worthwhile not only to know about students' funds of knowledge, but also to understand that *using* them can actually improve students' academic success (e.g., Dworin, 2006; Schrodt, Fain, & Hasty, 2015).

Educators who have a strong understanding of students' funds of knowledge can interpret and plan for a variety of assessments that may account for diverse perspectives and out-of-school knowledge. For example, if the reading assessment for comprehension focuses only on the cultural background of white middle-class students, educators may overlook their other students' comprehension abilities owing to their lack of knowledge on the topics being tested. In addition to interpreting assessments, knowing students' funds of knowledge can assist teachers as they plan their own classroom-based assessments (e.g., Cowie, Jones, & Otrel-Cass, 2011).

Windows, Mirrors, and Sliding Doors and Assessment

The asset-based pedagogies we've outlined stand by the claim that students' cultural and linguistic funds of knowledge and identity should be used and maintained through teaching practices. Since teaching materials and resources are a significant part of instruction, it's important for students to see themselves represented in the curriculum materials. Renowned children's literature scholar Rudine Sims Bishop (1990) affirms the notion that students need to see themselves reflected in the curriculum (mirrors), experience the curriculum through which they can see the perspectives of others (windows), and also walk through a door to imagine and become part of another world. Advocates for diversity in children's literature have recognized that there are there are still too few picture books that include the diversity of children represented in classrooms (*www.weneeddiversebooks.org*). Recently, the International Literacy Association (2017) affirmed this concern and published a position statement that described culturally sustaining pedagogies with the metaphor of windows, mirrors, and doors. We believe that the International Literacy Association's (2017) position is relevant for language and literacy assessments. When students take a language or literacy assessment—whether it be to read a passage and answer comprehension questions, or write a short essay to show how they can develop an argument—it is important that aspects of these assessment practices pertain to part of their knowledge. In order to ensure that students have doorways in which to access the world and opportunities, the position statement notes:

> Literacy educators tailor their instruction to accelerate student growth in reading, writing, speaking, and listening. These practices occur daily and are marked by the frequency, intensity, and duration needed to accelerate learning. The academic trajectory of every student is carefully monitored so that literacy educators can respond in a timely fashion, propelling student learning. (p. 3)

Educators can tailor instruction to accelerate student growth by creating assessment practices that leverage student knowledge.

WHAT DO CULTURAL AND LINGUISTIC RESOURCES HAVE TO DO WITH ASSESSMENT?

In order to engage in culturally and linguistically sustaining practices in instruction and assessment, an educator must know where to start. To do so, an educator can inquire about students' resources, skills, and knowledge. Simply stated, a resource is something that people use in order to function effectively. In classrooms, these resources can be tangible items, such as books, writing materials, or anchor charts. Intangible resources that students use in classrooms include background knowledge, identity, and motivation. Students in classrooms use tangible and intangible resources in order to understand what an educator is saying, engage in classroom activities, or communicate with classmates. If educators encourage students to use both tangible and intangible resources, students have a chance to participate more fully in classroom learning. Once educators have a working knowledge of students' resources, they can plan their instruction and assessment to include opportunities for students to incorporate their outside-of-school resources to achieve academic success. Knowing how important these cultural and linguistic resources are for emergent bilinguals begs the question, "Where does an educator look to identify them?"

Literacy Events and Practices

Literacy extends beyond reading and writing and encompasses more than the books students read and the stories students write. A literacy event can involve speaking and listening and can demonstrate the ways people communicate and how they read the world. The concept of *multiliteracies* (New London Group, 1996) broadens the concept of literacy to encompass not only reading and writing, but also visual, digital, technological, spatial, audio, and other multimodal representations of communication. Researchers concerned with the literacies of emergent bilinguals extend this notion by stating that *pluriliteracies* (García, Bartlett, & Kleifgen, 2007) include all of these forms of communication, whereas multiliteracies can be in two or more languages. Encouraging the development and assessment of pluriliteracies gives students a variety of ways to show mastery of academic content.

For example, one literacy standard in kindergarten in the area of speaking and listening is "Ask and answer questions in order to seek help, get information, or clarify something that is not understood" (CCSS.ELA-LITERACY.SL.K.3). This standard is a potential avenue for students to use their out-of-school knowledge to engage in a literacy practice of discussion with a kindergarten peer. An educator might ask students to "teach a friend to do something that you know how to do at home." This type of purposeful assessment could reveal students' interests and abilities and boost their confidence. Moreover, it could be an opportunity for students to use translanguaging to convey their messages. Other literacy practices and events that happen both in school and in out-of-school contexts in elementary settings may include:

- Storytelling
- Dramatic play
- Chanting, singing, rapping, and creating new words to songs or poems
- Using and describing visuals and photos
- Explaining games or activities
- Giving directions
- Recommending books at the library

- Teaching a friend how to do something
- Switching among various languages or dialects (translanguaging) orally or in writing
- Viewing and discussing

With an expanded view of literacy, a whole host of meaning-making events and practices become available to educators as they seek to understand students' cultural, linguistic, and affective resources. When educators partner students' funds of knowledge with an expanded view of literacy, they can look beyond traditional academic activities and assessments (e.g., worksheets, quizzes) to find indicators of their knowledge. These suggestions are not designed to ignore important academic skills, but to encourage educators to gather information with an asset-based mindset to be better informed about students' capabilities. With expanded notions of literacy, there are more ways of looking for what students *can* do.

Cultural Resources

Culture represents the ways of being and knowing and ways of talking and doing that each student carries into the classroom. Culture is a complex web that involves stories about family, history, religion, nationality, and geography. Cultural resources can be out-of-school informal knowledge that is accumulated through lived experiences. Culture is manifested in practices, beliefs, and values, and is also represented in artifacts and objects.

Culture is inextricably linked to language and literacy. Many cultural practices are present in speaking, reading, writing, and listening. Narrative practices, such as storytelling and singing, are some of the ways that families and communities express their culture. In classrooms, students who are able to tap into these cultural resources can make connections between in-school and out-of-school knowledge. For example, literacy standards outline the importance of students learning how to read and retell events that happen in narratives as well as how to write narratives. Educators can help students to make direct connections to their cultural knowledge; students call upon their experiences to create narratives, read narratives, and ask questions.

Educators can use students' cultural resources during language and literacy assessment. In the classroom vignette that opened this chapter, we shared an example in which Ms. Carl did not have a firm understanding of her students' culture and experiences. Ms. Carl could have used students' knowledge of gift giving in their culture to find an appropriate opportunity to write thank-you notes. As much as tangible tools, such as books and writing materials or other curricular resources, help students make sense of new material at school, students' cultural resources also serve as an important conduit to understanding.

Linguistic Resources

Linguistics is the study of language. As outlined in Chapter 1, it includes the following components:

- Formation of sounds (phonology)
- Parts of words (morphology)
- Meaning of words (semantics)
- Putting words together to make sense (syntax)
- Appropriate usage of words in context (pragmatics)

Students who are multilingual can often apply aspects of one language to new language learning. For example, students use what they know about sounds in their first language to sound out words in another language. As we described in Chapter 1, this theory is referred to as the interdependence hypothesis (Cummins, 1979), in which students' knowledge of their first language provides insight into learning the new language. One example is derived from research conducted by Helman et al. (2016). In their research they describe a student, Tong, who used knowledge of his first language, Hmong, to sound out words in English. Since Hmong is a tonal language with more frequent nasal sounds such as /n/ or /ng/, Tong used the phonology of his first language to spell the word *dream* as *ging*. Although this spelling of *dream* was not correct, it illustrates his ability to progress from sounding out words to writing them in a new language. Tong's teachers had a working knowledge of the sounds and structures of the Hmong language, which allowed them to see that what Tong was doing was using his linguistic resources in a writing task. This example shows how getting to know a student's language could help an educator analyze assessments. When educators analyze assessments, they ask themselves, "Is what I am doing working? Is the child able to show what they know?" In Tong's case, the answer is, "Yes!" Tong did learn how to move from sound to print. Now, based on data from his writing, the educators know that they should work on explicitly teaching difficult sounds in English with focused instruction. More examples of how students use the sounds they know in their first language to read and write words in English are presented in Chapter 5.

In the next section we highlight other opportunities that teachers can use to look for cultural and linguistic resources as they enact assessment practices that utilize what students bring to the classroom.

Cultural and Linguistic Resources Found in Classroom Moments

There are many opportunities to find and draw upon students' cultural and linguistic resources. Helman et al. (2016) suggest that educators find out about students' resources and connect their funds of knowledge to the language and literacy curricula. Once educators know about students' resources, they can be used as they plan instruction and assessment. Read the following dialogue that demonstrates how a teacher uses a student's cultural knowledge to plan an informal classroom-based assessment. The story takes place in Ms. Fredell's third-grade classroom on a Monday morning as students are walking in and getting their things situated for the day.

Ms. Fredell: Angelita! Good morning! How was your weekend? What did you do?

Angelita: This weekend I got to make tamales with my grandma! We made hundreds of them for our church celebration of La Posada!

MS. FREDELL: Wow, that's a lot of tamales. Did your grandma teach you how to make them?

ANGELITA: Yes, she showed me how to measure the masa and cook the pork and roll them up so we could steam them. They were so delicious!

MS. FREDELL: Cool! Do you think you could teach someone else how to make them? Maybe even write out a recipe or instructions for how to do it?

ANGELITA: Sure! I could try. I might have to ask my grandma to help me.

MS. FREDELL: Well, today during writer's workshop we will be finishing our unit on writing informational texts. Do you think you could write a text about making tamales for your final writing piece?

In this example, a third-grade student was excited to talk to her teacher about her weekend when she arrived at school. The student shared that she and her grandmother spent time over the weekend cooking a special meal that they brought to a family cultural celebration. She discussed what they cooked and offered to write instructions for making the dish. As the teacher listened to this story, she started making connections to the standard that they had been working on: "Write informative/explanatory texts to examine a topic and convey ideas and information clearly" (CCSS.ELA-LITERACY.W.3.2). The teacher encouraged the student to use that story in a final assessment of the standard.

The highlighted experience between the student and her grandmother is a rich opportunity to connect reading, writing, speaking, and listening in the classroom. Potential academic learning in the areas of reading, speaking, and listening include recipe reading, sequencing of events, vocabulary building using descriptive adjectives related to the aromas and touch of food, procedural language involving consequences ("If you cook this too long, then . . ."), and more. In connection with assessment, there are literacy standards that can be aligned as well—for example, "Write narratives to develop real or imagined experiences or events using effective technique, descriptive details, and clear event sequences" (CCSS.ELA-LITERACY.W.3.3). Ms. Fredell leveraged Angelita's cultural knowledge to demonstrate mastery of this standard.

Taking a step back to get to know students' experiences highlights the knowledge and skills they are acquiring at home. Educators can also tap into these experiences at school. Figure 3.2 is a collection of classroom examples in which educators ask questions to find out more about students' resources. We suggest literacy standards that can be connected. An educator can informally ask these questions as they get to know students at the beginning of the year, or they can keep these kinds of questions in mind as they introduce specific language arts objectives and standards. When the time comes to assess students' knowledge of standards, educators can use this background information as they ask them to independently speak, read, or write for assessment purposes.

To gain an understanding of students and who they are, educators can work toward including these moments of sharing and talking into the content of their classrooms. Students must have opportunities throughout the day to share what they know and who they are. Classroom routines, such as sharing circles or morning meetings,

Topics	Example language and literacy standard connections	Example assessments of literacy standards
What kinds of stories are told in your family?	Compare and contrast two or more versions of the same story by different authors or from different cultures.	Ask students to complete a Venn diagram or other graphic organizer.
What kinds of outings do you go to on the weekends? Do you get to help your family go to the grocery store? Or to other stores?	Describe people, places, things, and events with relevant details, expressing ideas and feelings clearly.	Listen to students describe people, places, and things while using an oral language rubric.
Do you have any special recipes for cooking? Or how do you take care of someone when he or she is sick?	Reading and writing informational/explanatory texts.	Write a story or develop a recipe and include important details for explaining your topic. Create a short video explaining how to make a dish that your family makes at home.

FIGURE 3.2. Getting to know students' cultural and linguistic resources and links to assessment.

allow students to have moments to talk and respond to others in a purposeful and positive manner. These moments can give educators insights into students' cultural and linguistic resources.

WHAT DO AFFECTIVE RESOURCES HAVE TO DO WITH ASSESSMENT?

The word *affective* refers to feelings, attitudes, and motivations. Affective resources in literacy are the students' feelings, attitudes, and motivations that students bring to literacy events and practices. Each of these components is complex and interconnected. Students' feelings about a particular topic may be related to their attitudes and motivations. For example, a student who has fond feelings about a specific video game, let's say Minecraft, may have a positive attitude when it comes to reading a book about a character who plays Minecraft. The student's motivation to finish the book could be influenced by her positive feelings and attitudes. The student may be more motivated to read and write in the final assessment if she is allowed to write about the character who plays Minecraft. Educators understand that these feelings, attitudes, and motivations are resources, because they are tools that students can use to successfully engage in literacy practices. Educators who understand their students' affective resources can provide specific reading materials, resources, and individualized support. Knowing a student's affective resources can also help to anticipate difficulties and obstacles in instruction and assessments.

Recent research related to motivation in reading makes connections to the affective domain (Conradi, Jang, & McKenna, 2014) and highlights recommendations in the area of reading assessment (McKenna & Stahl, 2015). Some aspects of the affective domain include motivation, interest, self-concept, and self-efficacy. In Figure 3.3, we present questions adapted from the Burke Reading Interview (Goodman, Watson, & Burke, 1987) and the Reading Interview for Linguistically Diverse Students (Kim & Goodman, 2011) that can be asked of students to capture some ideas about their affective resources. In Figure 3.4 we present several questions that educators can ask themselves as they consider their assessment practices.

Motivation

Educators generally think of motivated readers as those who read and engage in reading tasks quite easily. Typically, motivated readers read for pleasure and find purpose in reading. When students are engaged and motivated in their reading, they are more likely to understand what they read. Students who are given choices in what they read increase their effort and commitment to reading (Guthrie et al., 2004). In fact, students' motivation to read is one of the most important factors in their reading achievement, especially in their ability to comprehend (Guthrie & Wigfield, 2000).

Motivation is multifaceted (Guthrie et al., 2007; Wigfield & Guthrie, 2000), which means that there are several factors that make up the construct of motivation. Among the components are interest, self-concept, and self-efficacy. Educators have the ability to encourage students and plan instruction and assessments that align with any of the facets of motivation that we describe in the next sections. For example, one common assessment that educators give to students is a running record (see Chapter 5 for how to conduct a running record). In a running record, a student reads a portion of a text (or a whole text) aloud while an educator listens and records reading behaviors. Before conducting a running record, an educator might say, "I would like to listen to you read. Would you like to choose a book that you like to read to me?"

Affective component of literacy	Guiding questions
Motivation	When do you read? What makes you want to read? Do you prefer reading in English or in another language?
Interest	What do you like reading about? What do you like writing about? What do you like talking about with your friends? What do you like to read about in your home language?
Self-concept	Do you like reading and writing? Can you think of someone (in either English or in your home language) who is a good writer? A good reader? A good storyteller? Would you like to be like that person? In what ways?
Self-efficacy	What do you do when you come to a word you don't know? What do you do when you read something and you don't understand it?

FIGURE 3.3. Questions to ask multilingual students that help identify affective resources.

Affective component of literacy	Guiding questions
Motivation	Is the assessment I am using part of something that motivates students? Do students know the reason for the assessment? Have they been partners in the creation of the assessment?
Interest	Do the assessments I use reflect the interests and cultural knowledge of my students? If not, can I add to them or modify them?
Self-concept	In what ways do my students' responses to assessment reflect their self-concepts? If a student's self-concept is negative, is there anything that I can do to enhance the positive?
Self-efficacy	What are some ways that I can build student self-efficacy during assessments?

FIGURE 3.4. Reflective questions for educators regarding students' affective resources and assessment.

Interest

When considering whether to take into account students' *interests* in conducting assessments, the first step is for educators to ask students to describe their interests either inside or outside of school (see Figure 3.3 for questions to ask students in an *interest interview*). Educators should be careful not to assume to know what students are interested in based on their cultural background. Each person's ways of being in the world flow from his or her culture, but take shape in one's own unique and individual stories. Simply because students emigrated from a specific country or region or belong to a cultural or religious group does not mean that they want to read books related to certain topics. There are likely to be many topics that an individual student might be knowledgeable about or interested in. It is the role of the educator to discover these interests and give students opportunities throughout their school day to read, write, and talk about them.

After conducting interest interviews, educators can tailor some assessments that draw on students' interests. For example, one literacy standard that appears across elementary grades focuses on elements of constructing and writing an opinion: "Write opinion pieces on topics or texts, supporting a point of view with reasons" (CCSS.ELA-LITERACY.W.3.1). Students' interests could be potential topics for opinion writing. Informal assessments of opinion writing, such as graphic organizers or drafts of writing, can indicate students' understanding of how to formulate an opinion. Students are more likely to write more reasons that support their point of view relating to the topics of interest.

Self-Concept

An individual's overall self-perception as a reader, including one's sense of competence, is a part of one's personal identity (Chapman & Tunmer, 1995). This aspect of the affective domain is especially important because it may affect performance on assessments. If students have low self-concepts regarding reading and writing, chances are that they may feel similarly about reading and writing assessments. A student's self-concept can be revealed when he says things like, "I'm bad at taking tests" or "I'm not a good reader." These are invitations to an educator to help build a positive self-concept. Before administering an assessment, a teacher might reassure a student of his strengths. For example, "One thing I know you can do is identify the main idea in reading a paragraph. That is one thing that makes you a good reader."

Recently, Protacio and Jang (2016) studied EL educators and their beliefs about the reading motivation of their EL students. The EL educators in the study believed that self-concept was especially important to ELs' reading motivation. Their EL students saw a connection between their English proficiency and their reading abilities. When they felt that their English proficiency was not strong, their motivation to read was affected. The EL teachers understood that this correlation was a constant challenge that could influence student's self-concept. This is important to take into consideration as students are engaged in an assessment. If educators sense that students have a negative self-concept, they should work toward improving it by being positive and explicit about students' capabilities.

Self-Efficacy

Do students believe they can be successful in a given task? Self-efficacy relates to the belief that one has the ability to achieve (Conradi et al., 2014). In relationship to assessment, students may lack the confidence to answer questions or show what they know. This hesitancy may affect how they perform academically. When students succeed in reading tasks, they start to believe that they can achieve, and this self-efficacy may help them to continue to succeed (e.g., Bandura, 1977; Schöber, Schütte, Köller, McElvany, & Gebauer, 2018).

Educators can capitalize on students' interests in building motivation for reading and writing and engaging in other literacy events. Moreover, when students read more books that they are interested in and have a purpose for reading, they become stronger readers (Guthrie, 2004).

BUILDING SELF-EFFICACY IN LITERACY TASKS

Self-efficacy can be nurtured throughout the day at school. During instruction and guided practice, educators get to know what their students are capable of. Educators who use specific feedback strategies to reinforce what students do correctly can help foster self-efficacy. For example, an educator might guide a student through sounding out a word he doesn't know by using a "chunking" strategy. When the student uses this strategy correctly, it's important to not just say, "good job!" but to provide more specific feedback. Comments that highlight what a student has done well can contribute to the student's self-efficacy overall and also reinforce the literacy practice that is being mastered. For example, "Good job, Mohamed, you used the chunking strategy to look at the word parts and it helped you to sound out the whole word."

CALLING UPON FAMILIES AND COMMUNITIES

Creating and sustaining relationships with families can be pivotal for student success at school (Jeynes, 2012). Families and communities are home to students' cultural and linguistic knowledge. Reaching out and letting families know that they are welcomed and valued in the school is one way that educators can start building bridges. Epstein and Sheldon (2006) suggest that we reconsider the notion of parental *involvement* and replace it with the notion of a *partnership* among families, communities, and schools. In partnerships, schools learn from families and communities, and there is a shared responsibility between home and school (Borrello, 2016). García and Kleifgen (2018) state, "Parents of emergent bilinguals have a great deal to teach teachers about knowledge and skills that originate in their household that can, and should, be translated into academic success in schools" (p. 139).

Finding Out about Families and Communities

One trusted approach to finding out about students' cultural, linguistic, and affective resources is through family interviews and/or home visits. Educators interested in tapping into their students' funds of knowledge conduct home visits and interviews with a specific purpose—to learn from their students' families and communities. Although home visits are sometimes used to teach families about a school and what goes on in the classroom, the funds of knowledge perspective acknowledges that a home visit is a useful approach for increasing educator knowledge (Moll et al., 1992). The goal of building relationships with families and communities in this approach is one of reciprocity and of encouraging trust (Gonzalez et al., 1995). When educators approach home visits with the purpose of learning about students' resources (what students have), they dispel notions that families have insufficient knowledge (what students lack) to support school.

Partnering home visits with reflective practices is one way that educators can further learn from families and communities and apply their learning to the classroom. Gonzalez et al. (1995) suggest that after participating in home visits, educator study groups should meet and reflect on what they observed and envision ways to tailor classroom practices so that they incorporate what was learned from the home environment (see Figure 3.5).

Using the School Community

There are many advocates for emergent bilingual students in schools. EL specialists can often help find out more about individual students. When students enroll in schools, their families fill out a **home-language survey,** and EL specialists usually have access to this information (see Figure 3.1). These surveys are good sources of information for educators about what languages are represented in classrooms or in the entire school. EL specialists can also be part of educator study groups that discuss the progress of emergent bilinguals. Educators can create a *multiperspective team*

- Conduct home visits with an asset-based approach, then meet in a teacher study group to discuss, reflect, and inform instruction (Gonzalez et al., 1995).
- Talk with school staff who have similar cultural and linguistic backgrounds as the students in the classroom.
- Attend community events in the areas where students live.
- Read local newspapers.
- Invite families and communities to share stories in the classroom.
- Learn some of the characteristics of the languages that students speak.
- Build relationships with community-based organizations.

FIGURE 3.5. Ways to find out about students' cultural, linguistic, and affective resources with families and communities.

(WIDA, 2013) of school personnel with various expertise areas related to multilingual students. Multiperspective teams can include, but are not limited to, general education educators, special education educators, EL educators, cultural liaisons, administrators, school psychologists, speech pathologists, and others. The perspectives of this varied group can bring to the surface a greater awareness of how to ensure learners' success. Multiperspective teams are especially important when emergent bilinguals are the focus of conversations about reading interventions, special education, and other services. In Chapter 8, we discuss ways in which these teams can help evaluate language and literacy assessment data in making instructional decisions for emergent bilinguals.

ALIGNING LINGUISTIC AND CULTURAL RESOURCES WITH INSTRUCTION

Educators can create instructional practices that leverage students' funds of knowledge in language and literacy activities. By accessing students' resources through the methods we've described (interviews, relationship building, etc.), educators can include approaches that allow students improved access to language and literacy. There are several instructional approaches for culturally relevant and sustaining pedagogies that we share at the end of each chapter. These examples are just a small sample; we are not able to name them all (there are enough to fill a whole volume!), but we now share a few that are noteworthy.

One educational researcher who builds on connecting culture with the classroom is Katherine Au (1980). In her work with native Hawaiian students, Au uses a cultural speech event called "talk story." One part of the conversational structure of talk story includes more than one person talking at a time or a variety of people take turns leading the conversation. Au (1980) studied how a teacher could use talk story in a reading lesson. Au found that the Hawaiian students who used talk story in reading lessons fared better on reading achievement tests than those students who did not have the opportunity to use their cultural structures of conversation during literacy events at school. By means of talk story, Au and a colleague facilitated academic conversations through an approach that was familiar to their students, matching instruction to students' backgrounds.

Another way to bring family literacy practices and resources into the classroom is to invite students to tell and write stories using their language of choice. Students can tell and write stories about how they got their names (Nash, Panther, & Arce-Boardman, 2018), about family memories (Dworin, 2006), or any other engaging writing activity (Lee & Handsfield, 2018). Educators who facilitate students' text creations in the languages that students choose send a message to students that all of their language resources are valued and honored.

SUMMARY

When educators leverage the cultural, linguistic, and affective resources of emergent bilinguals to access language and literacy, they work toward helping students achieve academic success. In this chapter, we discussed asset-based pedagogies that include designing assessments that use students' diverse cultural and linguistic knowledge. Doing so enables educators to see students' knowledge as a resource for learning, not as a barrier.

Educators can learn about students' cultural and linguistic resources through approaches such as conducting interviews, visiting students in their homes and communities, and learning about the languages that are represented by students in the classroom. In the classroom vignette described at the beginning of the chapter, Ms. Carl and Mr. Abdirahman used their teaching partnership to discuss the cultural background of students. As Ms. Carl becomes more knowledgeable about the culture and language of her students, she can integrate this knowledge into planning, teaching, and assessing. Educators can also leverage students' interests and motivations—the affective resources that students have—to design literacy instruction and assessment. Finally, we considered the importance of building and promoting family, school, and community partnerships as a trusted approach to furthering academic achievement.

CHAPTER 4

The Growth of Oral Language

Mr. Rigby, one of two EL specialist teachers at Riverview Elementary, uses his knowledge of English language development to collaborate with his colleagues to plan instruction and assessment for the emergent bilinguals at the school. Part of his job includes administering the annual standardized language assessments to students who are classified as ELs to document their progress toward full proficiency, conducting English language development lessons with small groups of emergent bilinguals in both push-in and pull-out settings, consulting with teachers about how to best differentiate their instruction for students at various levels of English proficiency, and coplanning and coteaching lessons with the general education teachers. Mr. Rigby also sees himself as an advocate for informing students' families about language-learning aspects of schooling and forging strong school–home relationships.

For one 6-week period in the late winter, Mr. Rigby spends most of his time at Riverview assessing the school's emergent bilingual students on the standardized assessment of yearly progress in English. Times vary for administration, but Mr. Rigby finds that he spends around 15 minutes per student for the speaking component of the test, and also conducts group-administered sessions on reading, writing, and listening. When he added up the time preparing for the test, administering it, completing the pre- and post-paperwork, and implementing other logistics, Mr. Rigby feels that he has given a third of his teaching year to the assessment. Nonetheless, he feels that this allocation of resources is worth it, because it is important to monitor the long-term growth of English for emergent bilingual students. The information he gets from the standardized assessment, even though it is not received until the fall of the following school year, helps him plan for his English language development (ELD) groups, identify students who may not be making sufficient progress, and in consulting with teachers, school leaders, and students' families. Each fall, Mr. Rigby provides the results of the standardized language proficiency test to the teachers of students who took the test.

He assumed that teachers would also find the data informative and that it would help them tailor their instruction to better meet students' learning needs.

Recently, however, Mr. Rigby was disheartened by something he heard in a child-study team meeting. As the team discussed the progress of a specific student, it became clear that the teacher who was participating in the meeting had not consulted the standardized language assessment scores for her students and didn't realize they might be helpful for her teaching. Most important, the teacher did not know exactly what the proficiency scores on the test meant, nor how they might influence the type of classroom instruction that could support students' success. Although Mr. Rigby knows how busy the daily life of a classroom teacher is, he began to wonder if all the time and resources put into administering the test was worth it. He wondered how he might help teachers who aren't EL specialists to do more than file the results in their cabinets. How could this valuable information from the yearly assessment, as well as the year-to-year data indicating progress in English, be better integrated into the teaching practices of the staff at Riverview Elementary?

This scenario highlights a common tension in educational assessment: What is the right balance between the time spent assessing students and the time spent teaching them? And how do educators ensure that assessment results inform instruction in systematic ways? Mr. Rigby was able to make the most of the assessment data highlighting students' yearly progress because he was deeply involved in the data collection process and had strong background knowledge in language development. Unfortunately, because general education teachers did not have the same opportunities to dig into the data and uncover what it revealed, the assessment results were only helping those who were already "in the know." In this chapter, we discuss formal and informal assessments of English language development, and how teachers, EL specialists, reading specialists, and school leaders can better understand and use them to support emergent bilinguals' literacy growth.

Any discussion about assessment and instruction with emergent bilinguals needs to take into account students' current development of language as well as the language resources they have at their command in particular educational settings. All literacy learning involves a symbiotic relationship between the oral language knowledge a person has and the ability to decode (or encode) that language from (or into) text. What makes this process different for bilinguals is that they have more than one oral language system to work with, and these systems inform and interact with each other. To reconnect with our analogy of reading as a smoothly operating automobile, a bilingual person is something of a hybrid—there are multiple systems contributing to the regular functioning of the engine. In the same way that a hybrid engine has the potential to be more efficient on the highway, a reader who is bilingual has the potential to streamline her decoding of text by calling upon more approaches, structures, and vocabulary when using her linguistic and literate knowledge.

As we described in Chapter 1, learning language is a developmental process, whether it is one's first, second, or sixth language. With each new language a person learns, the process becomes more streamlined because the learner has additional background knowledge *about* language learning and how languages work in general.

Learners move from a period of little oral understanding or communication of the new language to a period of basic understanding and interpersonal communication (Cummins, 1979), to being able to increasingly engage with more decontextualized academic content, especially when language supports are provided, to a well-developed capacity to use academic language with similar supports used by a native speaker. Later in this chapter we share the descriptors used by several standardized language assessments that highlight this developmental continuum.

Despite the entwined nature of language learning and literacy development, at times emergent bilingual students are given assessments without consideration of their language competencies, as if the two strands of development can be separated. In reality, even basic word recognition and decoding processes rely in part on language knowledge. For example, the number of words students know in English affects the ease with which they develop an awareness of sounds (phonemic awareness) or letter–sound correspondences (phonics) (Walley, 1993). More advanced literate processes, such as reading comprehension or composing text, are even more reflective of language knowledge. Still, educators may not look deeply enough into their students' assessment results to connect the dots back to the continuum of language development. If emergent bilingual students are to be successful at school, they need to have the language that will help them understand and engage with academic content. For this reason, every educator needs to consider their students' language development, based on formal and informal assessments, when designing meaningful and comprehensible instruction.

In this chapter, we hone in on English language development—what it consists of, how it is assessed both formally and informally, what language assessment results mean for instructional practice, and how language development emerges and impacts all areas of the language arts. Following our discussion of the assessment of English language development, we share examples of literacy activities that will help teachers advance students' language capabilities, whether they are at a beginner or more-advanced level. We begin with several conceptual ideas that undergird this topic.

FOUNDATIONAL IDEAS

It is important to uncover the foundational assumptions that often go hidden in the day-to-day workings of school settings, so that students are not unintentionally undervalued or underserved. For example, as we put forward early in this book, when students are labeled "English learners" or "limited English proficient" they are positioned according to what they lack academically, rather than by what language knowledge they bring to school (*deficit based*), and these labels have real-world consequences, as noted in Chapter 3. If students are described instead as "multilingual" or "emergent bilingual," they have the potential for exceptionality (asset based). As described in Chapters 1 and 3, when educators uncover and explore the language resources that students bring to school, the *linguistic interdependence* between languages—how they use various structures and processes to accomplish similar goals (Cummins,

1979)—can be acknowledged and put to use. Then, the home language is recognized as contributing to a complex *communicative repertoire* that aids students in learning and interacting with others (García, 2009).

Emergent bilinguals are often given the message that their language resources other than academic English are not welcome or important in school. Imagine if they received a different message, one that invites all students to strive to become literate bilinguals and highlights the positive cognitive and social outcomes of being bilingual. Many researchers have outlined the *bilingual advantage* as including:

- Maintaining relationships with extended family members.
- Opening doors to new people and ideas.
- Gaining cognitive flexibility and increased executive functioning.
- Increasing one's knowledge about the world and its populations.
- Becoming more knowledgeable about languages in general (metalinguistic skills).
- Learning additional languages more easily.
- Being more marketable in the job pool.
  (Bialystok, 2017; Rodríguez, Carrasquillo, & Lee, 2014)

Bilingual people are more than two monolingual speakers residing in the same body. In juggling multiple language systems, they gain practice in purposely meshing and switching among tasks, interacting with a greater range of people and cultural systems, and comparing how languages operate. Shouldn't educators want these benefits for every student? If so, a first step is to validate the progress that emergent bilinguals who come to school with a home language other than English have already made on the path toward bilingualism.

In setting the stage for our discussion about the growth of oral language, another important notion to keep in mind is that that the oral and written language learning needed to be successful in schooling goes beyond having basic interpersonal communication skills and involves the ability to understand and use complex academic language—individual words as well as sentence- and text-level structures (Cummins, 1991; Nagy & Townsend, 2012). Figure 4.1 provides a simple overview of what is meant by academic language. We explore this topic in depth in Chapter 6.

Many students learn the language of social interactions relatively quickly in a new language and can appear to be fairly proficient. However, the language of schooling consists of textbook-type information and is often abstract, technical, and decontextualized. Language learners are likely to be challenged by advanced vocabulary usage, complex grammatical structures, and meaning-changing discourse connectors, as well as dense discourse and opaque themes (Helman, 2012). When educators gauge language proficiency only through surface-level measures, they may not perceive that students need support with the academic language embedded in the curriculum. Students may then become inundated with large amounts of academic language and not receive the additional support they need to learn the material. In Chapter 6 we take a deep dive into assessing academic language as it surfaces within

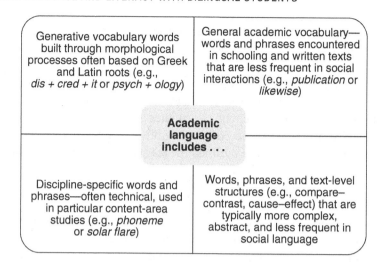

FIGURE 4.1. An overview of academic language.

subject-matter learning in the classroom. In this chapter, we begin with a survey of frequently used standardized language assessments, of how these assessments are used, and what their results tell educators about their students.

PART ONE: THE FORMAL ASSESSMENT OF LANGUAGE AT SCHOOL

The first step in identifying students who may qualify for EL services takes place when they enter school. Typically, the school or district asks the enrolling family to fill out a home-language survey or language-use survey, as described in Chapter 3. In this brief questionnaire, an adult family member is first asked whether the student speaks a language at home other than English. If the answer to this question is "yes," the respondent is asked which languages are spoken, with whom, and in what contexts. A "yes" response on the home-language survey triggers the use of a district-based screening assessment to determine whether the student will be classified as "English learner" or "proficient" in English. Depending on local criteria, students who score under the threshold for fluency in oral English will receive the designation of EL and potentially receive support services and assessments mandated by local and state guidelines if the parents sign consent forms for their child to participate.

The descriptions of language assessments highlighted in the next sections include those designed for students who have been classified as EL in their district and state. Although specific measures and processes vary among states, there are common federal accountability policies that regulate what types of assessments may be used and how often they need to be administered. In the 2016–2017 school year, 39 U.S. states and territories used the WIDA ACCESS test (WIDA Consortium, 2018) to formally assess students' English language progress, whereas several states with the highest population of students identified as ELs (e.g., California, New York, and Texas) used a state-adopted measure. In the next section, we answer some basic questions about language proficiency assessments and their use in K–12 classrooms.

Standardized Language Assessments

As we described in Chapter 2, standardized assessments have typically been developed by researchers or test designers and are implemented using specific, delineated procedures that must be followed. These measures often take into account accumulated data that have been collected about various student populations (i.e., "normed") and show evidence of producing reliable and valid results. In this way, standardized assessments provide a comparison of one student's performance with others within specific age or developmental bands.

Why Are These Assessments Used in Schools?

Current federal regulations require that state accountability systems include measures of English language proficiency for students who have been identified as ELs based on state guidelines (in the manner noted previously). The *Every Student Succeeds Act* (2015) outlines requirements for documenting students' progress in English, sets guidelines for students' entrance into and exit from EL programs, provides greater inclusion of ELs' academic achievement as part of accountability laws, and monitors the number of students who are reclassified out of the EL designation. In order for education agencies to receive Title I funds (provided to schools with high proportions of children from low-income families) or Title III funds (provided to schools to support ELs' achievement goals), these agencies must administer English language proficiency assessments (ELPAs) to these students. Within this national accountability context, individual states use their state-adopted language assessments to both initially identify a student as needing EL services and to monitor year-to-year growth on a standardized measure. Based on the information from the assessment results, state agencies may allocate funds and resources to schools, districts, and other organizations to support the achievement of EL students.

At the local level, the yearly standardized language assessment is used to monitor the long-term progress of individual students in developing English language proficiency. The ELPA should also inform school planning so that the success of EL students is prioritized and addressed systematically. For example, data from the ELPA may help administrators plan for the hiring of EL specialists. Finally, results from the ELPA should inform instructional practices to best support individual students, including assigning supplementary services based on their current linguistic proficiencies. Data on EL students' language proficiency growth should be included as an integral component of a school's MTSS plan and contribute to a holistic picture of the core instruction, supplemental support, or individualized instruction that each student requires in a tiered intervention model.

What Do These Assessments Measure?

Standardized tests of English language proficiency typically measure all four aspects of the language arts, including speaking, listening, reading, and writing skills. In the area of speaking, students must produce English words, sentences, and longer forms of discourse as they are asked to discuss an illustration, retell a narrative, give examples about or interpret academic information, or present their opinions. Students are assigned a score in this area based on the criteria of the specific ELPA being used. Typically, the assessment gauges students' ability to communicate in English in meaningful ways, their use of increasingly advanced and specific vocabulary, and the quality of the grammar, sounds, and word meanings within their utterances. The listening component of the proficiency assessments measures students' ability to correctly understand the content of a passage read to them and to select the correct answer to a question. Students receive a higher score if they are able to follow more advanced directions, comprehend more complex details and content-related ideas, and use higher-order thinking skills in English. Some states combine the speaking and listening sections of their language proficiency assessments into a global oral-language score.

ELPAs also evaluate students' written language skills related to both reading and writing. To assess reading, tasks are scaffolded so that students in the early grades read along with words or stories and read and choose words for answers. Later, students read a passage and choose sentence answers. Students in the upper elementary and secondary grades are required to read increasingly complex informational passages and solve problems. In the writing domain, students respond to a narrative or informational passage that has been presented to them and are prompted to create their own text. Their writing is evaluated based on the quality, quantity, and complexity of language use; the piece's coherence and clarity; and the accuracy of its mechanical aspects.

How Do ELPAs Guide Program Planning?

The annual ELPA results provide important data for a number of stakeholders. For accountability purposes, oversight may rest at the state, district, or school level. Annual goals that have been set for overall EL student learning should be evaluated and adjusted, depending on whether there has been sufficient improvement at each level. If student progress is not up to expectations, steps should be taken to improve the services that are provided to EL students. Following data analysis, specific areas for improvement are outlined and included in site- or district-based plans. These plans are constructed by leadership teams that include administrators, teachers, EL specialists, interventionists, school psychologists, and special educators. These plans should also take into account input from the families of students and school personnel who serve as community liaisons.

At the individual level, information about a student's annual growth is shared with the parents through a score report. This report informs parents about their child's score on the assessment as well as what overall language-level descriptor has

Measure	→ → **Greater Proficiency** → →					
WIDA ACCESS	Entering	Emerging	Developing	Expanding	Bridging	Reaching
ELPAC (California)	Beginning		Somewhat developed		Moderately developed	Well developed
NYSESLAT (New York)	Entering		Emerging	Transitioning	Expanding	Commanding
TELPAS (Texas)	Beginning		Intermediate		Advanced	Advanced high

FIGURE 4.2. Steps in second-language development in common language assessments.

been assigned to their child (see Figure 4.2). The score report may also contain suggestions for how parents can assist in their children's language development at home. Since score reports are available in many different languages, they can be understood by the families of all students.

Results from the annual ELPA should also inform the instruction that students receive in their classroom program and supplementary services. The vignette at the beginning of this chapter highlighted the fact that in many settings there are a lack of systematic and ongoing ways in which students' English language development scores are taken into consideration and built upon to provide them with systematic language instruction. This problem should be addressed at both the leadership level, for example, with principals and instructional coaches instituting structures that ensure dialogue among all personnel who work with emergent bilinguals, and at the classroom level, where all personnel who work with emergent bilinguals coordinate services and match them to students' identified language proficiency. We discuss this topic in greater depth in Chapter 8.

Discretion in the Use of Data from Standardized Language Assessments in Schools

There are several precautions that should be taken into account when using information from ELPAs to guide the instruction of individuals or groups of students. First, the ELPA is given once a year, and the results are typically available within 5 months or later. Thus, the assessments provide a snapshot of long-term growth, but do not reflect the student's actual language capabilities at any moment. Second, many students have difficulty showing all that they know in a high-stakes assessment setting. Both computer-based settings and/or unfamiliar personnel can influence a student's feelings of comfort and cause a weakened test performance. Test items that represent unfamiliar cultural values or unknown previous experiences or vocabulary may also cause a student to receive a lower score, despite his knowing the construct that is being assessed (Pitoniak et al., 2009). It is important that ongoing, formative assessment that documents students' English language development is included in decision making related to their instruction and inclusion in supplementary service programs.

COMMONLY USED STANDARDIZED LANGUAGE ASSESSMENTS AND PROFICIENCY LEVELS

As previously noted, the most common standardized language proficiency measure is the WIDA ACCESS test, used in 39 states. California, New York, and Texas have their own ELPAs that identify and monitor the progress of students identified as ELs. Figure 4.2 outlines the steps delineated in each of these assessments that show progress in English language development from the initial entry level (entering or beginning) to the most advanced level. The assessments vary in the number of steps used to show progress in language development, with the WIDA ACCESS test dividing the continuum into six steps, the ELPAC four steps, the NYSESLAT five steps, and the TELPAS four steps. Therefore, it is not possible to construct a step-by-step comparison across the four tests. In this section we describe the categories they use to document student progress in English language proficiency at various points along the growth band.

- **Entering/beginning-level proficiency.** At the earliest language proficiency level students have minimally developed skills in oral English. Students develop skills for following one- to two-step directions, point to pictures or objects, and begin to identify common objects. Students repeat words and phrases, name objects, and participate chorally in class (WIDA Consortium, 2019). They are highly dependent on language supports to advance their learning. They may have difficulty understanding conversations or separating words and phrases from the rapid flow of conversation and rely on a limited body of learned words to communicate (California Department of Education [CDE], 2014). Students may use their home language, gestures, drawing, or pointing to fill in gaps in oral English. As students start to acquire more words in English, they show less dependence on visual supports and modified language structures. They repeat, locate, sequence, compare, and describe short oral statements (WIDA, 2019).

- **Somewhat developed/developing/intermediate proficiency.** Depending on the ELPA used, the next step toward proficiency in English is known by a variety of names, but all imply developmental progression toward a midpoint. This step is characterized by greater listening and speaking skills; students use English for basic communication needs with limited linguistic support. However, they need substantial scaffolding to help them communicate about decontextualized or academic topics (CDE, 2018–2019). Students typically use simple sentence structures, often in the present tense. They ask questions and describe feelings in social contexts. At the academic-language level, students sort and then explain their reasoning, make predictions, and identify basic characteristics of subject matter within their content area studies (WIDA, 2012).

- **Expanding/moderately developed/advanced proficiency.** Three-fourths of the way along the ELD continuum, students show substantial growth in their academic language skills. They ask and answer questions in social and academic settings with supporting details; retell stories and identify main ideas; participate in class discussions; and identify, compare and contrast, and interpret oral information (WIDA, 2012). Students at this level still need moderate support to understand and communicate about decontextualized and less familiar academic topics (CDE, 2018–2019). Students are developing a broader range of syntactical proficiency and communicating in present, past, and future tenses. They are likely to be challenged by long sentences that have complex grammatical structures and unfamiliar words.

- **Reaching/well-developed/commanding/advanced high proficiency.** The top category of English language proficiency on the ELPA exams clearly highlights that the student has met proficiency expectations and is likely ready to be reclassified out of the EL designation. Students at this level may require minimal language support to be successful in academic settings on less familiar tasks and topics (CDE, 2018–2019). EL students at the highest level of proficiency are able to meet grade-level language standards, including giving presentations of subject matter information, defending opinions with evidence, and conducting and describing the results of scientific inquiry (WIDA, 2012). Students communicate using abstract vocabulary and use grammatical structures at a level very comparable to their monolingual English-speaking peers.

ASSESSMENTS OF STUDENTS' HOME LANGUAGE PROFICIENCY

Additional information that may prove helpful to educators as they attempt to gain a holistic picture of students' oral language strengths involves learning more about their multilingual capabilities. If educators have concerns about linguistic challenges students may be experiencing, they should meet with the school psychologist or speech and language professional to dig deeper into students' language background. At this point, the specialist will be able to identify a standardized language assessment that is available in the student's home language. A native speaker of that language may be available in the district or region to administer such an assessment. If the results point to a language delay in the home language, this information will be crucial in setting goals with the student.

For the most part, however, educators ought to know as much as they can about the oral and written language resources that students already have because this knowledge makes instruction more powerful. Information about students' linguistic backgrounds helps educators to be attentive to potential cross-linguistic transfer, to cheer on students' multilingual capabilities, and to arrange for peer collaboration in learning settings. A number of informal assessments that can inform educators' understanding of students' linguistic resources include the following:

1. Educators can survey students, or conference with younger students in small groups, about what languages they understand or hear in their lives outside of school. They invite students to share *with whom* and *in what ways* students use various languages.
2. Educators can ask students to write in another language they know. If they do

not know how to write in that language, educators ask them to draw a picture of what that writing looks like to them.

3. Educators can fill out a bilingual student identification and profile form (García, Johnson, & Seltzer, 2017), interviewing students about their bilingual use at home and with friends, about their travels to a country where the language is spoken, and about whether they can read and write in the language. Educators should be sensitive to not pry into the students' personal lives, but instead express enthusiasm for their bilingual assets.

4. Based on the bilingual student identification forms, educators can create a classroom bilingual profile (García et al., 2017), highlighting the language backgrounds of students in class, whether they are designated EL or not, and what their proficiencies are in listening, speaking, reading, and writing.

5. Educators can have conversations with parents or other family members to better understand students' multilingual capabilities outside of school, since students' families can often provide additional insights into their linguistic strengths. Parents can also share how one child's language growth compares to other children in the same family.

6. Educators can meet with school staff, community members, or groups of students who speak the same language and ask for information about how that language functions. Being in a group setting can often help students to think of new ideas that might not surface in a one-on-one conversation.

PART TWO: CLASSROOM-BASED ASSESSMENTS TO GUIDE INSTRUCTION

In this section, we present a number of quick, informal assessments for teachers to fold into their classroom routines that uncover students' receptive and expressive language capabilities, that spotlight students' emerging syntactic skills in the new language, and that help them to analyze reading and writing products for cross-linguistic influences. These informal assessment opportunities, most of which occur naturally throughout the classroom day, provide opportunities to capture students' use of the five key areas of language—phonology, semantics, syntax, morphology, and pragmatics—that can later be used to support their advancing linguistic capabilities.

Learning about Students' Receptive Oral Language

Because oral language does not always go hand in hand with a physical product, most opportunities for classroom-based assessment in this area will come from on-the-spot observations that educators make in class or through audio or video recordings they make of their students using language. A clipboard with a class list attached or an electronic tablet that is set up for note taking is essential for documenting the oral language behaviors of students in class during a number of classroom activities and routines.

COMMON CORE LISTENING STANDARDS (RECEPTIVE LANGUAGE), K–5

- ◆ Follow agreed-upon rules for discussions.
- ◆ Listen to others with care.
- ◆ Use knowledge of language when listening.
- ◆ Determine the meaning of unknown words or words and phrases that have multiple meanings.
- ◆ Understand figurative language, word relationships, and nuances in word meanings.
- ◆ Acquire general academic and domain-specific words.

Sharing Picture Books

During read-alouds or shared reading time in class, educators can look for visual cues as to whether emergent bilinguals are able to stay attuned to the content being presented. Although looking at the illustrations of a book does not necessarily guarantee that students understand what is being shared, it is an indication that they are trying to gain visual information that will help them follow the story or learn the information. Students who understand the flow of oral language being presented are more likely to have eyes on the material, have an engaged posture toward read-aloud material, and have emotional reactions to the content (e.g., laughing at humorous passages, showing concern with facial expressions during intense drama). Nonengaged behaviors can also be noted, for example, focusing on other things going on in the classroom, seeming to be overwhelmed or dazed, having unrelated sidebar conversations, or asking to be doing something else, such as using the restroom or other classroom materials. Educators can document their students' participation in read-aloud sessions by jotting notes onto an observation sheet that can be as simple as a list of emergent bilinguals' names, followed by a line or box to write anecdotes. It is also easy to create a short form, such as the one in Figure 4.3, that allows an educator to easily write a checkmark next to the behaviors the student demonstrates.

When educators discover that emergent bilinguals in class are exhibiting more behaviors that demonstrate distraction and disconnection, rather than engagement and active response during read-aloud time, steps can be taken to increase the

Student	Focuses attention on the book	Responds to content	Engaged body language	Distracted	Appears uninterested	Finds entertainment elsewhere
Mari	✓		✓			
Veronica				✓	✓	

FIGURE 4.3. Sample observation form for read-aloud lessons.

accessibility of the content. Consider finding books that help students experience the content in a stronger visual way. Look for shorter books in a new language that don't require as much extended attention. Allow students to preview books either by listening to them on tape in their home language or getting a preview of important new vocabulary words and ideas. Also, finding topics that are of special interest to students or relate to their everyday lives can increase their motivation to put forth the energy needed to stay focused through difficult new language content.

Following Directions

Observing emergent bilinguals as they participate in classroom activities is another way to informally assess their receptive oral language. Once again, it is helpful to have a list of students being observed on a clipboard or electronic note-taking device. If there is a coteacher or educational assistant in the room, that person can take over the role of observer and note taker to make data collection easier and more comprehensive. Observing students as they follow directions can be as simple as playing a game of "Simon Says" and hesitating before demonstrating the requested action. Are students able to follow the directions simply from hearing them spoken? Or do they look to see what their peers are doing before taking action? In a similar manner, educators should be attentive to the reactions of emergent bilinguals when directions for classroom activities are given orally. Which students seem to understand and begin the activity? Which students look for visual cues, such as procedure charts, or follow the lead of their peers? Which students ask for clarification in their home language? Having an awareness of which students need more specially designed or scaffolded instruction in order to keep pace with the procedural information being shared in class will be crucial to their effective participation and self-confidence in class.

The teaching practices that help emergent bilingual students to more easily follow oral instructions in class also happen to be excellent general practices for effective classroom management. They include:

- Using clear and straightforward language in procedural directions, stressing key action words.
- Facing the listeners.
- Creating procedure charts that combine written language with visual icons that students can follow along with.
- Previewing and practicing new and novel routines.
- Allowing students to call upon all of their linguistic resources, including asking questions of peers who can interpret directions in their home languages.

Another practice that educators can take to assess their students' receptive oral language and support those who need help is devising a way for students to show that they do not understand what was said. This signal could be a small card with a question mark or other symbol on it, it could be a body cue, such as a cupped hand on the ear, or it could take any convenient form that is understood by both the educator and student. In the moment, the educator knows to repeat or clarify directions. Over the long term, the educator learns which students are having trouble keeping up with the flow of oral English throughout the day.

"Point-to" Activities

Before emergent bilinguals have developed many expressive skills in English, they are likely to have some receptive language skills. Receptive skills can be informally assessed using pictures or real objects, as students are asked to point to what is being described. For instance, to assess students' knowledge of classroom vocabulary words an educator could make a copy of an illustration of a classroom scene and say, "Point to the pencil. Point to the trash can. Point to the stapler." In this way, educators can get a quick idea of which words the student already understands and which ones should be explicitly taught. Picture dictionaries that include scenes such as the classroom, the market, the city, and much more are readily available from booksellers or on the internet. In a related activity, educators can use "point-to" activities to check for students' understanding of key concepts in literature studies, social studies, mathematics, or science. In a particular setting the educator might say, "Point to what you think will happen next in the story"; "Point to the main character"; "Point to a librarian"; "Point to an addition problem"; "Point to a living thing."

As students work to expand their vocabulary knowledge in English, they can also create their own picture dictionaries by finding and printing pictures from the internet, cutting out pictures from magazines, or illustrating words that they feel will be useful to their learning. Until sufficient oral fluency is developed, these picture dictionaries can serve as a way to communicate with others when English words are not readily accessible to them. Students' picture dictionaries provide clues to the educator about their interests, capabilities, and the next steps in using English. Students should be encouraged to add labels to their pictures as well, ideally in both English and their home language.

Identifying the Sounds and Rhythms of English

Before students can express themselves comfortably in English, they begin to listen in conscious ways to phonological aspects of the language. After explaining what rhyming means to students (ideally with examples from their home languages), educators can present pairs of words that either rhyme or don't rhyme and ask students to tell them which words rhyme. Students can share their opinion either through a physical motion, such as a thumbs-up, or by holding up a card signifying "yes"—perhaps a happy face—or "no"—perhaps a sad face. For example, an educator might show students pictures of the following words, say the words out loud, and ask students to decide if they rhyme or not:

cat–hat [yes]
red–bed [yes]
ten–run [no]
tree–bee [yes]

Of course, helping students echo the words or chant them together presents a nonthreatening way for them to extend their receptive language skills into expressive ones.

In a similar manner, students can help refine their phonological recognition skills by listening for alliteration. Showing pictures, an educator might ask, "Do *boy* and *bus* start with the same sound?" Again, students can respond with bodily actions or by showing a card that represents "yes" or "no." Educators should take note of which sound contrasts seem to come easily to students and which are trickier for them to distinguish. We present many more examples of informal assessments of students' understanding of the phonological properties of English in Chapter 5.

Learning about Students' Expressive Oral Language

Expressive oral language is the language that students speak out loud in class to friends, partners, in large and small groups, and to school personnel. Once again, this type of student behavior does not always lead to a physical product that an educator can analyze, so a conscious effort must be made to capture the language through observation checklists, audio or video recordings, or dictation activities. The following informal assessments will help educators identify which students are speaking in class and to whom and how complex their language is and point to potential next steps for extending their expressive oral language.

COMMON CORE SPEAKING STANDARDS (EXPRESSIVE LANGUAGE), K–5

- Participate in collaborative conversations about grade-level topics and texts with peers and adults in small and large groups.
- Describe key ideas from information.
- Ask and answer questions about what a speaker says.
- Tell a story or recount an experience with facts and details and by speaking audibly in coherent sentences.
- Orally summarize information, and show how each claim is supported by evidence.
- Adapt speech to a variety of contexts and tasks, including using formal English.
- Demonstrate command of the conventions of standard English grammar and usage when speaking.
- Use general academic and domain-specific words.

Classroom Discussions

Most classrooms afford opportunities for students to contribute to group discussions in either small- or large-group settings. Educators can keep track of who is speaking on a regular basis in class using paper or electronic checklists with students' names on them. Tally marks can help the educator to become aware of who is speaking in class the most and whose voice is not yet present. While this quantitative data collection does not speak to the quality of the expression, it does alert the educator to a student's willingness to venture a public response. This first step is critical in helping the student become a proficient speaker in academic contexts. The educator can also take note periodically of how many and which students are raising their hands for the opportunity to speak. This information can help the educator get a quick picture of students' confidence and willingness to express their ideas in the presence of other students.

Speaking in front of the whole class can be intimidating to many emergent bilingual students, so it is important for educators to conduct observations as students participate in small group and partner conversations as well. Once again, educators will need a form for recording what they see, including which students are speaking, how often, and, if possible, the complexity of the language they are using. If a coteacher or educational assistant is present in the room, one person can collect language data, while the other leads the group. Later, the educators can meet to analyze the data that were collected and plan for instructional adjustments.

Audio or Video Recording Classroom Activities

Given life in a busy classroom, one effective way to capture students' language for later analysis is to audio or video record group activities that involve interaction. An educator can simply set up a recording device during an activity in which student talk is expected, perhaps with an eye to learning more about students who rarely speak up in whole-class settings. At a later time, perhaps in collaborative conversations with fellow educators, the team listens to the recordings to find out (a) if students are able to participate in group activities with their peers and teachers, (b) what strengths or challenges emerge in their communication skills, and (c) what structures seem to help all students participate equitably during interactions.

Students can also be mentored to record themselves individually or in partnerships as they tell stories, share reflections, respond to academic questions based on content-area learning, or conduct interviews with others. The recorded language samples serve three purposes: (1) they become artifacts of accountability for successfully completing an assignment, (2) they are data that educators can use to investigate students' linguistic strengths and challenges, and (3) they provide oral language practice and motivate students to talk more.

It is very common for educators to filter what students say through their own thinking processes, for example, making assumptions that students know specific vocabulary words when they use circumlocution (i.e., talk around words) to express themselves or use terms such as "this one" or "that." When speech is concretized by being recorded, educators have more than opinions about the kinds of linguistic skills students have—they have data. Language samples can be analyzed in a variety of ways: by how many words students put together in an utterance, by how many unique or academic words they use, by the pace of their speech and its coherence, and more. Recorded language can also help educators identify phonological challenges that may be holding students back from expressing themselves in English more clearly.

Transcribing Student Stories

A well-known activity, based on the language experience approach (Stauffer, 1980), is to write down students' oral storytelling before they have the academic skills to do that writing themselves. In this endeavor, students receive some kind of stimulus that inspires them to create a story, then they tell their story to a scribe such as a teacher, who writes it down word for word. Creating this artifact of students' expressive language can be analyzed in similar ways to a recorded sample, for example, by its coherence, complexity of language use, syntactical and morphological development, and length of phrases. Student stories can be elicited in some of the following ways:

- Participate in a real-world experience and then have individuals share stories about it. Some examples are taking a field trip, visiting a museum or business, attending a concert, cooking something to eat, and so on.
- Tell a story to get a story (McCabe & Bliss, 2003). The educator tells a dramatic story to students, sometimes with the help of props or visuals, such as a time they were lost, had an accident, interacted with an animal, or went on a special trip. After listening to an enthusiastic telling of the story, students are asked to share one of their own.
- Watch a video or listen to a powerful picture book that elicits personal connections.
- Create a piece of art (drawing, painting, sculpture, etc.) and share what was made and why.
- View a wordless picture book and construct a story to go along with it.

Once an experience has taken place, the student is asked to tell a story about it. Students then dictate their thoughts to a scribe, who writes them down or types them into a word-processing program using the students' exact language. An example from Ubah, a 9-year-old Somali American immigrant student, is highlighted in the box below. In addition to being analyzed to better understand students' expressive language, the written pieces can become texts for students to read and reread in future literacy activities.

> **UBAH'S STORY**
>
> On Eid me and my cousins go on my aunt's car, only the girls. And the boys go on my mom's car. And all the boys go to the movies upstairs in the mall. And the big girls go shopping, but starting from 15 years old don't like rides in the mall. But, 15 and younger like rides. But only my family 15 year olds don't like rides, but other people do. So, all of us go on the rides 15 and younger. The parents sit and talk; they sit on the benches. We have fun.

Learning about Students' Language from Their Reading

A regular part of informal literacy assessment involves obtaining information about students as they read their classroom texts. This data can be collected in more- or less-formal ways. For example **miscue analysis** and, in particular, taking running records are procedures for listening to students read texts and tracking their behaviors in terms of what is correct and incorrect, what kinds of approximations are made, and whether or not the student comprehends the material. In Chapter 5 we provide an in-depth explanation of running records and how to conduct them with beginning readers. Here, we introduce the idea that, whether through a running record or a less-formal observation process, listening carefully to students as they read provides a window into their linguistic development related to English phonology, morphology, syntax, and semantics. In a manner similar to what happens in a retelling, emergent bilinguals take in the printed words of their texts and filter them through their language lenses. Thus, a student at a certain level of English language development may read the sentence *Her father sang a song and played the guitar* as "Her father sing a song and play the guitar." For this reason, using a language lens while listening to students read may help educators better understand students' linguistic resources and help them take steps forward in their language learning (Briceño & Klein, 2018). The following reading events in the classroom provide opportunities for educators to get a peek at students' developmental progress in English language development.

Tracking Students' Syntactical and Morphological Approximations

Whether listening to an individual student read one-on-one or working with a small group in a reading session, an educator can tune into the language-related errors of emergent bilinguals. We suggest having a small notepad nearby in which specific student approximations can be jotted down. For instance, in an example guided reading lesson the featured book alternated between three verb tenses (*There are _____. I looked at _____. It was _____./There are boats in the lake. I looked at a boat sail by. It was sailing fast.*) For a school-age native English speaker, this series of verb tense changes may not stand out as especially difficult. For an emergent bilingual student, however, these tense pivots require a lot of foundational knowledge of the English language. Educators working with emergent bilinguals can find ways to support their students' language development by noting their specific language use and then embedding support for the language pattern in question, whether during that lesson or a future one.

Informal Use of the Cloze Procedure

The *cloze* test has been used in a variety of settings and for a number of purposes over the past half century (Taylor, 1953). During a cloze test, a student is given a reading passage and asked to fill in the blank for every *n*th word (e.g., every seventh word), or blanks are identified for specific words within the text that would highlight the reader's comprehension. In addition to giving educators information about readers' understanding of the text, the cloze procedure also provides insight into students' awareness of sentence syntax and the breadth of their vocabulary knowledge, both of which are necessary aspects of language development. For example, in the sentence *Plants need water and sunlight to _____*, students would need to not only understand the concept that living things grow, but also need the vocabulary word *grow* (or *get bigger* or *develop*, for example). A student who did not perceive the grammatical need for a verb in the blank spot might offer words such as *big* or *flowers* that demonstrate a connection to the topic, but would not be syntactically correct. This information about students' use of language will once again help educators to provide them with focused instruction in needed areas.

One instructional activity that expands on the cloze procedure was introduced by Cunningham and Hall (2008) and is called "Guess the Covered Word." In this activity, the educator presents a sentence that all students in the group can see with one word covered over. Students read the sentence with the teacher and discuss what the missing word might be, brainstorming ideas that the educator adds to a list. For example, in the sentence *Every day the teacher gets to school by* _____, a realistic idea could be a noun (bus, car, bicycle, etc.) or a present participle (walking, running, skating, etc.). As students begin to make suggestions for the covered word, the educator notices which students are able to suggest grammatically correct words and how varied the students' vocabularies are. To continue the activity, the first letter of the covered word is shown, and the educator crosses out words from the suggested list that would no longer work. For example, if the covered word begins with the letter *b*, the educator puts a line through any word on the list that does not begin with *b*. At this point, students are given an opportunity to brainstorm additional words they can think of that would now be possible for the missing word, and the activity continues letter by letter until the word is completely uncovered. This informal cloze activity provides helpful information to the educator and improves students' vocabulary and syntax knowledge.

Using the Maze Procedure with Reading Passages

In a manner similar to the cloze assessment, the *maze procedure* (e.g., Fuchs & Fuchs, 1992) leaves every seventh word in a reading passage blank, and students are provided with the correct word, along with two alternates that do not correctly express the intended meaning. For example, in the sentence *You can use your talent for* _____ *things than making so much noise,* the three options for the missing word might be: *better, finding,* and *longer.* The correct answer (*better*) demonstrates that the student understood the meaning intended within the passage.

When the maze procedure is used as an informal classroom-based assessment, it begins with a reading passage aimed at the reading level of a group of students. Passage length varies by reading level, but is likely to range from 120 to 400 words. The educator types up the passage or makes a copy from a page in a book, and inserts a blank for every seventh word. Next, three choices for the missing word are provided: the correct word (in the previous example, *better*), a word from the same part of speech (in the example, *longer*), and a distractor that does not necessarily represent the same part of speech but is at the students' reading level (in the example, *finding*). It is best if the answers are listed in alphabetical order so that an unwitting preference for the position of the correct answer does not occur.

Students read the passage to themselves and select the missing word in each seventh position. The educator can score each student's paper and take note of comprehension issues, confused vocabulary, and knowledge of correct syntax. The assignment can also be discussed in a small group so that students can ask questions and the language can be clarified for improved understanding. In addition, students can work in pairs to review their choices and talk about why one word is best suited to be the answer. This activity will get students talking about word meanings, grammar, and what the text attempted to communicate.

Learning about Students' Language from Their Writing

Because writing typically leaves a physical or digital artifact behind in the classroom, it is also a source of helpful data for learning about students' language development. Writing done by students on their own provides insights into their understanding of the sound system of English, their familiarity with its syntax, their vocabulary knowledge, and their use of morphological processes, such as inflectional endings (e.g., -s, es, -ed, -ing). In Chapter 7, we provide a thorough description of writing development and assessment, including classroom-based assessments and how they can be used with emergent bilinguals. In this section, we introduce several informal ways to look at and analyze students' unedited writing from a language-development perspective.

Analyzing Writing through Different Language Strands

Student writing may be elicited in similar ways to the storytelling ideas on page 78 of this chapter. For example, students can write stories based on an experience they had or a trip they took, as a response to a book or film they saw, as an explanation of a piece of art they have created, or as text for a wordless picture book. Students can write in response to a prompt that allows them to share their thoughts and feelings about their families, interests, friendships, and experiences. Once a piece of written text has been created, educators can look at it with an eye toward students' language use. Figure 4.4 highlights several examples of what educators might look for in students' writing using a language lens.

To highlight the usefulness of looking at students' writing through a language lens, we share one brief example. Even though this writing consists of only one sentence, it offers many possibilities for how to identify a student's language skills and potential next steps. Kevin, a 7-year-old Spanish-speaking student, has written the following sentence: I WUS PAYNWETHMAY FRANSHAKRS (*I was playing with my friend checkers...*): Using a language lens to analyze Kevin's writing, a thoughtful educator would be able to make the following observations that could help propel Kevin's language learning forward:

- **Phonology:** Kevin's words run together, so it would be helpful for him to practice separating words in speech before writing them on paper. He is doing a nice job of sounding out words, since most of the sounds are represented in his spelling. One cross-linguistic confusion that Kevin demonstrates is the substitution of *sh* for *ch* in the word *checkers*. This is a difficult sound contrast, because the digraph *sh* is not used in Spanish.
- **Semantics:** Kevin has meaningfully used all of the words in his sentence.

Area of development	Looking at language through students' writing
Phonology	• Do students accurately cluster parts within a word and perceive correct word boundaries? • Do students accurately represent sound–symbol correspondences in English? • What, if any, cross-linguistic confusions are evident? • What phonological clarifications do students need to support their writing at this time?
Semantics	• Do word meanings make sense for the writer's purpose? • Are students able to use grade-level specific and descriptive words? • Is circumlocution evident when a student does not know the exact meaning of a word? • What content words does the student need to learn to be successful in class?
Syntax	• Are sentences grammatically correct? • What, if any, cross-linguistic confusions are evident? • What syntactical structures would be helpful for students to learn and use in their writing at this time?
Morphology	• Do students correctly use inflected morphemes, such as words with -s, -es, -ed, and -ing? • Do students correctly combine word elements, such as prefixes, suffixes, and base words, to create more advanced words? • What, if any, cross-linguistic confusions are evident? • What morphological processes would be helpful for students to learn and use in their writing at this time?

FIGURE 4.4. Analyzing students' language development through their writing.

- **Syntax:** In English, the correct syntax for this sentence would be *I was playing checkers with my friend*. A syntactical structure that might be helpful for Kevin, and potentially his peers, would be *playing (a game)*. For example, the terms *playing basketball, playing soccer, playing cards, playing computer games* all fit in this structure. A sentence frame could be created for him and others to practice: *I like to play _____ with my _____ (e.g., I like to play hide-and-seek with my cousins).*
- **Morphology:** Kevin used the word *playing* but wrote it as PAYN. Since he is using words with the -ing ending in his oral language, he may be ready to work with that inflected ending in small-group language lessons. What other words could he think of that end with -ing? How would those endings be written?

Investigating Similarities and Differences among Languages

In various chapters of this book we discuss the importance of educators having background information about the languages that their students speak. Often, educators who work with students who speak many different home languages are concerned that it would be impossible for them to become knowledgeable about the ways that such a variety of different languages compare to English. We recommend that educators take small steps to learn about the home languages of their students, perhaps by starting with the language that represents the highest percentage of emergent bilinguals in the school. By learning some of the ways that this one language is the same or different from English, educators will become knowledgeable about cross-linguistic transference in general, and this information will be helpful in meeting the needs of all of their emergent bilingual students.

A helpful book that should be in every teacher resource library is Swan and Smith's *Learner English* (2001). This book outlines the ways that the phonology, spelling, punctuation, syntax, morphology, and verb tenses of a variety of world languages differ from English. The authors clearly spell out what kinds of predictable errors might occur for speakers of specific languages other than English, and with this knowledge educators can assist students in identifying the confusions. A quick web search about the characteristics of a specific language and its comparisons to English can also be helpful to educators who want to learn what may be tricky for these students as they learn English. Family and community members who speak English and the students' home languages are excellent resources for learning about how the two languages differ, what can be built upon, and what will need to be explicitly identified as causing interference during English literacy learning.

Multilingual students themselves are an often neglected resource for educators who wish to learn about what is the same or different between their home language and English. Students should be encouraged to share what they know about their home language, including how it is written and read, what sounds the letters or symbols make, how sentences are put together, what specific words mean, and the fact that often words have unique meanings that don't translate well into English. During writing time, consider inviting students to do some or all of the following activities:

- Show what you can write in your home language.
- Create an illustration of what writing in different languages looks like.
- Use some words from your home language in your writing assignment.
- Create a bilingual piece of writing.
- Write first in your home language and then translate your piece into English with help.
- Fill out a graphic organizer that shows what is the same or different about writing in English and in your home language.
- Create charts of the many ways to say common phrases (e.g., "Hello," "Goodbye," "How are you?," "Good wishes") in the languages of students in the class. Use these phrases in your personal writing.

PART THREE: INSTRUCTIONAL APPLICATIONS

In this section we present tips for intentionally planning literacy instruction so that students have opportunities to learn new language skills and practice using them in the classroom. First, we share a number of universal instructional actions that can be embedded into a variety of literacy lessons that support language learning. We then present a flowchart that highlights which instructional enhancements may be most appropriate for emergent bilinguals at each step of their language development progression.

Teaching That Supports Language Development

A classroom that encourages language learning gives students the opportunities to verbally engage with others, to receive comprehensible language input, and to be challenged and supported in taking the next step forward in their understanding of English phonology, syntax, morphology, semantics, and pragmatics (see Chapter 1). Learning a new language is influenced by a number of factors, including linguistic ones, such as the closeness or distance between a student's home language and English in relation to its sound, syntax, and semantic characteristics (Helman, 2016). As we discuss throughout the book, the more overlap between a student's home language and English, the easier it will be for students to transfer what they already know about sounds, word building, sentence building, and vocabulary. For students who have less of an overlap, explicit and systematic teaching is even more important. Sociocultural factors, such as how the home language and English are positioned and valued in relation to each other, the interpersonal reasons for learning a new language, and opportunities to practice English affect students' language identities and motivation to use English. Other factors that influence students' language learning are more personal, such as their outgoingness and willingness to risk trying out a language that they are in the process of learning. As described in Chapter 3, these affective factors can present pathways or roadblocks to learning a new language.

Given that many factors influence language learning, it behooves educators to take a multilayered approach to fostering English language development in the general education classroom. Through the following examples of teaching practices, we suggest ways for educators to create a language-learning community, to provide clear and explicit language instruction, to help students make connections to what they already know, and to use instruction that helps students to be active and engaged (Helman, 2016).

Creating a Language-Learning Community

If students are to be willing to try out their new language, classroom norms must uphold a set of values that guides collaborative and empathetic behavior. If students are laughed at when they mispronounce a sound or incorrectly use a word, they are not likely to risk speaking up again. Since oral language is learned through speaking and listening, when students don't talk, they don't get the practice they need. To ensure that a classroom is a welcoming language-learning environment, educators should demonstrate many of the following behaviors:

- Uphold classroom norms that do not allow put-downs of others based on linguistic background or any other identifier.
- Develop personal relationships with students.

- Encourage students to learn about each other, collaborate, and value their shared qualities as well as each other's uniqueness.
- Be conscious of adequate wait time and equitable turn taking so that more voices in the room can be heard.
- Learn about and encourage sharing of multilingual assets that students bring to school.
- View each student as essential to the classroom community, and hold all students to high expectations.
- Explicitly value bilingualism and multilingualism through classroom decorations and materials, the content of assignments, asking students to make connections across languages, and responding positively to students' multilingualism and language-learning efforts.

Providing Clear and Explicit Language Instruction

Students who receive regular, systematic, and clearly defined English language instruction do better than students who are not provided that instruction or perhaps only receive language instruction through their grade-level content studies (Saunders, Foorman, & Carlson, 2006). Whenever possible, emergent bilinguals should receive both instruction of academic content with language supports (see Chapter 6) and sanctioned time for English language development (ELD). Ideally, ELD time is taught and overseen by a trained EL teacher who understands the complexity of the English language and all of its component areas. In addition, the EL teacher should use regular formative assessment practices, based on a clear scope and sequence of language skills, to monitor students' growth in developing school-based language skills. The EL teacher also serves as a liaison to the general education teachers so they understand emergent bilinguals' current levels of English language proficiency and what types of lessons and activities will help them to flourish in class.

Whether ELD instruction at a particular school takes place with an EL teacher, an educational assistant, the classroom teacher, or other school personnel, the following practices will help emergent bilinguals receive the kind of clear and explicit language instruction that will best serve them:

- EL specialists, classroom teachers, and others who work with emergent bilinguals should communicate regularly about student learning targets, assessment results, and the alignment of language instruction across general education and supplementary instruction settings.
- ELD instruction should be based on state standards and address the many layers of language development that lead to school success.
- Explicit ELD instruction involves the use of visuals and other clarifying materials, teacher modeling while thinking out loud, guided practice, vocabulary instruction, moving from simple to more complex tasks, and clustering related information (Helman, 2016).
- The use of procedure charts, visual directions, and regular routines allow students to work with comprehensible information that they can follow.

Connecting Instruction to What Students Already Know

New learning builds on what a person already knows. For example, a person who knows something about gardening is aware that plants are living things that often begin with a seed and have specific needs such as water, sunlight, and the right temperature. A schema for how plants grow has been created within the person's knowledge repertoire and each time new learning happens in the area of plant growing that information expands and is refined. A carrot seed looks and acts differently from an acorn, but what is the same about the way they grow? Schema theory posits that abstract knowledge structures are developed in learners' brains, and that new information that is related to an already existing schema will join that schema and be more easily remembered and drawn upon (Anderson & Pearson, 2002).

Emergent bilinguals have many existing schemata about how language works in their home language. If encouraged to reflect on how their new language connects to what they already know, students will be farther along on the path of language learning. In Figure 4.5, we provide examples of how home language learning provides a foundation for learning a new language at school.

A first step in helping students to connect school learning to their existing knowledge is for educators to find out what background knowledge and experiences students bring to the classroom. Educators can learn this information by visiting with families and community members, surveying students and family members about students' strengths, sharing digital photo stories, and encouraging students to draw

Language learning at school	Can connect to home-language learning
Language represents concepts that are studied in all of the content areas—language arts, science, mathematics, social studies, and more.	Many concepts have been developed in students' home languages that are foundational to disciplinary knowledge, for example, labels for colors, shapes, sizes, measurement, weather, living things, and emotions.
Language involves interaction between people through sharing, asking questions, listening, taking turns, and responding to others.	Students have capabilities and experiences using their home language for a variety of communicative and interpersonal purposes.
Language can be written down for creative and communicative purposes. Written language can also be read to gain information, follow directions, or to experience enjoyment.	Students see their families and community members using written language in culturally familiar ways and for specific purposes.
Written language represents oral language through a systematic code, often an alphabet, that must be deciphered in order to be used.	Students may have experiences with the written code of their home language. By learning to read and write in a first language, students may have developed many literacy behaviors that can be transferred to reading and writing in a new language.

FIGURE 4.5. Home-language learning supports language learning at school.

and write about experiences they have outside of school. Once educators have a more holistic awareness of their students, it becomes easier to value their bilingual potential and build bridges to their home languages. This is the first step in helping students realize how what they are learning at school connects to what they already know.

Helping Students Stay Active and Engaged

Being immersed in a language outside of one's comfort zone can be an exhausting experience. Listening while only partially understanding what is being said can induce boredom, confusion, and tiredness. Even with their best intentions for learning, emergent bilinguals often experience a zoning-out feeling, and perhaps even doze off if they are asked to sit and listen for extended periods of time. Educators who work with language learners acknowledge that "sitting and getting" is not the most effective strategy. Students need to not only use language, they need to get up and move, interact socially, and "do" things that involve language objectives. Whether they seek to communicate through oral or written language, emergent bilinguals need opportunities to engage in authentic and purposeful activities as they learn.

"Teacher talk" monopolizes the vast majority of time in classrooms, squelching opportunities for students to use their own voices and practice their growing language skills (Flanders, 1970; Pianta, Belsky, Houts, & Morrison, 2007). Classroom activities that involve partner or small-group collaboration by their very nature embed occasions to use language for communication and academic purposes. When clearly organized, collaborative activities give each student a role and a reason to participate. As teachers lead instruction in a whole-class setting, it is important for them to stop at frequent intervals to ask students to share their thoughts and questions with a partner. Partner sharing gets 100% of students using their expressive and receptive language skills, which is a much larger percentage than when the teacher is doing all of the work. Figure 4.6 presents a variety of simple ways to get students using their voices in the classroom.

In addition to getting students talking, educators can also structure active engagement through physical movement, artistic creation, singing, dancing, using music, building, sorting and classifying, taking pictures, illustrating, asking open-ended questions, and through many other activities. The key is to break up the auditory messaging with physical or creative activities, time for reflection, and opportunities to make the information come to life.

Example Instructional Enhancements for Students from Beginning to Advanced English Proficiency

In the previous section, we outlined teaching practices that enhance students' language development in the core classroom. No matter the grade level or content area taught, there are ways to incorporate these support strategies into classroom routines. Of course, instructional practices change in specific ways depending on the maturity level of students; nonetheless, educators who are knowledgeable about the developmental qualities of the age group they teach will be able to apply the foundational

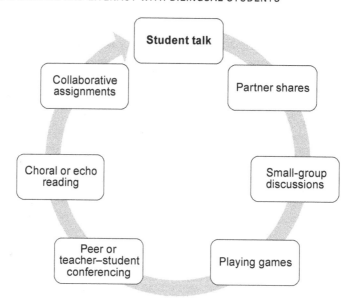

FIGURE 4.6. Informal structures to encourage student talk.

idea of each set of strategies appropriately. For example, a 5-year-old student and a 12-year-old student at the beginning level of English language development will need to be motivated differently to be actively engaged, but both will need to be involved and understand the content. Similarly, a language-learning community looks different as the grade levels progress, yet it always involves acceptance of language differences, inclusion, curiosity, and a low-anxiety environment where mistakes are considered a part of learning.

In Figure 4.7 we have shared a planning form that could be used by individual teachers or teams of educators to embed additional support strategies into their instructional programs. A blank copy of the form is available in Appendix A (p. 197). Figure 4.7 features examples of some enhancements that can be created, organized by the types of support they represent. In this example, educators have brainstormed a variety of ways to increase their use of clear and explicit language instruction by providing visuals; preteaching vocabulary; using sentence frames; selecting, modeling, and practicing language structures based on grade-level standards; and providing explicit feedback on students' writing compositions. Additionally, the planning form is designed to help educators think about which strategies might be most critical for students at each level of English language development. For example, students at the entering/beginning level are likely to need more basic enhancements, whereas developing and advanced/reaching students still need support, but at a finer-grained level. There is no hard line separating the support that students at various language proficiency levels could use; however, it is helpful to plan for tailoring support as students' language proficiency grows so that they take on more and more of the work at a higher and higher level.

Planning Form for Strategies to Support Language Development

Support strategies	Entering	Beginning	Developing	Developing	Expanding	Bridging	Reaching
	Beginning				Moderately developed		Advanced
A language-learning community	"Buddy up" new students with peer partners.		Create bilingual charts for important content-area words in class.		Implement a writing assignment involving English and the home language.		Have students interview multilingual community members and share in class.
Clear and explicit language instruction	Have visuals for content and preteach unknown vocabulary.		Provide sentence frames to expand student language.		Select, model, and practice language structures based on grade-level standards		Provide explicit feedback of students' writing compositions.
Connect to what students know	Find out about students' language and literacy backgrounds.		Use textual materials that represent students' experiences.		Encourage writing that shares home and community experiences.		Help students take leadership roles on collaborative projects.
Active engagement	Use movement and rhythm to learn new vocabulary.		Give frequent processing time such as partner shares.		Structure collaborative work on a regular basis.		Have students create vocabulary notebooks for keeping track of advanced academic language.

FIGURE 4.7. Embedding language development strategies across proficiency levels.

A planning guide such as this one can serve a number of purposes: (1) it can guide an instructional improvement conversation among EL specialists, interventionists, and general education staff; (2) it can serve as a plan for setting individual or group professional-learning goals, potentially with data collection and coaching support; and (3) it can be used to increase collective knowledge about what enhancements are currently being implemented at the school site. There is much to learn professionally when educators have focused conversations about how to improve instruction for emergent bilinguals as they progress in their language proficiency.

SUMMARY

This chapter focused on assessing the growth of oral language through standardized and informal measures. Since language is foundational to all aspects of literacy learning and its use in the world, understanding students' linguistic skills in both English and other languages is crucial to planning for instruction that propels them forward. In this chapter, we shared information about standardized assessments of English language proficiency that are used to monitor the long-term growth of emergent bilinguals, including what aspects of the language arts they measure and what the proficiency levels mean. We described a number of ways to learn more about students' skills in the five key areas of language—phonology, semantics, syntax, morphology, and pragmatics—by analyzing their expressive and receptive oral language, their reading abilities, and their writing skills. Once educators have a good understanding of their students' language strengths and needs, they can summon a range of teaching ideas that we offered for supporting language development in the classroom, including creating a language-learning community, providing systematic and explicit instruction, connecting to what students know, and helping students stay active and engaged.

CHAPTER 5

Assessing Beginning Reading for Emergent Bilinguals

After winter break, Ms. Peterson, the first-grade teacher, and Ms. Guest, the reading specialist, administered their school's universal screening measure to the entire class. As part of the school's MTSS process, they gave the screening measure a few times a year in the fall, winter, and spring. Once it was administered to the whole class, Ms. Peterson, like other classroom teachers at the school, met with the reading specialist, the special education teacher, and the EL teacher to discuss the results and make a plan for needed interventions.

For the winter screening period in first grade, the district plan calls for two assessments: one in sentence reading and one in decodable word reading. At this point in the year, Ms. Peterson expects her students to read sentences with easily decodable words and common sight words with good fluency and accuracy.

During the administration of the screening measure, Ms. Peterson realizes that Amal, one of her students who has beginning proficiency in English, is unable to read many of the words accurately. The results of Amal's universal screening measures aren't a complete surprise to Ms. Peterson, as she has conducted formative assessments in her class up to this point.

Amal arrived in the United States from Ethiopia the previous summer. Her first full year in a U.S. school began in first grade. Amal is an outgoing and talkative child, and she jumped right into playing with friends on the playground and using Arabic to communicate with her Arabic-speaking peers. Her parents work hard to make sure that Amal keeps up with Arabic by teaching her how to read in Arabic at home. Amal is a risk taker when it comes to learning English, always repeating what the teacher says and asking her friends to help her during class time to explain what the teacher is saying.

During the data meeting to discuss screening results, Ms. Peterson voices her concern.

"Although Amal's screening scores are below benchmark, I've seen a lot of growth in Amal's reading in English since she arrived. According to some assessments I conducted before winter break, she could identify 15/26 letter sounds and started to sound out simple CVC words. Actually, after doing some research on the Arabic language, I found out that Arabic and English share some sounds, such as /m/ and /n/. I've been trying to use these two sounds often, because Amal is becoming more proficient in reading CVC words."

The EL specialist, Mr. Rigby, nods his head in agreement and chimes in, "I agree! I've noticed a similar thing. In some of the oral language rubrics I have been using to keep track of Amal's English language development, she is now using more complete sentences to communicate for social purposes. The other day she asked very confidently, 'Can I sharpen my pencil?'"

The reading specialist, Ms. Guest, wonders, "Since we are seeing great growth in both language and reading, I want to make sure we continue keeping track of that progress."

Mr. Rigby agrees. "Yes, too often our students get a lot of work in phonics and become strong decoders, but they lack the vocabulary to comprehend what they are reading."

Ms. Guest suggests, "Let's make sure to bring several pieces of evidence of Amal's beginning reading and beginning English language to our next meeting to make sure we keep good track of her progress. Also, let's make sure to use a phonics diagnostic assessment that tells us exactly what sounds and decoding Amal has mastered, and where we can best focus her instruction."

As you have already read, students possess resources in their home language that assist them in learning how to read in English. In the previous classroom example, the educators discussed at least two important pieces of information that helped them understand Amal as a beginning reader. First, the classroom teacher talked about the linguistic resources that Amal brings from Arabic, her home language. Amal's teacher pointed out that there were phonological similarities in both Arabic and English that could be built upon—the sounds /m/ and /n/. Also, the educators talked about motivation, an affective resource that Amal brings to her studies. They delved into how comfortable Amal felt in the classroom taking risks using English words and asking her peers questions in Arabic. The conversation among the educators was rooted in several important theoretical underpinnings that can help educators understand how emergent bilinguals learn how to read in another language.

In this chapter, we discuss the assessment of three crucial components of beginning reading success: phonemic awareness, phonics, and fluency. First, we outline some theories that help describe how students use their home language to learn how to read in a new language. Then, we define phonemic awareness, phonics, and fluency. From there we launch into Part One, an explanation of several types of formal assessments of phonemic awareness, phonics, and fluency that are commonly used in schools today. In Part Two, we provide ideas for creating classroom-based informal assessments of these components. We make recommendations for administering assessments and suggest questions that educators can ask for guidance when analyzing and interpreting assessment data for emergent bilinguals. Finally, in Part Three, we share recommendations for how to provide instruction in phonemic awareness, phonics, and fluency in the classroom.

FOUNDATIONAL IDEAS

Learning how to read in another language is a complex endeavor. As we described in Chapter 1, there are many things going on "under the hood" to keep the process working well. This is true for all students learning how to read, but for students learning to understand the language at the same time, there are additional factors that come into play, such as the linguistic features of their home language. We described linguistic features in Chapter 1 as phonology, semantics, syntax, morphology, and pragmatics.

One reason that literacy in a home language influences learning how to read in a new one is because sometimes there are commonalities in the linguistic features of the two languages that make alternating between them smoother or more difficult. This bridging is called *language transfer,* defined as "cross-language relationships found in structures that belong exclusively to the linguistic domain (e.g., phonology), as well as skills that involve cognitive and language abilities (e.g., reading comprehension)" (Genesee, Geva, Dressler, & Kamil, 2006, p. 157). Sometimes there is a positive transfer; that is, the commonalities of the known language and the new language have similar features, making the new language more easily accessible. At other times, there is a negative transfer; that is, there are differences in the linguistic features of the known and the new language. In this case, the features of a known language don't apply to the new language and may confuse new readers as they apply what they know in a new context. Of course, language transfer depends on the specific two languages being considered. For example, there are similarities between Spanish and Italian that would be different from the similarities between Spanish and English or English and Chinese.

Language transfer is important to consider when teaching and assessing phonemic awareness, phonics, and fluency, the subjects of this chapter. When languages share phonological features, students can sound out or spell words in a more straightforward way. When languages vary greatly in their phonological features, additional explicit instruction and practice are needed to successfully make sound-to-print connections. For example, when some emergent bilinguals read aloud, the grammar of their home language may emerge as they process the new language. As a case in point, if a student's home language does not use -s to create plurals, there is sometimes a tendency to drop the -s from plural words in English. Students make sense of a new language by taking what they know from their home language.

Another related theory that helps explain how students use what they know from their home language when learning a new one is **common underlying proficiency** (**CUP**; Cummins, 1991), a shared knowledge base that applies to any language-related activity. Students draw on this underlying pool of knowledge that is based on what they know in their home language as they navigate learning the new language. In this way, the commonalities among languages can facilitate learning a new language.

When it comes time for assessment, educators should be aware of the linguistic characteristics of students' home languages to identify the ways that students use what they already know, or their CUP, to facilitate their understanding of the new language. As mentioned in Chapter 4, this process could help educators better analyze assessment results and plan for focused instruction.

Theories such as language transfer and CUP help explain the complexities of learning to read in a new language. Keeping these theories in mind will support educators as they plan, teach, and assess phonemic awareness, phonics, and fluency; each of these components is crucial to successful reading.

Phonemic Awareness, Phonics, and Fluency: Essential Components of Learning to Read

What Is Phonemic Awareness?

Phonemic awareness is the ability to distinguish and manipulate sounds in spoken words. For emergent and beginning readers, phonemic awareness might sound like word play. Educators working on developing phonemic awareness in their students might show a photo of a cat and ask students, "What is the beginning sound in the word *cat*?" Or, they might ask, "What word do you know that has the beginning sound /b/?" Phonemic awareness tasks require students to listen and respond orally. Pure phonemic awareness activities do not involve written letters (graphemes), although many early literacy tasks do combine phonics (letter–sound knowledge) with phonemic awareness. Besides identifying beginning sounds, such as in the previous examples, additional tasks associated with phonemic awareness include sound blending, sound segmenting, and sound manipulation. For the most part, isolation tasks are usually taught and mastered before manipulation tasks. Figure 5.1 shows phonemic awareness tasks with definitions and examples. Sound isolation is the first task, because it is less complex than manipulating sounds.

COMMON CORE FOUNDATIONAL SKILLS STANDARDS: PHONOLOGICAL AWARENESS

Kindergarten

- Isolate and pronounce the initial, medial vowel, and final sounds (phonemes) in three-phoneme (consonant–vowel–consonant, or CVC) words. (This activity does not include CVCs ending with /l/, /r/, or /x/.)
- Add or substitute individual sounds (phonemes) in simple, one-syllable words to make new words.

First Grade

- Isolate and pronounce initial, medial vowel, and final sounds (phonemes) in spoken single-syllable words.
- Segment spoken single-syllable words into their complete sequence of individual sounds (phonemes).

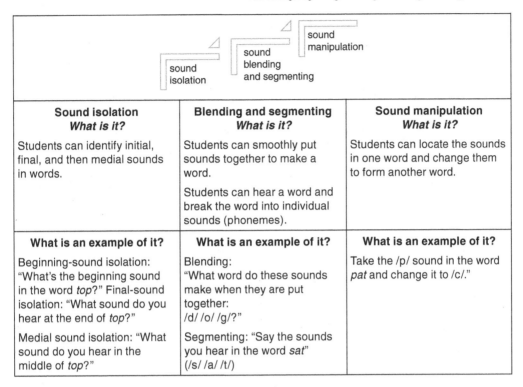

Sound isolation *What is it?*	Blending and segmenting *What is it?*	Sound manipulation *What is it?*
Students can identify initial, final, and then medial sounds in words.	Students can smoothly put sounds together to make a word. Students can hear a word and break the word into individual sounds (phonemes).	Students can locate the sounds in one word and change them to form another word.
What is an example of it?	**What is an example of it?**	**What is an example of it?**
Beginning-sound isolation: "What's the beginning sound in the word *top*?" Final-sound isolation: "What sound do you hear at the end of *top*?" Medial sound isolation: "What sound do you hear in the middle of *top*?"	Blending: "What word do these sounds make when they are put together: /d/ /o/ /g/?" Segmenting: "Say the sounds you hear in the word *sat*" (/s/ /a/ /t/)	Take the /p/ sound in the word *pat* and change it to /c/."

FIGURE 5.1. Phonemic awareness definitions and examples.

For monolingual English-speaking students, phonemic awareness is highly predictive of later reading achievement (Lyon, 1995). Students who show strong phonemic awareness abilities early on are more likely to become successful readers. However, the same may not be true for emergent bilinguals. Even those emergent bilinguals who learn phonemic awareness and phonics at the same rate or outpace their English-only speaking counterparts (August & Shanahan, 2006; Lesaux & Siegel, 2003) are not likely to automatically become successful readers without receiving explicit instruction in vocabulary and comprehension skills (e.g., Mancilla Martinez & Lesaux, 2011). Therefore, it is crucial that educators get an early start in both teaching the vocabulary involved in phonemic awareness and phonics and in administering ongoing assessments to determine how students are learning these vital skills. We show several ideas for these informal assessments in the Part Two.

What Is Phonics?

Phonics is the method of teaching letter–sound correspondences and the decoding of sounds to construct words. The *alphabetic principle* is the understanding that written letters represent sounds in spoken language. Once students know the sounds that letters represent, they begin to *decode* (read sounds to make words) and *encode* (write sounds to make words).

There are several approaches to teaching phonics, and certainly, one size does not fit all. For emergent bilinguals, researchers recommend a systematic and explicit approach where letters, letter sounds, and letter combinations are taught directly to students alongside oral language development (e.g., Vadasy & Sanders, 2010, 2011). In the systematic and explicit instruction approach, educators connect letter sounds and combinations to the words in text or in the context of sentences. Oftentimes in this approach, letter sounds and combinations are connected to visuals so students can easily remember the sounds. For example, *or* in the word *corn* may be represented with a visual of corn.

Figure 5.2 illustrates a simplified version of the sounds and sound patterns associated with phonics skills. Outlining this continuum helps to make the teaching approach systematic; that is, there a starting place and a path forward. This continuum can be used in assessment when teachers work to identify which sounds students have mastered and which sounds need further instruction. Diagnostic phonics assessments or learning needs assessments (such as those in Figure 5.6) generally follow a similar progression. For the most part, the continuum begins with the skills mastered first, such as letter sounds, and progresses to simple words, to words with more complex spelling patterns, and concludes with the decoding of complex multisyllabic words. In between, letter sounds and multisyllabic words can also be

Letter names and sounds
Short vowels (VC, CVC)
Consonant digraphs *sh, ch, th, wh*
Consonant blends *bl, br, ch,ck, cl, cr, dr, fl, fr, gh, gl, gr, ng, ph, pl, pr, qu, sc, sh, sk, sl, sm, sn, sp, st, sw, th, tr, tw*
Long vowels with silent *e* *a–e, i–e, o–e, u–e*
Complex consonants clusters *-tch, -dge, kn, gn*
***r*-controlled vowels** *ar, er, ir, or, ur*
Advanced vowels Diphthongs: *oo, oa, ou, oi, oy, au, aw* Digraphs: *ea, ee, ai, ay, oe, oa, igh*
Multisyllabic words two-, three-, and four-syllable words
Prefixes and suffixes

FIGURE 5.2. Continuum of phonics skills. VC, vowel–consonant; CVC, consonant–vowel–consonant.

considered along an easy-to-hard gradient, but it is not unusual for students to be able to recognize or sound out some "harder" words from time to time.

What Is Fluency?

Fluency is the ability to decode and understand text at the same time (Samuels, 2006). Three related components of fluency contribute to comprehension (Figure 5.3). *Accuracy* is the ability to read words correctly in a text. *Rate of reading* refers to the speed or pace at which a student reads aloud. *Expression* refers to how a student reads the text with meaning, using appropriate pauses, and emphasizing specific words. Starting in first grade and continuing through fifth grade, the Common Core State Standards include these three separate skills related to fluency.

COMMON CORE FLUENCY STANDARDS

Kindergarten

♦ Read emergent-reader texts with purpose and understanding.

First Grade and Second Grade

♦ Read with sufficient accuracy and fluency to support comprehension.

Third–Fifth Grades

♦ Read grade-level prose and poetry orally with accuracy, appropriate rate, and expression on successive readings.

Fluency is a significant reading skill because of its connection to comprehension. Most students who are fluent readers are more likely to be able to comprehend what they are reading; fluent readers do not have to spend too much time on decoding words and can allocate more time working to comprehend text (Kuhn, Schwanenflugel, & Meisinger, 2010). However, for emergent bilinguals, the assumption that fluency by itself leads to comprehension does not always tell the full story (Goldenberg, 2011). As stated earlier in the chapter, sometimes emergent bilinguals gain the skills they need to decode words and can read at a good rate and with good accuracy, but lack the vocabulary knowledge needed to comprehend (e.g., Vadasy & Sanders, 2010; 2011). Educators can remedy this problem by having a strong focus on oral language

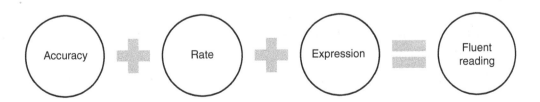

FIGURE 5.3. Components of fluency.

and vocabulary instruction and assessment throughout the reading development process.

In the next section, we explain the system of assessments that are commonly used in schools to measure how students are progressing with respect to these three crucial components.

PART ONE: THE FORMAL ASSESSMENT OF BEGINNING READING AT SCHOOL

Educators should use a balanced system of assessments to identify the beginning reading behaviors of emergent bilinguals in order to elucidate both their strengths and the opportunities for growth. In Chapter 2, we described the purpose for each type of assessment—universal screening, progress monitoring, learning needs assessments, eligibility for services, and accountability—in a balanced system. We focus now on the content of each type of assessment. Take, for example, universal screening, whose purpose is to identify which students in a school or classroom may need further support. Universal screening includes reading tasks that are essential to a student's literacy progress. At the beginning of kindergarten, or shortly thereafter, universal screening assesses students' knowledge of letter sounds, an essential component of beginning reading. Figure 5.4 illustrates recommended areas of formal assessment that capture significant components of reading development at each grade level, as well as the purposes for each assessment.

It's important to note that, at the current time, there is an incomplete research base for an assessment framework for emergent bilinguals in the area of reading (August & Shanahan, 2006; Hopewell & Escamilla, 2014). Furthermore, most of the research on emergent bilinguals in the area of reading assessment has been conducted with Spanish-speaking students. Although these students account for a large proportion of emergent bilinguals in U.S. schools, the existing knowledge base is hardly representative of all the languages spoken in classrooms today. Mindful of this situation, many researchers, educators, and policy makers attempt to use research about monolingual English speakers and apply it to their understanding of literacy development with emergent bilinguals. Next, they overlay the knowledge base for educational practices that support and sustain the learning success of multilingual students. Here, we provide a brief overview from the National Literacy Panel on Language-Minority Children and Youth (August & Shanahan, 2006) and other recent research on the topic of appropriate assessment in PA, phonics, and fluency for emergent bilinguals.

Recommendations for Beginning Reading Assessments for Emergent Bilinguals

In the early 2000s, a panel of researchers and experts in reading and second-language acquisition convened to answer the question: What does the research say about learning how to read in another language? The panel, called the National Literacy Panel on

Screening:	Purpose: Identify students at risk; identify baseline reading level.
Are there any students who require extra support?	**Kindergarten:** Phonemic awareness, letter names, letter sounds, decoding (end of kindergarten)
	First grade: Decoding oral reading fluency (mid-first grade)
	Second–fifth grades: Oral reading fluency
Progress monitoring:	Purpose: Determine responsiveness to instruction and need for instructional changes.
Are students progressing in the extra support given?	**Kindergarten:** Phonemic awareness, letter names, letter sounds, decoding (end of kindergarten)
	First grade: Decoding oral reading fluency (mid-first grade)
	Second–fifth grades: Oral reading fluency
Learning needs assessment:	Purpose: Determine focus and content of instruction.
In what area might my students need more teaching?	**Kindergarten:** Phonemic awareness, letter names, letter sounds, decoding (end of kindergarten)
	First grade: Decoding oral reading fluency (mid-first grade)
	Second–fifth grades: Oral reading fluency

FIGURE 5.4. Formal assessments of reading screening, progress monitoring, and learning needs in reading.

Language-Minority Children and Youth (August & Shanahan, 2006), made recommendations based on the body of research that had been conducted up to that point. Although these recommendations were made nearly 20 years ago, educators in the field still use them to design curriculum, plan instruction, and administer assessments.

One important finding from the panel is that both ELs and monolingual English speakers have been shown to have the potential to develop equivalent word recognition and decoding skills (August & Shanahan, 2006). This means that if a student is learning English as a second or third language, learning how to *decode* in English is generally achieved at about the same pace as students who speak English as a first language. ELs, however, will likely find the other two components of reading, vocabulary and comprehension, much more difficult (August & Shanahan, 2006). This finding is important for assessment of language and literacy, because it reaffirms for educators that assessments are needed to keep track of the progress of students' vocabulary and comprehension. Emergent bilinguals gain no advantage when educators spend copious amounts of time on phonemic awareness and phonics skills *without* building vocabulary and comprehension at the same time. As shown in Figure 5.4, it is recommended that educators assess and teach vocabulary, comprehension, and oral language in all grades. In Chapter 6, we focus on assessments of vocabulary and comprehension.

In order to fully understand the progress of emergent bilinguals, it is important to review data from a comprehensive system of assessments. Students who operate in multilingual worlds may have different reading "achievement" trajectories. Educators should take these varying trajectories into account as they review language and literacy data, while being careful not to assume that students are at risk because they do not progress at the same rate as monolingual English-speaking students. As Hopewell and Escamilla (2014) state, "incorrect understandings of bilingual students' reading achievement lead to costly and unnecessary reading remediation initiatives that limit students' opportunities to learn" (p. 69). This sentiment serves as a warning to educators that one assessment is not enough to determine the reading achievement of bilingual students.

For beginning readers, a comprehensive system of formal assessments includes phonemic awareness, phonics, and fluency (and oral language, comprehension and vocabulary, the areas of focus in other chapters). Each of these three reading components have several connected and interrelated skills that can be assessed and taught in a systematic and explicit approach. In the next sections, we outline the screening, progress monitoring, and learning-needs assessments that educators can use to pinpoint areas of mastery and decide on the next steps for teaching. All of these formal assessments should be accompanied with classroom-based informal assessments that are performed frequently and give educators information about daily teaching objectives.

Screening and Progress Monitoring Assessments for Phonemic Awareness and Phonics for Emergent Bilinguals

Screening measures are intended to determine which students might need supplementary support. They generally have agreed-upon cut scores. A *cut score* is a specific score on an assessment that communicates proficiency. For universal screening measures of reading, the cut score lets educators know if the student may be falling behind and require intervention. When considering this assessment system for emergent bilinguals in beginning reading, educators are cautioned to reconsider the standard cut scores (Linan-Thompson, Cirino, & Vaughn, 2007) when making consequential decisions such as placement into special education. As we continue to provide information on several of the screening and progress monitoring assessments used in many school districts, we reaffirm our position stated in the previous chapters that multiple measures should be used when making decisions about student support and placement.

PAYING ATTENTION TO PHONOLOGY WITH EMERGENT BILINGUALS

In letter–sound assessments, pay attention to sounds that may be difficult for students to produce. Are these sounds represented in students' home languages? Be careful not to focus on having students producing the "perfectly correct" sound. It's OK if the sounds that the student produces are not similar to DAE (dominant American English). For example, the /v/ sound (called a *voiced fricative*—where the top teeth touch the bottom lip) is not represented in sounds in Mandarin Chinese. Therefore, Chinese-speaking students may say words like *very* as "wary." It's not that students don't know the /v/ sound, it's just that the representation of the sound for them is /w/.

Nevertheless, screening and progress monitoring measures can be used with emergent bilinguals (e.g. Klingner, Artiles, & Barletta, 2006; Vanderwood & Nam, 2008). For students in bilingual programs, in which part of their instruction is in a language besides their home language, researchers suggest that home-language literacy assessments be administered as well (Esparza Brown & Sanford, 2011; Lesaux & Marietta, 2012). The screening and progress monitoring assessments noted in Figure 5.5 are not an exhaustive list of all universal screening measures, but are used with great frequency among schools in many states.

Learning Needs Assessments for Phonemic Awareness and Phonics for Emergent Bilinguals

As stated in Chapter 2, a learning needs assessment can help teachers determine the focus and content of instruction. There are two types of learning needs assessments that can help determine the focus of instruction (Figure 5.6). A diagnostic assessment in phonemic awareness and phonics will inform an educator about where to begin instruction on the continuum of skills. Then, once instruction is under way, educators use formative assessments to determine whether or not instruction is working and how they can move on to the next skill.

There are several diagnostic learning needs assessments available online. An online search will yield several free assessments to download and use in the classroom, such as those listed in Figure 5.6.

Screening and Progress Monitoring in Fluency for Emergent Bilinguals

Universal screening of oral reading fluency usually begins in the middle of first grade and continues through the upper elementary grades. In an MTSS framework, universal

Assessments	Phonemic awareness	Phonics			
	Phoneme segmentation	*Letter names*	*Letter sounds*	*Nonsense words*	*Decodable words*
Dynamic Indicators of Basic Early Literacy (DIBELS) Next*	Grades K–1	Grades K– beginning first grade		Grades K–3	Grades K–3
FastBridge Learning*	Grades K–1	Grades K–1	Grades K–1	Grades K–1	Grades K–1
aimswebPlus*	Grades middle K– middle first grade	Grades K– beginning first grade	Grades middle K– beginning first grade	Grades middle K–first grade	

FIGURE 5.5. Selected screening and progress monitoring assessments for phonemic awareness and phonics. *Also available in Spanish.

Areas of diagnostic assessments	Name of website and link
Phonological awareness	Literacy Resources, Inc. 2015 *www.literacyresourcesinc.com/resources/assessments* Includes some Spanish assessments
Phonemic awareness	Really Great Reading 2015 *www.reallygreatreading.com*
Phonics	Scholastic RED 2002 *www.scholastic.com/dodea/module_2/resources/dodea_m2_tr_core.pdf* Read Naturally Sounds for Signs 2010 *www.readnaturally.com/knowledgebase/documents-and-resources/26/346*

FIGURE 5.6. Examples of diagnostic learning needs assessments in phonemic awareness and phonics.

screening scores are used in data-driven decision making. That is, educators use the cut score of a universal screening measure in fluency to decide if a student needs further support in reading from the second through the through upper-elementary grades. If the student falls below the cut score, it is recommended that the student receive an intervention (Tier 2). To determine whether the intervention is effective, educators monitor students' progress using a fluency measure (e.g., Dynamic Indicators of Basic Early Literacy [DIBELS] Next, FastBridge Learning, and aimswebPlus). As we have stated previously, although the process of using cut scores to determine intervention eligibility for emergent bilinguals is recommended, it is important to take additional measures into consideration as well. Educators should gather information from measures of vocabulary and comprehension to get more information about how well students understand what they are reading. It could be detrimental to overall reading success if a student "passes" the cut score on the fluency measure but does not understand the text. For this reason we advise against only using a fluency measure to decide if a student needs an intervention.

For first graders, assessment of fluency begins at midyear, because that is when some monolingual English speakers and/or some emergent bilinguals are able to read at the sentence level. For monolingual English speakers, the ability to read fluently at the sentence level is a benchmark that identifies whether the student may need other support. That is, first-grade monolingual English speakers who have a difficult time reading first-grade-leveled sentences in the middle of first grade *may* warrant a reading intervention. We make the point here about monolingual English speakers, because it's important to remember that not all emergent bilinguals in the midyear of first grade (or other grades) can read at the sentence level in English. It's not that they are necessarily at risk; however, there are potentially other factors that affect their reading progress at this point. For example:

- Students in bilingual, dual immersion, or other language programs are developing reading skills in both languages.
- Students who are newcomers and have started school in kindergarten or at the beginning of first grade may still be learning letter sounds and decoding.

Despite the need to be cautious regarding the use of cut scores for emergent bilinguals, educators can use fluency norm charts to identify whether students are reaching benchmarks. Fluency norm charts outline fluency benchmarks for each grade. For example, a second-grade student who reads a second-grade text at 109 words per minute is in the 75th percentile (Hasbrouck & Tindal, 2017). It is very possible that emergent bilinguals would meet the same benchmarks on the chart, especially those students who are at more advanced levels of English proficiency. For students at one of the first two levels of English proficiency, or for students in dual language or immersion programs, educators should consult bilingual instruction experts at the school or district level to consider how to read and interpret the standard cut scores. Many bilingual programs set their own reading benchmarks based on their curriculum.

The purpose of progress monitoring is to determine responsiveness to instruction. We believe that progress monitoring of fluency is appropriate for emergent bilinguals if they are reading at the sentence level. That is, if students are struggling to decode simple one-syllable words and/or don't know all their letter sounds, assessing their reading fluency is not an appropriate use of instructional time. We also recommend that a team of teachers (e.g., reading specialists, EL teachers, special education teachers) decide when it is appropriate to administer progress monitoring in fluency for newcomers. The following example might best describe this situation. If a student is a newcomer at the beginning of third grade and has emerging English skills, it is not appropriate to assess her with third-grade oral reading fluency passages. The score would likely be zero for several weeks or months or even a year. Instead the student's progress can be monitored using other assessments, such as letter sounds, decoding, and sight words. At this point oral language assessments (see Chapter 4 for examples) are an important addition to the data collection for emergent bilinguals who are newcomers in the mid to upper elementary grades and are considered beginning readers.

Learning Needs Assessments of Fluency for Emergent Bilinguals

Educators can conduct a learning needs assessment to determine which area of fluency should be a focus of instruction. By paying attention to the three components of fluency, they can answer the following questions:

- Does the student need to work on increasing accuracy?
- Does the student need guidance in reading at a good pace?
- Does the student need modeling of how to read with expression?

Educators can use an accuracy calculation (see Figure 5.7) and a fluency rubric (see Figure 5.9 on p. 103) to determine which area to focus on for fluency instruction.

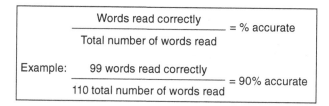

FIGURE 5.7. Determining accuracy in a students' reading.

To determine an area of focus for fluency, students read a passage from a text. Using curriculum-based measurement (CBM), the educator listens for expressive reading, marks words read incorrectly, and counts the total number of words read. To do an accuracy calculation, educators count the total number of words read correctly and divide the number by the total number of words read in the passage. For example, if a student reads 99 words correctly and he reads a total of 110 words, then 99 should be divided by 110. This percentage is 90%.

A student's accuracy rate can also help determine if the text being read is too difficult. For example, if a student reads a text with an accuracy rate of 70%, it's possible that this low accuracy score could affect the student's comprehension of the text. If 30% of the words are errors, the student is likely to be missing some important details about the text. Therefore, it is commonly agreed that educators use these percentages (see Figure 5.8) to help determine a suitable text for students to read independently. It is *not* recommended that students *only* read instructional level texts; difficult texts present plenty of literacy learning opportunities if they are read with appropriate supports to minimize frustration (Brown, Mohr, Wilcox, & Barrett, 2018).

In addition to determining a student's accuracy rate while reading, it is important to pay attention to the expression a student uses. Expression refers to the patterns of rhythm, stress, and emotion that are communicated while reading a text. Does the student read dialogue as if someone is talking? Does the student take breaks at a period, and raise his or her voice at the end of a question? Although it isn't always the case that expression can tell an educator if a student comprehends a text, it can be a good indicator. For example, if there is a point in a story at which there is a problem, the dialogue between the characters tends to change. Fluent readers will change their voices to show changes and shifts in the story line.

Independent level	95–100% accuracy Students can read the text with very few errors.
Instructional level	90–94% accuracy Students can read the text with few to several errors.
Frustration level	Below 90% accuracy Comprehension of text may be affected by low accuracy.

FIGURE 5.8. Accuracy rate and text reading.

PAYING ATTENTION TO THE SYNTAX AND MORPHOLOGY
OF EMERGENT BILINGUALS

Sometimes emergent bilinguals will use the syntax (how words are ordered in a sentence) and morphology (the components of individual words) of their home language when they read aloud in English. In some languages, for example, the adjective follows the noun, as in *dress red,* instead of *red dress.* This syntactical error should be noted as one way in which students are influenced by their home language. Educators can think out loud with students about these cross-linguistic influences and try to be especially aware of them. Similarly, morphological errors, such as deleting an ending like -*ed,* are not unusual for students whose home language does not use this morphological process to indicate the past tense.

In addition to asking comprehension questions, assessing expression in reading can be a good way to determine comprehension of text. Educators can use a fluency rubric (Figure 5.9) to assess the expression and pace of a student's reading. The rubric can be used in a variety of ways:

- **Self-assessment:** Students can rate themselves on the rubric. To begin, choose one area of assessment. For example, focusing just on expression and volume is a good start. After several lessons and practice in expression and volume, students can record themselves and listen again to do a reassessment of their reading.

Student name: _____   Name of text: _____

Date: _____

	1	2	3	4
Expression and volume	Reads in a quiet voice with **no** expression.	Reads in a quiet voice with **some** expression.	Reads with volume and expression throughout **most** of the reading.	Reads with varied volume and expression during the **entire** reading.
Phrasing	Reads word-by-word with **no** attention to punctuation.	Reads in phrases, pays attention to **some** periods.	Reads with good phrasing for **most** of the reading with good intonation.	Reads with good phrasing for the **entire** reading with good intonation.
Smoothness	**Frequently** stops to sound out words, repeats words, or repeats phrases often.	**Sometimes** stops to sound out words, repeats words, or repeats phrases often.	Reads **most** of the words with no errors.	Reads smoothly the **entire** reading.
Pace	Reads slowly.	Reads somewhat slowly.	Reads at a good pace throughout most of the reading.	Reads at an appropriate pace throughout the entire reading.

FIGURE 5.9. Fluency rubric.

- **Peer assessment:** Students can listen to each other read a text and rate each other on the rubric. In order for students to be successful at rating each other, we recommend modeling behaviors of how to give a peer helpful feedback.
- **Feedback:** Educators can use the rubric to score a student's fluent reading and give specific feedback. Keep track of each rubric by providing the date and the title of the text. Review student progress over the course of instruction.

PART TWO: CLASSROOM-BASED ASSESSMENTS FOR GUIDING INSTRUCTION

In Part One, we described an assessment system that is typically in place in most schools. We considered assessments in phonemic awareness, phonics, and fluency and how they are used for decision making. In Part Two, we describe how to create informal assessments related to the daily instruction of phonemic awareness, phonics, and fluency. In addition, we provide recommendations for how to administer beginning reading assessments with emergent bilinguals and suggest ways that educators can analyze and interpret beginning reading assessments from a perspective that values the uniqueness of bilingual literacy development.

Informal Assessments for Daily Instruction of Phonemic Awareness

Part of a balanced assessment system includes informal reading assessments. We defined informal reading assessments in Chapter 2 as those assessments that educators use to assess their students' performance and progress toward daily learning targets. Some informal assessments that could be used in phonemic awareness and phonics are:

- Educator-made quizzes
- Work samples of classroom activities
- Observations and anecdotal note taking
- Checklists

RECEPTIVE AND PRODUCTIVE LANGUAGE SKILLS IN PHONEMIC AWARENESS

As described in Chapter 4, the four language arts skills are listening, speaking, reading, and writing. Of those four skills, listening and reading are receptive language skills. They are receptive because they are taken in by a person. Language learners can show that they understand by responding with a yes or no, instead of producing spoken words or letters on a page. Speaking and writing are productive skills; students say sounds and words as they verbalize and form letters, words, and longer texts as they write. For the most part, the receptive skill of listening is a good place to start with students who are new to English when assessing beginning reading skills.

Example of a receptive phonemic awareness task

Show a picture of a cat and a car.
Ask: Do these words have the same beginning sound?

Example of a productive phonemic awareness task

Ask: Can you tell me three words that begin with the /l/ sound?

In the following figures (Figures 5.10 and 5.11), we provide additional examples of informal assessments of phonemic awareness that can be used in the classroom. We also provide the corresponding templates for the informal assessments of sound isolation tasks, segmenting, blending, and manipulating in Appendices B and C (pp. 198–199). These templates can be used to tailor assessments to individual students. The examples feature targeted letter sounds as guides for how to record the progress of students. A targeted letter sound is a specific sound or set of sounds that an educator is teaching during the lesson(s). Other sounds can be easily substituted to individualize this informal assessment. Additionally, for informal assessments, it is up to the educator to determine how many sounds are assessed. In the example assessments, we show a variety of attempts at each task. For example, Figure 5.10 shows four pictures that students need to look at to identify the beginning sounds. More pictures can be

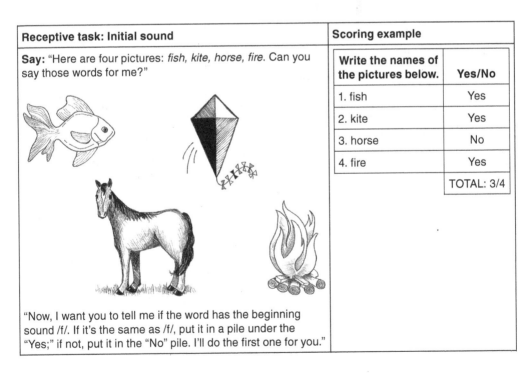

Receptive task: Initial sound	Scoring example	
Say: "Here are four pictures: *fish, kite, horse, fire*. Can you say those words for me?"	**Write the names of the pictures below.**	**Yes/No**
	1. fish	Yes
	2. kite	Yes
	3. horse	No
	4. fire	Yes
		TOTAL: 3/4
"Now, I want you to tell me if the word has the beginning sound /f/. If it's the same as /f/, put it in a pile under the "Yes;" if not, put it in the "No" pile. I'll do the first one for you."		

FIGURE 5.10. Sound isolation tasks: Receptive and productive assessment and scoring example. Drawings used by permission of Path to Reading Excellence in School Sites (PRESS).

Segmenting task	Scoring example	
Say: "I am going to say a word. I would like you to tell me the sounds you hear in that word. For each sound put a chip in a box. I'll do the first one for you. *big.* /b/ /i/ /g/. "Now it's your turn: *sun, fun, lit, had.*" 	**Words**	**Sounds said by student**
	1. *sun*	/s/ /u/ /n/
	2. *fun*	/f/ /o/ /p/
	3. *lit*	/l/ /i/ /t/
	4. *had*	/h/ /e/ /m/
	TOTAL: 10/12	
	When scoring segmenting, give 1 point for each sound.	

Blending task	Scoring example	
Say: "I am going to say four sounds. I would like you to put those sounds together to make a word. For each sound I will put chip in a box. I'll do the first one for you. /s/ /n/ /a/ /p/. The word is *snap*. "Now it's your turn: *clap, clot, clip, slip.*" 	**Words**	**Sounds said by student**
	1. *clap*	/cl / /a/ /p/
	2. *clot*	/cl / /o/ /p/
	3. *clip*	/c/ /l/ /i/ /p/
	4. *slip*	/s/ /l/ /i/ /p/
	TOTAL: 12/16	

Manipulation task: Initial sound	Scoring example	
Say: "We are going to do a game where we switch around some sounds in a word. Let's do the first one together. What is the beginning sound of the word *happy*? /h/. Now, I am going to take the /h/ off the word *happy* and add an /s/ sound. The new word is *sappy*. "Now you try. Take off the first sound from the word *love* and add a /d/. What's the word?" Student says: "*Dove.*" *mike* add /b/ . . . *bike* *can* add /f/ . . . *fan* *log* add /f/ . . . *fog* *lake* add /m/ . . . *make*	**Words**	**Sounds said by student**
	mike add /b/	*bike*
	can add /f/	*fat*
	log add /f/	*flog*
	lake add /m/	"I don't know."
	TOTAL: 2/4	

FIGURE 5.11. Segmenting, blending, and manipulation examples.

added if students show increasing independence in the task or decreased if they are new to the task. Figure 5.11 has simple directions for doing segmenting, blending, and manipulation tasks and recording what the students are able to achieve.

In Figure 5.12 we provide an example of how an educator might keep track of the phonemic awareness tasks practiced each week (a blank template is provided in Appendix D). In the example shown, the educator gave one or two informal assessments per week. Once the student got closer to mastery of the task, a new task was introduced. For example, on 9/12/2018 the student scored 8/10 on an initial sound isolation task. This score indicated to the educator that the student had a good grasp of this concept, and so the following week he practiced isolating middle sounds. It should be noted that a few phonemic awareness tasks can be taught and practiced at the same time. For some students, blending sounds to make a word is an easier task than isolating middle sounds. Educators should take care not to get "stuck" on one skill.

Informal Assessments for Daily Instruction of Phonics

Earlier in the chapter, we provided a continuum of phonics skills (Figure 5.2). This continuum is not exhaustive of all phonics sounds, and within each category there are a variety of sounds and sound combinations. For example, there are *many* blends in

Task	Date 9/4/2018	Date 9/10/2018	Date 9/18/2018	Date 9/25/2018	Date 10/11/2018
Sound isolation: Initial	3/4	8/10			
Sound isolation: Medial			3/4	3/10	
Sound isolation: Final					8/10
Blending				8/10	
Segmenting					7/10
Manipulation: initial					
Manipulation: medial					
Manipulation: final					

FIGURE 5.12. Keeping track of student progress in classroom-based assessments of phonemic awareness.

the English language, including *st, sk, sm,* and so on. In the next section, we provide some informal assessment activities that can be used with a variety of phonics skills listed on the continuum.

Sound Boxes

Sound boxes are a suitable assessment for students who have mastered letter–sound correspondences and are working on putting sounds together to read words. Sound boxes are best used with students learning CVC, CCVC, CVCC, and digraphs (*sh, th, wh* with short vowels). There are a few options for assessing students using sound boxes.

In the first example, the educator writes each letter (or places letter tiles) in the box, and then the student decodes the word. Additionally, the educator can write words on a whiteboard and ask the student to read them. In the second example, the educator says a word, and then the student uses the letter tiles to make the word. Then the educator records the number of correct sounds and the sounds that are missed (Figure 5.13). This record provides a clear indication for reteaching, because it shows what the student has mastered and what is still being worked on. Instructional ideas for using sound boxes are shared in Part Three.

Like the phonemic awareness examples of informal assessments, an educator can provide more than four attempts at the skill for an assessment. If the student is new to the task, it may be a good idea to start with assessing a lesser number of total words. Since these are formative assessments, they should closely match the instruction.

Sound boxes: Decoding consonant blends	Scoring example	
Say: "You are going to build some words using these sound boxes and letter tiles. You will put the letter tiles on each sound box and read the word. I'll do the first one for you. /s/ /t/ /e/ /m/ stem." *stop, step, tip, tap, map* (letter tiles: e, m, t, i, p, a, o) (sound boxes: s, t)	1. stem *s t e m*	4/4
	2. stop *s t a p*	3/4
	3. step *s t i p*	3/4
	4. tip *t i p*	3/3
	5. tap *t a p*	3/3
	6. map *m a p*	3/3
		TOTAL: 19/21

FIGURE 5.13. Example of a phonics classroom-based assessment using sound boxes.

Word Sorts

Compile a list of targeted words on index cards or small pieces of paper. For example, if students have been working on reading words with vowel teams, such as *ee* and *ie,* make several cards that have a word written on each card. Then, ask the students to sort them into two piles: words with *ee* and words with *ie* (see Figure 5.14). Make sure that students read each word out loud before sorting it. Once the words are sorted, ask the students to read the words again.

As a formative assessment, educators can tally the words sorted and read correctly. Keep track of these results throughout the process of teaching the sounds (see the tracker form in Figure 5.15; a blank template is provided in Appendix E). Once students have mastered reading words with sets of sounds or patterns, begin working on the next sound or pattern combination(s).

Running Records

A running record is method of recording the reading behaviors of a student while she reads a text aloud. *Running records* are informal and can be prepared at any time during instruction. For an emergent bilingual, running records are an opportunity to see how a student's linguistic resources may be contributing to reading development in English (or other languages of instruction). The steps for conducting a running record are as follows:

1. Select a reading passage (from a book) long and difficult enough for an individual student. Either type or write the text of the reading passage on the template.
2. Ask the student to read the text. Say, "I would like to listen to you read today. While you read I am going to take some notes. These notes will help me see

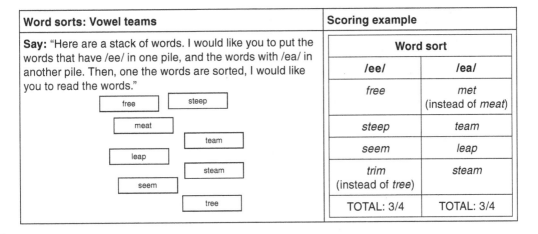

FIGURE 5.14. Example of an informal assessment of phonics using word sorts.

Task	Date 10/3/18	Date 10/7/18	Date 10/14/18	Date 10/21/18	Date 10/28/18
Letter sounds					
CVC words					
Digraphs with short-vowel words	10/12				
Consonant-blend words		6/12	8/12	11/12	
Silent-*e* words					3/10
Vowel-team words					
Complex consonant-cluster words					
r-controlled words					
Advanced-vowel words					
Multisyllabic words					
Words with prefixes and suffixes					

FIGURE 5.15. Keeping track of student progress in classroom-based assessments of phonics.

how to help you in your reading. Do you have any questions?" While the student is reading, mark the text on the prepared passage with the suggested markings (shown in Figure 5.16).

3. At the end of the reading, ask a few comprehension questions and take notes in the following areas:

   a. Retell: "What happened? Can you summarize?"

   b. Evaluate/analyze/critique: "What did you think about? What would you do?"

   c. Motivation: "Did you like reading about . . . ?"

4. Analyze the reading behaviors on the template using a *miscue analysis* (see Figure 5.17). While doing a miscue analysis, consider the linguistic features of the student's home language when analyzing the errors. Take notes about the student's use of the linguistic resources from the home language.

When deciding on the student's overall comprehension of the text, consider the context of the story. Is this story similar to or different from stories that reflect the

Reading behavior	Example
Correct	✓ ✓ ✓ ✓ ✓ ✓ ✓ My mom walked me to school yesterday.
Substitution	✓ ✓ *walks* ✓ ✓ ✓ ✓ My mom walked me to school yesterday.
Omission	✓ ✓ ✓ ✓ ✓ ✓ _____ My mom walked me to school yesterday.
Insertion	✓ ✓ ✓ ✓ ✓ ✓ ✓ *morning* My mom walked me to school yesterday∧.
Told	✓ ✓ T ✓ ✓ ✓ ✓ My mom walked me to school yesterday.
Appeal	✓ ✓ ✓ ✓ ✓ ✓ *y . . . yes . . .* My mom walked me to school yesterday.
Repetition	✓ ✓ ✓ ✓ ✓ ✓ ✓ My mom walked me to school yesterday. ┃ R
Self-correction	*always/* ✓ ✓ ✓ ✓ ✓ ✓ <u>SC</u> My mom walked me to school yesterday.
Attempt	✓ ✓ ✓ ✓ ✓ ✓ <u>*y . . . yes . . .*</u> My mom walked me to school yesterday.

FIGURE 5.16. Recording the reading behaviors on a running record.

Meaning: Does the error tell you that the student is understanding the meaning of the story?	**Example:**				
	Pg.	E	SC	E: MSV	SC: MSV
	Mi mamá ✓ ✓ ✓ ✓ ✓ My mom walked me to school yesterday.	II		M	
	When students use linguistic resources from their home language during a running record as in the student example ("Mi mamá" instead of "My mom"), decide how this might be recorded as an error. In this case, the meaning of the sentence is still upheld.				
Structure: Does the error tell you that the student is following rules of grammar in English or in their language?	**Example:**				
	Pg.	E	SC	E: MSV	SC: MSV
	✓ ✓ _walking_ ✓ ✓ ✓ ✓ My mom walked me to school yesterday.	I		S	
	In this example, the student applied a rule of English grammar by adding the -ing at the end of the verb.				
Visual: Does the error tell you that the student is seeing a word that is visually similar to the word in the text?	**Example:**				
	Pg.	E	SC	E: MSV	SC: MSV
	✓ ✓ ✓ ✓ ✓ _dishes_ I washed my hands before dinner.	I			V
	The student did use the knowledge of the beginning sound of the word and the words are visually similar, with their first two letters being the same.				

FIGURE 5.17. Questions for a miscue analysis with emergent bilinguals.

sociocultural background of the student? Could this issue affect the how the student understands or reads the story? Does the story contain metaphors, similes, or other figurative language that the student might not be familiar with and thus impede his comprehension?

Use the procedures in Figure 5.16 and Figure 5.17 to conduct a running record with the emergent bilingual students' literacy development in mind.

Administering Assessments in Beginning Reading

There are several approaches for differentiating the administration of assessments for emergent bilinguals. Educators should take into account the level of a student's English proficiency, the affective factors (e.g., "Is my student nervous about test taking?"), and the type of assessment being administered. For example, when administering summative assessments, it is necessary to follow the standardized directions in order to ensure the fidelity of test taking. Suggestions for differentiating assessment administration for emergent bilinguals include:

- Make sure that students understand the language in which the directions for the assessment is written.
- Model assessment tasks ahead of time.
- Use routines and procedures for administering assessments.
- Give students additional time to complete assessment tasks.
- Make sure students feel comfortable and relaxed in the assessment environment.

Directions for phonemic awareness and phonics tasks may be difficult for emergent bilinguals to understand. For example, consider the instruction "Can you tell me the middle sound of the word *pen*?" A student who is new to English may not understand the academic language of the directions. If possible, educators should give directions in the home language of the student. If this is not possible, consider using manipulatives, such as cubes or small markers, to help the student make the connection between the word and its individual sounds. Another way to differentiate the directions for students is to model the tasks ahead of time. For classroom-based informal assessments, daily phonemic awareness activities can be thought of as informal assessments. Educators should do similar things in assessment that were done during instruction, but be sure to ask students to perform the task independently so they can show what they can do without assistance. Educators should take anecdotal notes and record their progress using a progress chart (like the one provided in Figure 5.15). Another suggestion for administering assessments for emergent bilinguals, especially those who are newer to English, is to give the students more time to complete the tasks.

Analyzing and Interpreting Assessments in Beginning Reading for Emergent Bilinguals

In addition to administering screening and progress monitoring assessments in beginning reading for emergent bilinguals, we recommend that educators ask the following questions while analyzing and interpreting assessments.

- **Are students progressing at the same rate as a "true peer"?** "True peers" are students with the same or similar levels of language proficiency, acculturation, and educational backgrounds (Brown & Doolittle, 2008). If there are two emergent bilinguals who arrived in the same school around the same time and had similar instruction, yet one student is still lagging behind considerably, this outcome could be an indication that the student may need a different instructional approach.

- **Where is growth occurring?** Use a variety of assessments to find areas of growth. Early reading assessments commonly used for screening and progress monitoring typically ask educators to calculate the rate of sounds or words read in a minute. Educators track this over the course of the school year (screening) and every other week (progress monitoring). Table 5.1 illustrates letter–sound fluency data collected

TABLE 5.1. Example of Letter–Sound Fluency Progress Monitoring

Week	1	2	3	4	5	6	7
Letter sounds correct/ Total sounds read	4/17	5/16	4/15	4/14	10/21	11/23	20/28
Accuracy	23%	31%	26%	40%	47%	50%	71%

on one kindergarten student over the course of 9 weeks. The educator recorded the letter sounds read correctly/total number of sounds read. Then, the educator calculated the accuracy of the letter sounds read—similar to the method for calculating the accuracy of words read correctly. In this example, the student was progressing in both total sounds read correctly and the accuracy of the sounds read.

- **Is instruction explicit and systematic?** In the area of beginning reading, research highlights the importance of systematic and explicit instruction for emergent bilinguals (e.g., Goldenberg, 2013; Lesaux & Marietta, 2012). Explicit instruction includes modeling of skills and objectives, guided practice with immediate and specific feedback, and independent practice. Systematic instruction follows a sequential approach with room for differentiation. Explicit instruction is important, because students need to hear and practice with support the skills required to successfully decode and comprehend text. Systematic instruction is necessary to ensure that all of the skills are taught and that students don't receive instruction in one area, but not in another. If an emergent bilingual student is not showing progress, it is important to reconsider the instructional approach that has been used to teach early literacy skills.

- **Are all factors of language and literacy development being considered?** When tracking progress for emergent bilinguals, we have reiterated the importance of using multiple measures, since one assessment is not likely to capture the complexity of bilingual language and literacy development. Moreover, some factors of development are not easily quantified in many commonly used reading measures. In Chapter 3, we mentioned several notable cultural and affective factors, such as prior literacy experiences and motivation in reading, that should be taken into account while describing student progress.

- **What is the affective filter like?** The **affective filter** (Krashen, 1982) refers to how comfortable a student feels about learning the new language in a specific environment. Students who have a low affective filter feel comfortable in taking risks in learning language. Students with a high affective filter feel anxious and nervous, and sometimes feel bored or uninspired about language learning. If students are not showing progress in reading skills, it would be wise to consider whether the affective filter is the cause. As we described in Chapter 3, the affective resources of a student, such as motivation and engagement, are crucial to reading development. Moreover, educators can take specific steps to change the atmosphere of a classroom so that students feel positive and comfortable in their learning environment.

PART THREE: INSTRUCTIONAL APPLICATIONS

Phonemic Awareness Instruction in the Classroom

Phonemic awareness instruction in the classroom can be embedded throughout the literacy block and the school day. Educators in grades K–2 should schedule 15–20 minutes (not necessarily consecutive) of explicit instruction and guided practice per day. For students who are in the upper grades and new to learning English, phonemic awareness is a practice that can be integrated into explicit language instruction taught by the classroom or EL teacher. In any of these cases (and ones not mentioned here), phonemic awareness activities are most effective when used within a context; that is, they should fit into parts of the curriculum that are already being taught, such as children's literature, thematic instruction, classroom field trips, or community-based activities. When emergent bilinguals have a stronger sense of the vocabulary used in phonemic awareness activities, they gain deeper understandings of the letters, sounds, and meanings of the words. For example, if a kindergarten classroom visits an apple orchard on a field trip, the educator can capitalize on some of the words used to describe and tell the story of the trip.

> Educator models: "I am going to say two words that have the same first sound. I'll do the first one: *apple, ant*. The first sound I hear in those words is /ă/: /ă/ *apple*, /ă/ *ant*. Both those words begin with the sound /ă/.
> Educator guides: "Now, let's try one together: *sort, seed, cider*.* What is the first sound you hear in all of those words?"
> *Even though cider begins with the /c/ sound, it is a soft /c/ and has the same sound as /s/. In this case, it is OK to use it along with other /s/ words.

In the following phonemic awareness activities, it's important to make sure that emergent bilinguals know the vocabulary being used in the activity. If they don't, preteach the words before playing the game. As mentioned in previous sections of this chapter, building vocabulary alongside beginning reading skills is crucial to students' overall literacy development.

Sound Isolation: What's in the Box?

In two versions of this activity, students identify the beginning (or ending) sound of photo cards or small objects.

Version 1. Gather small objects that have the same beginning (or ending) sound. Place them in a box or a bag. Ask the students, "Can you name the objects in the box and tell me the beginning (or ending) sound?"

Version 2. Gather small objects that begin with two different beginning (or ending) sounds. Provide two small boxes or containers. Place the objects on the table. Ask the students, "Can you place the objects that begin with /m/ in this box and the objects that begin with /p/ in this box?"

Sound Isolation: Find Your Match!

In two versions of this activity, students match beginning sounds to photo cards or small objects.

Version 1. In this activity, gather two photo cards and a selection of small objects or other visuals for several targeted sounds. Pass one object out per student. Tell the students to identify the beginning (or ending) sound of the object in their head. Model as follows:

> "Everyone has a small object. First, you will say what the beginning sound of your object is, then you will find someone in the room that has an object with the same beginning sound. For example, I have a *mug*. The first sound in *mug* is /m/. Now, what you will do is find the person in the room who has the same beginning sound as you. Since I have a mug with the first sound /m/, I need to find someone who has the /m/ sound. When I say, 'Find your match!' you will walk around and find another student who has the same sound."

Version 2. Pass out the two photo cards, small objects, or other visuals for several targeted sounds. As in Version 1, tell the students to identify the beginning sound of their object.

> Educator models: "I am going to say a sound. If your object matches the sound I have, please stand up! [or line up at the door]. For example, if I called the sound /m/, I would stand and line up because I have a *mug* and the first sound in *mug* is /m/. If you have the beginning sound /m/, please line up!"

Sound Blending and Segmenting: Sound (Elkonin) Boxes

For both blending and segmenting tasks find an image (see Figure 5.18), draw three connected boxes, and provide students with some type of chip (such as the small circles used in a bingo game).

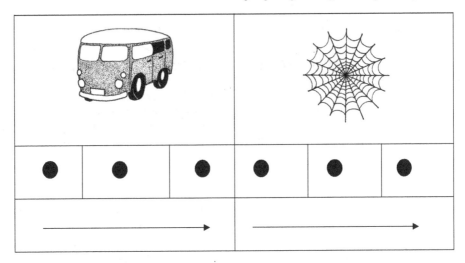

FIGURE 5.18. Sound boxes for blending and segmenting. Drawings used by permission of Path to Reading Excellence in School Sites (PRESS).

Sound Blending

Educator models: "I am going to say three sounds. As I say each sound, I will put a chip in the box, then I will follow my finger across the arrow and say the word. /v/ /ă/ /n/—*van*."

Educator guides: "Now it's your turn. I'll say the sounds, and you read the word. /w/ /ĕ/ /b/. What's the word?"

Sound Segmenting

Educator models: "I am going to say a word. Then, I will put a chip in each box for each sound. Next, I will follow my finger across the arrow and say the word. Watch. /v/ /ă/ /n/—*van*."

Educator guides: "Now it's your turn. I'll say the word and you put a marker in each box for each sound. *Web*."

Student says: "/w/ /ĕ/ /b/."

Sound Manipulation

For sound manipulation tasks, materials are not necessary.

I Say, You Say!

Educator models: "I am going to say a word. Then, I am going to take off one of the sounds and make a new word. The word is *cat*. Now, I'll take the /c/ off the word and instead add an /h/. What's the new word? *Hat!*"

Educator guides: "Now, it's your turn. I say the word *fan*. Take the /f/ off of the word and add an /m/. You say the new word!"

Student says: "*Man!*"

This game can also be played by manipulating medial and final sounds.

MAKING A CONNECTION WITH CHILDREN'S LITERATURE

There are lots of opportunities to use children's picture books for assessment of phonemic awareness. For example, educators can show students a picture book that is familiar to the students. Show a page to students and play "Phoneme Pop." Say: "When I say the word of a picture on the page of this book, tell me the first sound you hear!"

Phonics Instruction in the Classroom

Like phonemic awareness instruction, phonics is best taught and reinforced in authentic contexts in which students have an opportunity to make connections to the words they are decoding, not on isolated tasks in which students need to sound out and read long lists of words without visuals or explanations. Systematic and explicit instruction is strongly recommended for emergent bilinguals (Goldenberg, 2013; Leseaux & Marietta, 2012). Systematic phonics instruction should follow a continuum of skills similar to the one introduced earlier in this chapter. Although it is possible that students can read some words farther along the continuum than others, it's best to use assessment data to determine which phonics skill area needs the most work and teach explicitly beginning there. Explicit instruction of phonics involves a gradual release of responsibility (Fisher & Frey, 2008; Pearson & Gallagher, 1983), in which the educator models a sound (or sound combination), provides guided practice reading the sounds in a word, allows students to collaborate and share as they practice reading words, and then offers them independent work time to read words that were modeled.

Usually, phonemic awareness and phonics are taught and assessed at the same time. Educators teach and assess phonemic awareness skills as they are teaching phonics skills. For example, a student who is working on initial sound isolation in phonemic awareness can also be learning letter names and sounds.

The following activities are just a *few* approaches for practicing phonics skills and should be explicitly taught.

Sound-Spelling Boxes

This activity is similar to the one presented in the earlier phonemic awareness section, except the chips are replaced with letter tiles, magnetic letters, or other movable letters or letter combinations (see Figure 5.19). Choose 8–12 letters. To do a productive task, ask students to use the letter tiles to create the word that is represented in the visual, *wave*. To do a receptive task, place the letters in the box and ask students to sound out each letter to make the word *wave*. Make a list of the words you have practiced and review them once you finished reading several words. Ask the student to talk about the words, making sure to incorporate oral language development throughout the activity.

FIGURE 5.19. Sound boxes and letter tiles for phonics activities. Drawing used by permission of Path to Reading Excellence in School Sites (PRESS).

Word Chains

Present the students with a decodable word written on a dry erase board. Have an eraser and dry erase marker ready. Read the word on the board (e.g., *cake*), and model how to sound it out and read it fluently. Then, erase just one letter of the word (erase the letter *c*) and replace it with another letter (add the letter *m*). Say: "If you can read *cake*, you can read *make*." Then, continue in a "word chain" by changing only one letter at a time. This word chain could continue in the following way: *cake, make, take, lake, like, pike, Mike, bike, bake.* All sound combinations on the continuum that the student has studied can be used.

Word Game Board

Gather dice, a game board, a marker for each player, and two to four players. Make a simple game board like the one in Figure 5.20 or draw your own. Write down targeted words that students have been learning during instruction. With the players, roll the dice and move the number of spaces that come up. Read the word where the piece lands. Encourage the students to talk about the word, say a sentence using the word, or tell what the word means.

START	cake	flake	shake	frame	lake
shame	frames	snake	brake	grape	fame
game	same	tame	take	gate	END

FIGURE 5.20. Example of a game board using silent *e*.

Integrating Oral Language Development into Phonemic Awareness and Phonics Instruction

Emergent bilinguals need plenty of opportunities to increase the number of words in their vocabularies. There are numerous ways to encourage language growth while explicitly teaching letter sounds, letter–sound combinations, and decoding words so that the teaching of these skills is not isolated, but there is a context for greater oral language development and vocabulary growth.

The graphic organizer in Figure 5.21 features several options for how an educator might spark a conversation about a particular word. One approach is to engage in conversations about the words that are being practiced. For example, while teaching the /o–e/ sound, an educator might introduce the word *rose*.

Fluency Instruction in the Classroom

Fluency instruction in the classroom can be embedded throughout the literacy block and practiced across content areas such as science and social studies. Fluency instruction should not just focus on reading rate; too often fluency practice becomes a race to see how many words can be read in a given time period. The following activities can be used to practice all three components of fluency: rate, accuracy, and expression.

Peer Learning Strategies

Peer learning is a well-researched approach to increasing fluency for all students, including emergent bilinguals. Much of the research in this area comes from peer-assisted learning strategies (PALS; Fuchs, Fuchs, Mathes, & Simmons, 1997), whereby students are strategically partnered and follow a set of procedures to read with each other.

Draw a picture of the word.	Give examples of the word in a sentence.
	I gave my mother a rose. *The rose has thorns that hurt my fingers!* *He rose from bed in the middle of the night.*
Do you know this word in your home language? *la rosa* (Spanish)	**Ask questions about the word.** *Where have you seen roses growing in your neighborhood?* *Who would you give a rose to?*

FIGURE 5.21. Ways to develop oral language during a phonemic awareness and phonics lesson.

To partner students in peer learning strategies, an educator chooses students who are more fluent (partner A) and pairs them with students who are less fluent (partner B). Partner A acts as the model of reading for partner B and helps him when he needs support. To do so, partner A reads a book or passage aloud that is at the reading level of partner B. Then, partner B reads the same text that was read by partner A, while partner A helps partner B with any words he does not know, using an error correction procedure. The partners alternate taking turns reading, asking comprehension questions, and making predictions about the text.

Repeated Reading

Repeated reading is an approach to increasing the accuracy, rate, and expression that helps improve comprehension (Therrien, 2004). To use this strategy, ask a student to read a text (a book or a passage) that can be read with 93–97% accuracy. In the first reading, the student reads the passage or portion of the book, while an educator sits nearby to correct errors. When he has finished reading, the educator asks simple comprehension questions, such as "Who was that story about?" Then, in the next reading, the student reads the exact same text, while the teacher corrects errors. At the end of the second reading, the educator asks a question, such as "What was the story all about?" In the third and final reading, the student reads the exact same text, while the teacher corrects errors. At the end of the third reading, the teacher asks a question, such as "What happened in the story?" or "What do you think about what you read?"

In some variations of this strategy, students use a graph to record how many words per minute they read at the end of each reading of the same text, so they can see that each time they read (it is hoped) they increased the number of words they were able to read. Some teachers also use a fluency rubric (such as the one shown in Part Two) to comment on the improvement of the student's expression during reading.

Readers' Theatre

In readers' theatre, a group of students read from the text of a script. Students do not concentrate on memorizing the lines, but work toward reading the script fluently and with expression. Each student is assigned a part in the script. Students practice their assigned parts with help from the teacher. There are many free scripts for readers' theatre to be found online.

SUMMARY

Learning how to read in a new language is a complex endeavor. Using a variety of formal and informal assessments of beginning reading can make this complex process more manageable. While formal assessments of beginning reading can help determine if a student may need additional support to progress in reading, diagnostic assessments and informal assessments can help an educator to pinpoint students' strengths and opportunities for growth. When educators take into account the linguistic features of a student's home language, they have a better understanding of how to support reading objectives. Like the classroom vignette in the beginning of the chapter, Ms. Peterson used Amal's knowledge of sounds in her home language to plan her instruction. This example shows how educators can capitalize on what students already know about language while developing English language and beginning reading skills.

CHAPTER 6

Assessing Academic Language and Comprehension in the Content Areas

Mohamed arrived at his fourth-grade classroom excited to share some news with his teacher, Mr. Hassan.

"Mr. Hassan! I heard some people on TV use the word *eliminate*—one of the words we are learning about in math! Can I put a star on our 'Words We See and Hear' chart?"

"Cool, Mohamed. Great work keeping your ears open for our words!" Mr. Hassan replied with excitement. "What was the word? How did they use it?"

"Well, I was watching the sports channel, and they were talking about all the soccer teams playing in the championship games. One of the guys on the TV said that my favorite team was eliminated."

"Oh, yeah! That's great you heard that," replied Mr. Hassan. "It's true—when we talk about sports and especially when we talk about championships, we use the word eliminate to mean that a team is no longer able to keep playing because they lost."

"Right, like yesterday in PE, Ms. Hoffman split us up into four groups to play badminton. When a team lost, they sat down because they were eliminated. Is that right?" Mohamed wondered.

"Yeah, you could say that," Mr. Hassan affirmed. "Our definition of *eliminate* is "to take out." So, the team that lost was eliminated from playing. Great work listening for that word that gets used everywhere—especially outside of school. Now, you can go place a star next to the word eliminate on our 'Words We See and Hear' chart. And keep your ears open for all the words we're learning."

Later that day, Mr. Hassan gathered a small group of students to conduct an informal assessment of the words they had been learning that week. After passing out a few blank pieces of paper, he gave the directions.

"I am going to use our words of the week to describe a situation. You will write a sentence responding to the situation and using the word. Let's begin."

Mr. Hassan said, "You go to the doctor and the doctor says, 'You need to eat more healthy foods. What is one thing that you will eliminate from your diet to be healthier?' Write a sentence using the word eliminate that answers the question."

This snapshot of a fourth-grade classroom provides insight into how one teacher at Riverview Elementary, Mr. Hassan, is building an awareness of words into his instruction and assessment. By encouraging his students to look outside the classroom for words they are learning in class, this teacher is making important links between the vocabulary students need to comprehend inside and outside the classroom. Mr. Hassan used the word *eliminate* in his vocabulary teaching, because it had been a part of a mathematics lesson in which the class learned about eliminating variables. He knew that this word had a similar meaning across different content areas and that it could be a good word for students to practice in several contexts both inside and outside the classroom. If Mohamed did not know the meaning of the word *eliminate*, chances are that he may not have known that his team didn't play in the championship games. This example highlights how crucial understanding language is for both listening comprehension (like the classroom example) and reading comprehension. It also illustrates two classroom-based assessments that can be used to measure word consciousness: a "Words We See and Hear" chart and an assessment that encourages students to come up with an example of how to use the vocabulary in context.

Up to this point in the book, we have described several components that contribute to overall reading and listening comprehension: linguistic, cultural, and affective resources (Chapter 3); the development of oral language (Chapter 4); and the ability to distinguish sounds, decode words, and read with fluency (Chapter 5). In this chapter, we discuss how to assess the language-based skills that help emergent bilinguals comprehend text across different content areas. Simply stated, if students do not know the meaning of words or the complex structure of academic language in what they hear or read, it can be very difficult for them to understand and know how to respond. Without vocabulary knowledge, students are likely to miss out on developing content knowledge (Templeton et al., 2015).

Making sense of language is the essence of comprehension (Catts, Hogan, & Fey, 2003). Language has many layers and, for this reason, comprehension of text can be quite complex. For managing both instruction and assessment, it can be helpful to think of comprehension as consisting of three components. In this chapter, we consider comprehension through these three language-based skills: academic language, morphological awareness, and word consciousness. Comprehension involves much more than the use of these three skills, but here we zero in on these three vocabulary-related areas. In the following example, we showcase the language-based skills needed to comprehend a specific sentence from a nonfiction text on skeletons: *In contrast to the endoskeleton, the exoskeleton of the grasshopper sheds 5 or 6 times over the course of the lifetime of the insect.*

Academic language is the oral and written language used to communicate for academic purposes (Nagy & Townsend, 2012). While the words *endoskeleton* and *exoskeleton* are academic vocabulary that the reader must know to comprehend the meaning of the sentence, the reader must also know academic syntax, such as "in contrast to." This phrase tells the reader that one thing is different from another thing. Moreover, in this sentence, the subject of the sentence, *grasshopper,* is also referred to as *the insect.*

Morphological awareness is an understanding that words are made up of parts that have individual meanings. The morphemes *endo* and *exo* are commonly used in science. These morphemes communicate to the reader that a skeleton can be on the inside or outside.

Word consciousness is an awareness of how words work in different contexts and reinforces word learning (Anderson & Nagy, 1992; Beck, McKeown, & Kucan, 2013; Graves & Watts-Taffe, 2002). The words *sheds* and *course* are multiple meaning, or *polysemous,* words. Knowing that the word *sheds* in this sentence is a verb that means "gets rid of" provides one of the meanings of this word. The word *course* is also used in many contexts in different, but related ways.

Assessing the academic language required to comprehend particular texts involves more than determining whether a student knows the academic vocabulary. Students may know that an *exoskeleton* is a hard covering on an insect or crustacean, but they also have to know how to use the word *exoskeleton* to communicate what they understand. Here are just a few phrases that include the word *exoskeleton,* which can be used to talk about these particular kinds of insects and crustaceans: "shed an exoskeleton," "produce an exoskeleton," "exoskeletons have evolved," and "a new exoskeleton is formed when . . ." Knowing the definition of the word is only part of vocabulary knowledge (Beck, McKeown, & Omanson, 1987). The goal is to encourage students to align academic vocabulary with academic syntax (Nagy & Townsend, 2012), as in *As a result of the cicada molting from its exoskeleton, the adult skin began to harden.*

In this chapter, we discuss the assessment of these three language-based skills that contribute to reading and listening comprehension across the content areas. First we lay a foundation for comprehension by introducing several theories that begin to explain how students comprehend text. Then we discuss academic language, morphological awareness, and word consciousness and give examples of what these processes may look like in a classroom. From there, we describe formal assessments of language and comprehension that are commonly used in schools. We provide several informal classroom-based assessments that are effective across grades and content areas. Along the way, we continue to share how to support emergent bilinguals through formal and informal assessment practices. We close the chapter with suggestions for some instructional ideas for the classroom.

FOUNDATIONAL IDEAS

In laying a foundation for the discussion of comprehension assessment with emergent bilinguals, we outline what is involved in this complex process. The way in which students acquire new knowledge that expands on what they already know can be explained by *sociocultural theories* (Au, 1998; Moll, 1994; Nieto, 2002; Vygotsky, 1978), which posit that students' culture, language, and social interactions are deeply tied to knowledge. Taking a sociocultural approach to facilitating students' acquisition of knowledge means using students' culture, language, and lived experiences as the conduit for new learning. Knowledge is, after all, the primary element of comprehension (Pearson, 2015). If educators are to work toward ensuring comprehension, focusing on knowledge building is essential.

A framework for the comprehension of text is the simple view of reading (SVR; Gough & Tunmer, 1986), which posits that word decoding and language comprehension are necessary for text comprehension. The SVR framework applies to emergent bilinguals (e.g., Hoover & Gough, 1990; Mancilla-Martinez, Kieffer, Biancarosa, Christodoulou, & Snow, 2011; Proctor, Carlo, August, & Snow, 2005), and aligns with what we have shared in previous chapters—that fluent word reading and vocabulary knowledge will help emergent bilinguals comprehend text. Decoding skills are necessary, but not sufficient (Gough & Tunmer, 1986) for comprehension. Oral language development is also a crucial factor for reading comprehension (e.g., Lesaux, Crosson, Kieffer, & Pierce, 2010).

To extend the understanding of comprehension to emergent bilinguals, it's important to think beyond the SVR. Students comprehend text when they can decode and know the meaning of the words *and* when they draw on their pool of knowledge and background experiences. Thinking beyond the SVR allows educators to take other factors into consideration, such as students' experiences, that are integral to reading comprehension.

In Figure 6.1, we place reading in an additional language at the intersection of three related and complex areas broadly defined as sociocultural, psychological, and linguistic (Helman, 2016). Funds of knowledge are located within the area of sociocultural factors, because they represent what students know from their community, home, school, and lived experiences. Another aspect of the web of knowledge are psychological factors that include the components of the affective and cognitive domains. The psychology of reading and comprehension include particular cognitive processes in the brain, such as **working memory,** that enable students to access the information that has been learned and to synthesize and make meaning from it. Psychological factors also include the affective domains of motivation and interest that readers have.

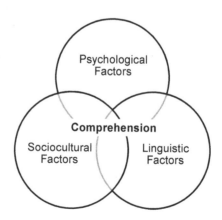

FIGURE 6.1. What influences comprehension for emergent bilinguals?

Also layered in the knowledge web are linguistic factors: *vocabulary*—what words mean; *semantics*—what words mean in context; *morphology*—the meaning of word parts; *syntax*—the order of words; and *phonology*—the sounds that make up words. To comprehend, students have to read the words, know how to use the words to make meaning, and connect their meaning in text to what they already know.

To illustrate these foundational ideas, we return to the classroom example of exoskeletons in science. The following science standard is an example: "Construct an argument that plants and animals have internal and external structures that function to support survival, growth, behavior, and reproduction" (NGSS Lead States, 2013). In order to make meaning of any science text (e.g., textbook, digital text, lecture) that addresses this standard, educators should consider the web of factors involved. Educators might ask: Do students have knowledge from out-of-school experiences about crustaceans, cicadas, or grasshoppers, and can they use this knowledge to construct an argument about exoskeletons? Are students interested in this topic? Are students able to synthesize the text that they have read? Do students have the language to talk about this topic?

What Is Involved in Comprehension of the Content Areas?

Contained within the linguistic factors of knowledge building is the concept of academic language. Academic language is the oral and written language that is used to communicate in academic settings (Nagy & Townsend, 2012). It is related to other concepts we described in Chapter 1—academic language proficiency and basic interpersonal communication skills (BICS; Cummins, 1979). Academic language requires language skills that are different from BICS, the language used for social interactions. Academic language is a unique register (Schleppegrell, 2001) characterized by specific features and structures within texts. Text structure, as we have read, is the way in which a text is organized. Understanding text structure can contribute to overall comprehension of a text (e.g., Williams & Pao, 2013). For example, poems, lab reports, narratives, and historical documents all have unique text structures.

Furthermore, each discipline utilizes its own academic language (Schleppegrell, 2001; Shanahan & Shanahan, 2008; Zwiers, 2013); science, mathematics, social studies, and literacy are but a few examples. Features of academic language across content areas include specialized vocabulary, words with complex morphology, dense and abstract text, and stylized grammar (Lesaux & Harris, 2015; Nagy & Townsend, 2012; Snow & Ucelli, 2009).

Another language-based skill related to comprehending text in the content areas is morphological awareness. **Morphemes** are the smallest cluster within a word that holds meaning; for instance, the word *books* has two morphemes *book* + *s*. Morphemes include affixes, such as prefixes and suffixes, that may be classified as derivational or inflectional. Morphemes also include base words and/or roots (also called free or bound morphemes), which are word parts that can or cannot stand alone. Figure 6.2 presents an example of the morphemes within one word.

Students who have morphological awareness can unlock the meanings of words by knowing the meanings of word parts. Teaching and fostering morphological

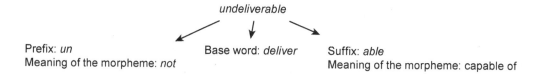

FIGURE 6.2. Morphemes in the word *undeliverable*.

awareness can support their comprehension of words, sentences, and larger chunks of texts. Students with morphological awareness look for patterns and word parts in a word, and they manipulate words by adding affixes to create their own new words. Morphological awareness can be cultivated across the content areas by teaching students morphemes that are common to the discipline. For example, Figure 6.3 includes a sampling of morphemes that are represented in specific content areas.

In order to comprehend complex text, students must be able to point out words they do not know or words that are used in multiple ways. Word awareness (or word consciousness) involves having an awareness of words and their uses. Silverman and Hartranft (2015) note that students with word awareness "notice words in the environment, recognize when they do or do not know a word, and exhibit excitement and interest in word learning" (p. 100). An integral part of being aware of words is knowing their definitions and being able to use words to communicate a message. Yet that process is complex. Beck et al. (1987) present word knowledge along a continuum (see Figure 6.4 for an example). This continuum explains the extent to which one can know a word by providing information about the breadth (how many words a student knows) and about the depth (how deeply the student understands a given word across contexts).

Word consciousness for emergent bilinguals is unique, as the knowledge and understanding of words in two languages represent more layers in this schematic. Unique considerations of word knowledge for emergent bilinguals include:

- Does the student know a **cognate** for the word? Cognates are words, such as *television* (English) and *televisión* (Spanish), that are similar across languages.
- Does the student know the concept of what the word represents and have a definition for the word in another language? For example, "I can describe what a word means in Chinese, but I can't think of the words used to describe it in English."
- Does the student have a general concept of a word, but not know the word itself? For example, "That is the thing that you put on your head to listen to music."

The three areas of language comprehension, morphological awareness, word consciousness, and academic language, contribute the many ways in which emergent bilinguals can access text—through reading, writing, or oral communication. Having a strong command of these aspects of language is necessary for comprehension, which is the ultimate goal of reading.

Examples of some morphemes commonly found in Mathematics	Examples of some morphemes commonly found in science	Examples of some morphemes commonly found in social studies
centi (hundred) centimeter	*anti* (against) antibodies	*anti* (against) antislavery, antitrust
circum (around) circumference	*arthro* (joint) arthritis	*counter, contra* (against) counterculture, contradict
equi, equa (equal) equilateral	*chloro* (green) chlorophyll	*inter* (between) intercontinental
hemi (half) hemisphere	*cide* (kill) pesticide	*ism* (state of) Communism
grad (step) gradient	*endo* (inside) endoskeleton	*ist* (person) Communist
kilo (thousand) kilometer	*hydro* (water) hydroelectric	*trans* (across) transcontinental
meter (measure) diameter	*micro* (small) microscope	*uni* (same) unilateral
tri (three) triangle	*ology* (study of) geology	
uni (same) unit	*tox* (poison) toxic	

FIGURE 6.3. Sample morphemes across the content areas.

PART ONE: THE FORMAL ASSESSMENT OF VOCABULARY AND COMPREHENSION AT SCHOOL

Starting in the earliest grades and lasting well into postsecondary settings, a majority of formal language and literacy measures consist of tasks related to comprehension and vocabulary. Moreover, when students are formally assessed across content areas, such as in science or social studies, success on the assessment relies on comprehending the text and knowing the specific content-area vocabulary.

	Word		
	sinister	*gradual*	*interfere*
No knowledge of the word.	x		
A general sense of what the word means.			
A context-based understanding of the word.			x
A knowledge of the word, but inability to use the word automatically and appropriately.		x	
Rich knowledge of the word and how it can be used in a variety of places and how it can be manipulated with morphemes.			

FIGURE 6.4. Example of a word knowledge continuum. Based on Beck, McKeown, and Omanson (1987).

Reading comprehension assessments measure students' ability to decode words as well as use comprehension skills and strategies, including the ability to compare and contrast, infer, summarize, find the main idea, and so on. Vocabulary assessments often ask students to identify the definition or meaning of words. Formal, summative assessments of comprehension in elementary schools are often administered two or three times a year (universal screeners) to keep track of student progress and to make decisions about whether intervention may be needed. High-stakes state standardized assessments in comprehension and vocabulary are administered once a year and are designed to evaluate school programming and overall reading achievement.

Standardized assessments of comprehension and vocabulary share similar features (see Figure 6.5). In these assessments, students often are asked to read and respond to a passage. Generally, it is a short narrative or expository passage, and sometimes a hybrid text (Afflerbach, 2018) that includes a graphic or visual representation that is integral to fully understanding the passage. After students have read the passage, they are asked to read questions presented in a multiple-choice format that range from literal to inferential-type questions. They are prompted to choose a corresponding choice to answer the question. These types of questions sometimes include response choices such as "none of the above," "all of the above," or "only A and B," "only A and C," and so on. Additionally, the question prompt may include language such as "Which one of the answers below does not . . ." Students at times are asked to provide a constructed response. In this response category, students are either asked to write their responses in a few lines that are provided (brief response) or are given a whole page or two (extended response). Usually, test items can be organized from easier to more difficult readings and test items. In computer-adapted assessments of comprehension and vocabulary, students read passages that are based on their performance on previous items. That is, they are presented with more difficult or easier passages depending on their success with the first few passages.

When administering formal assessments of vocabulary and comprehension to emergent bilinguals, consider the following ideas. First, emergent bilinguals (and all

Assessments	Vocabulary	Comprehension
Dynamic Indicators of Basic Early Literacy (DIBELS) Next* **	Grades K–3	Grades K–6
FastBridge Learning* **	Grades 1–8	Grades 1–8
easyCBM* **	Grades K–8	Grades K–8
Clinical Evaluation of Language Fundamentals (CELF)**	Grades K–12	Grades K–12
Measures of Academic Progress (MAP)**	Grades 2–12	Grades 2–12

FIGURE 6.5. Selected screening and progress monitoring assessments for vocabulary and comprehension. *Also include progress monitoring assessments. **Available in English and Spanish.

students) need to know the language of the test. For example, as described above, educators can explicitly teach the meanings of phrases such as "none of the above," or "choose the option that best describes . . . ," or "which one does NOT show . . . ?" Additionally, educators can provide accommodations or modifications, such as increasing the amount of time given to take the test, although many modifications are not evidence based (Gottlieb, 2012). Depending on the type of assessment and the language proficiency of the student, educators decide whether or not it is useful to administer the assessment at all. The decision not to use the assessment may be made if the student is a newcomer with beginning English proficiency and a difficult reading and writing or content-area assessment is involved. Educators should consider an alternative way in which newcomers can demonstrate their knowledge. For high-stakes tests, in some states, emergent bilinguals who have been in the country a year or less are not required to take the test. If they have lived in the United States longer, requirements state that they *do* need to take the assessment. Educators should check their own state's requirements for ELs and state-standardized assessments.

Administering standardized, universal screeners in comprehension and vocabulary for emergent bilinguals is recommended (Esparza Brown & Sanford, 2011; Klingner, Artiles, & Bareletta, 2006; Vanderwood & Nam, 2008) and should be used along with other pertinent data on language proficiency and instructionally informing assessments that have been gathered. Educators can use universal screeners in vocabulary and comprehension as a part of a system to track emergent bilingual students' progress in reading. In analyzing the progress of emergent bilinguals in vocabulary and comprehension according to the results of universal screeners, we recommended that educators think about several aspects related to the construction of the assessment. For example, in Chapter 1, we discussed the importance of recognizing bias in assessment. Often, comprehension measures include an assumed knowledge of topics. For example, if the comprehension assessment involves students reading a story with cultural references (e.g., cultural celebrations, cultural norms) with which they are not familiar, it's important to take this bias into consideration when analyzing assessment results. Educators can look for the specific questions that students were asked that may have depended on cultural knowledge, and consider how the results of these types of questions contribute to an overall statement of a student's comprehension knowledge.

Commonly Used Formal Learning Needs Assessments for Vocabulary and Comprehension

The selected learning needs assessments we present here are used as tools to determine which areas of language-based skills students have learned and which areas warrant additional teaching. The formal assessments listed in Figure 6.6 are typically given when students indicate that they may need a specific language intervention. In many cases, these types of diagnostic assessments are not administered by a classroom teacher, but by the school psychologist or speech and language specialist. These learning needs assessments can tell an educator about syntactic and semantic knowledge, pragmatics knowledge, morphological knowledge, expressive vocabulary skills, and receptive vocabulary skills. Administering these formal assessments in both languages (when possible) can gauge emergent bilinguals' overall vocabulary knowledge.

Reading and Academic Vocabulary Inventories: Informal Learning Needs Assessments of Comprehension and Vocabulary

Educators use inventories of academic vocabulary and informal reading inventories (IRIs) to determine where to focus instruction (see Chapter 7 for information on spelling inventories). Generally, IRIs are administered by the classroom teacher one to three times a year and can be considered an initial tool for determining placement into an instructional group. Once emergent bilinguals are placed in instructional groups, educators can use other informal classroom-based assessments to gauge whether they

Vocabulary assessments
Clinical Evaluation of Language Fundamentals, fifth edition (CELF-5; Wiig, Semel, & Secord, 2013)*
Peabody Picture Vocabulary Test, fourth edition (PPVT-4; Dunn & Dunn, 2007)*
Expressive Vocabulary Test, second edition (EVT-2; Williams, 2007)*
Comprehension assessments
Diagnostic Assessment of Reading Comprehension (DARC; Center for Applied Linguistics & University of Houston, 2002)*
Group Reading Assessment and Diagnostic Evaluation (GRADE™ Online; Williams, 2001)

FIGURE 6.6. Selected formal diagnostic assessments of vocabulary and comprehension. *Available in English and Spanish.

have made daily progress toward objectives. Instructional groupings should change frequently based on student progress.

Many inventories used in classrooms are provided by educational publishers who also include information and materials for administering and analyzing the inventory. It is also important to consider any information the publisher provides about validity and reliability studies that have been conducted to support the measure.

Informal Reading Inventories. IRIs are assessments of what students can do and what they cannot yet do in relation to reading and understanding particular reading passages. In an IRI, educators listen to a student read and record their individual reading behaviors. IRIs can give educators insights into a student's decoding, fluency, and comprehension skills, and are commonly used by classroom teachers in the elementary grades. Some common IRIs used in schools are the Developmental Reading Assessment (DRA2+; Beaver & Carter, 2006) and the Benchmark Assessment System (BAS; Fountas & Pinnell, 2011). Some IRIs are also available in other languages.

The purpose of this type of assessment is to determine a teaching point for individual students. Some classroom teachers administer IRIs to their entire class a couple times over the course of the school year, while other teachers administer the assessment only to those students whom they are concerned are not making progress. An IRI is an individually administered assessment that begins with the student reading a text at or around a 93–96% accuracy rate (instructional level). If the text is too hard, a teacher substitutes a text that the student can read with higher accuracy. The aforementioned published IRIs include specific books that are designed to be read with the student during the administration of the assessment. While the student reads, the educator listens and records the student's errors. At the end of the reading, the educator asks comprehension questions about the text, records fluency descriptors for the reading, and may also ask questions about vocabulary it contained.

IRIs can be useful tools for determining learning needs in reading instruction for emergent bilinguals. Once again, it is important to be mindful of the cultural as well as the specific linguistic knowledge (e.g., idioms and words with multiple meanings) required to comprehend the texts of IRIs and consider these areas when planning for instruction. Educators should be careful to not hold students back from moving forward in reading texts based on mismatches of cultural and linguistic knowledge.

Academic Vocabulary Inventories. An *academic vocabulary inventory* measures the extent to which students know academic words that are specific to a content area (e.g., *endoskeleton*) and general academic words (e.g., *procedure*) that are used across content areas. Stahl and Bravo (2010) suggest that educators work together to identify content-area- specific words and general academic words that students need to know to participate successfully in content-area studies. With these agreed-upon lists of academic words, educators can assess the degree to which students know the academic language of their content area. Educators can create their own inventories or can use inventories available from educational publishers. One such published academic vocabulary inventory suitable for the upper grades is the Academic Vocabulary and Spelling Inventory (AVSI; Templeton et al., 2015), which assesses students' academic vocabulary, morphological knowledge, and spelling development. In the AVSI, students are asked to spell a list of 20 words (e.g., source, economical, majorities). After the students spell the words, the students determine the extent of their knowledge about each word by rating themselves and whether they know any related words or are able to add prefixes or suffixes to the word. With this information, educators can determine the extent to which students have morphological awareness, general vocabulary knowledge, and orthographic (spelling) knowledge.

PART TWO: CLASSROOM-BASED ASSESSMENTS OF VOCABULARY AND COMPREHENSION THAT GUIDE INSTRUCTION

Classroom-based assessments can indicate student progress toward learning the daily or weekly comprehension and vocabulary objectives. Results from these informal assessments tell an educator what to reteach or review or when to move on. Administering classroom-based assessments of morphological awareness, word consciousness, and academic language, gives educators more than a general sense of what students are capable of, and they can then focus on specific areas in their teaching.

Informal Assessments for Daily Instruction of Morphological Awareness

In the following classroom-based assessments of morphological awareness, students show proficiency in knowing the meaning of word parts and understanding the definitions of words. In assessments of morphological awareness, students are expected to identify a morpheme, know what the morpheme means, and then know how the morpheme(s) and the word roots can be combined to make a word with a definition that makes sense. It is helpful to remember that there are several tasks or abilities associated with morphological awareness. For example, consider the word *disengage*. A student may be able to point out that *dis* is a prefix and that it means "not." The student could say, "Oh, that word means *not engaged*!" However, if they don't know what the word *engaged* means and how it appropriately fits with the morpheme *dis*, they may not have a complete understanding of what the word means. For instance, one common meaning of the word *engage* is to have a plan for marrying someone. However, if a person doesn't plan to marry, we would not say that he was *disengaged*. For this reason, it pays to assess to what extent a student knows a morpheme and how it is used with a base word.

Word Sorts

The following examples are easy to implement for any morphemes taught across content areas. To assess knowledge of morphemes, provide students with a set of words written on flash cards (small pieces of paper) that contain the morphemes that are the target of instruction. In Figure 6.7, there are eight words, each with one of three morphemes taught in mathematics: *tri, quad,* and *hex*.

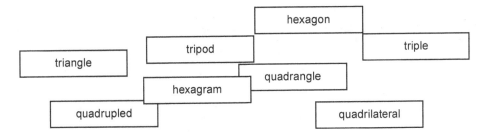

FIGURE 6.7. Sample word sort in mathematics.

A word sort can be done as an *open sort*. First, ask students to read all the words. Then, ask them to sort the words based on a pattern they choose. To do a *closed sort*, ask students to read all the words and sort them based upon specific morphemes. In the example in Figure 6.7, an educator may ask students to sort by prefixes (*tri, quad, hex*).

To keep track of student progress, use a chart like the one in Figure 6.8 that indicates the extent to which the students know the words. In this chart, the educator took notes in each section of the form in order to comment on the extent to which the student had a good grasp of word meanings.

Word Mapping

For words that contain several morphemes, word mapping is an assessment approach to investigate the extent to which students can identify the word parts and put them together to define a word that makes sense. For example, the word *unthinkable* has three morphemes and can be mapped onto three distinct morphemes, *un, think,* and *able* (see Figure 6.9). In this example, as is sometimes the case, a direct translation of the morphemes (not able to think) doesn't really make sense outside the context of a sentence. Things that are *unthinkable* are often also considered horrific or terrible. Given this sort of example, assessing knowledge through a word map is a good way to see if students know word parts *and* word meanings.

Date	Targeted morphemes	Sort morphemes	Define morpheme	Define word	Used in a sentence
10/16/2018	tri quad hex	Halima read 6/8 words accurately. Halima sorted all words accurately.	Halima knew morpheme meanings	Halima provided definitions for triangle, hexagon.	Halima used triangle in a sentence. She was not able to create a sentence with hexagon.

FIGURE 6.8. Sample assessment tracker for morphological awareness.

	Morpheme	Morpheme	Morpheme	What does this word mean?	Use it in a sentence.
unthinkable	un	think	able	not able to think, something horrible	Then, the unthinkable happened

FIGURE 6.9. Example of a word map.

Informal Assessments for Daily Instruction of Word Consciousness

Earlier, we introduced the continuum of students' word awareness, beginning with their having no knowledge of a word and approaching a full awareness of a word and how it can be used in varying contexts. For emergent bilinguals, educators should consider the extent to which students may know a word and be able to explain the word in another language. Allowing students to foster and access their word consciousness across languages through translation and translanguaging is a beneficial way for them to express their knowledge of words. For students using two or more languages, it is not uncommon to hear, "I know that word in _____, but I don't think I know it in English." This metalinguistic knowledge is an important indicator of what students *do* know about the word.

COMMON CORE WORD-CONSCIOUSNESS STANDARDS, K–5

Determine or clarify the meaning of unknown and multiple-meaning words and phrases based on kindergarten to fifth grade reading and content, choosing flexibly from an array of strategies.

◆ Use frequently occurring affixes as clues to the meaning of a word (K–first grade).
◆ Determine the meaning of the new word formed when a known affix is added to a known word (second–third grades).
◆ Use a known root word as a clue to the meaning of an unknown word with the same root (second–third grades).
◆ Use common, grade-appropriate Greek and Latin affixes and roots as clues to the meaning of a word (fourth–fifth grades).

Word Charts

Word awareness charts can be displayed in the classroom for the entire class to access, or they can be written in students' notebooks or writing journals. They can also be posted in hallways, so that multiple classes can interact with the words. The objective of the word awareness chart is to encourage students to see and listen for words that they are learning about in the classroom and be able to make connections to other content areas in the curriculum or in out-of-school contexts. Here's how one educator uses word charts (shown in Figure 6.10) to document students' ability to notice and identify words.

WORDS WE SEE AND HEAR		
Words (Include cognates and the word in other languages.)	**Where did you see or hear the word?**	**How was the word used?**
beneficial *beneficioso (Spanish)* *faa'iido (Somali)*	*I heard the word in a commercial about vitamins!* *I read the word in our science textbook.*	*Taking vitamins is very <u>beneficial</u> to your health.* *Finding the cure for polio has been <u>beneficial</u> to society.*

FIGURE 6.10. Example of a word chart.

"This week, we've focused on the words *beneficial, conclusions,* and *distinct.* I have written those words here on this chart, 'Words We See and Hear.' I also know that some of these words have cognates in some languages. If you know this word in another language, we can list it right here. Now, I would like you to listen for these words in the classroom, outside the classroom, or anywhere! When you hear one of those words, keep it in your mind or write it down so you can tell me about it. If you see the word while you are reading, you can mark the page with a sticky note. Then, when you come to class, tell me about the word and we will write about it on the chart."

Example/Non-Example

This assessment of word knowledge (Beck et al., 2002) can be administered orally, in writing, or visually. An educator provides examples of word meanings through an oral, written, or visual representation, and students respond by stating if the examples are accurate reflections of the words or if they are not. In the discussion below, an educator and students demonstrate how to administer this classroom-based assessment.

EDUCATOR: We've been learning a lot about the word *stunning.* Today, you are going to tell me what things are *stunning.* I am going to read a sentence aloud. If you think it is an example of something that is *stunning,* say the word *stunning.* If it is not, don't say anything at all. First, remember what the word *stunning* means and all the ways that we have talked about that word this week. Let's start.
The wildflowers in the mountains were colorful and smelled wonderful.

STUDENTS: Stunning!

EDUCATOR: Mr. Hernandez always wears a rain jacket to recess.

STUDENTS: (*silence*)

EDUCATOR: Even though it was pouring rain, Maddy ran the race faster than everyone else.

STUDENTS: Stunning.

In another version of this assessment, the educator hands out a form, such as the one in Figure 6.11, that includes several sentences that may or may not represent the word *stunning*. Students read the sentences and then write the word in the space to the side. Educators can also gather visuals or photos that represent the word *stunning*. Bear in mind that not everyone would agree with the statements provided. For example, while one person may think it's stunning to watch a tiger slowly cross a field, another may find it terrifying. Encourage students to defend their answers based on the definition of the word.

Situations

In this assessment (Beck et al., 2002), an educator presents students with a word, and students respond by identifying situations that may represent that word. For example:

Language arts example

"This week we have been learning about a few words: *vanish, devastated,* and *unforgettable.* Can someone tell me about a situation where something vanished? Can someone tell me about a situation where someone would be devastated? Can someone tell me about a situation that was or would be unforgettable?"

Science example

"This week we have been learning about new morphemes frequently used in science: *geo, hydro,* and *endo.* What would make a scientist say this: We have

Language arts example	
Read the sentences below. If the sentences describe something that is *stunning*, write the word *stunning*. If it is not stunning, leave it blank.	
The beautiful tiger walked slowly across the field.	
My muddy shoes left the carpet dirty and wet.	
The crown of jewels sparkled in the sunlight.	
Social studies example	
Read the sentences below. If the sentences describe something that is a *revolution*, write the word *revolution*. If it is not a revolution, leave it blank.	
Citizens of the city and countryside worked together to fight against the policies of the authoritative king.	
The representatives of the U.S. Congress pass laws during the session.	
Many of the citizens of the country were unable to access clean water, so they started protesting in front of the president's house.	

FIGURE 6.11. Example/non-example activity.

harnessed all this energy using this *hydro*electricity. Can someone tell me what a *geo*logist might study? What might you be looking at if a cicada shed its *endo-skeleton?*"

Vocabulary Knowledge Scale

The *Vocabulary Knowledge Scale* (VKS; Wesche & Paribakht, 1996) self-assessment (see Figure 6.12) provides students with the opportunity to think about the extent to which they know a word. As an extension of the original, this version of the VKS includes questions that may be useful for an emergent bilingual, because it draws on word knowledge in another language. Educators can encourage students to use the point system or provide another way of self-assessment, such as yes/no answers or symbols that indicate individual responses (e.g. checkmarks, smiley faces, stars).

Informal Assessments for Daily Instruction of Comprehension

Cloze Passages

We introduced cloze passages in Chapter 4 as procedures that can informally assess students' syntax and vocabulary knowledge. Cloze passages are also used to determine comprehension of key ideas in a text. After students have finished reading a text, an educator presents them with a version of the text in which several key words have been removed. The students read the passage and then fill in the blanks to show how well they understood what they read. For example: *The rough, outer shell of a crustacean is called a/an _____. It has the ability to _____ the body of the crustacean. This outer shell can _____ as many as 6 times throughout the lifetime of the crustacean.*

Response Logs

In a response log, students answer questions or take notes before, during, or after reading. In many cases, response logs are used during independent reading. Response

I don't remember having seen this word before. (1 point)	
I have seen this word before, but I don't think I know what it means. (2 points)	
I have seen this word before, and I think it means _____. (3 points)	
I know this word. It means _____. (4 points)	
I know this word and can describe it in another language. (4 points)	
I can use this word in a sentence. (5 points)	

FIGURE 6.12. Vocabulary knowledge scale for emergent bilinguals.

logs contain general or specific questions about the text. A teacher may encourage all the students to write about the same topic in a response log. For instance, if a class is working on the standard *Explain how specific images (e.g., a diagram showing how a machine works) contribute to and clarify a text,* an educator might ask students to write a response in a reading journal that explains one of the diagrams and briefly summarizes what was read.

Response logs can be used for many genres. In responding to narrative fiction, educators can prompt students to respond in ways such as, but not limited to, the following:

- Create or fill out a story map while they read.
- Create character descriptions.
- Ask questions about the text.
- Make predictions.
- Make connections.

A response log relies heavily on the ability to respond with written sentences, so beginning readers and writers can use alternate forms of responding, such as having a discussion with a peer about what they read or drawing a picture about what they read. To incorporate response logs into science and social studies, consider using two-column learning logs. On one side students write evidence from the text, expressed as either phrases or sentences. On the other side of the column, students respond using a variety of sentence frames: *I connect to this because . . . , This reminds me of . . . , I wonder about . . . ,* or *This is important because. . . .* Other sentence frames or question prompts can be used in two-column learning logs. Collecting learning logs and response logs frequently can give educators a good idea of how students are engaging with a text.

Reading Conferences and Anecdotal Notes

Conducting individual reading conferences is another informal way to keep track of a student's decoding, reading fluency, and text comprehension. In a reading conference, educators check in on how students are using specific strategies that were taught or on how they are applying their knowledge of the standards. Conducting a reading conference can take place once a week or more often if there are concerns about student progress. They also can be conducted in pairs or groups of three if a group of students has been working on a similar reading strategy. In a reading conference, educators can take anecdotal notes (see Figure 6.13) about a student's reading and the extent to which he or she is able to retell the story, describe its key details, or accomplish any other comprehension tasks. In the conference, it is a good idea to start off with a compliment about the student's reading in order to point out strengths. Then the educator should provide specific feedback and instruction in an area or two. Educators complete the conference by suggesting a next step for a student. For example, "The next time you read this text, put a sticky note next to a word you don't know. Try and figure out the meaning from the words around it. When we meet again, I'll ask you what strategies you used to figure that word out."

Student:	Date:	Book:
Strengths		**Opportunities**
Next steps		

FIGURE 6.13. Example of a reading conference tracking sheet.

Exit Slips

At the close of a lesson, educators use an informal assessment called "exit slips" to determine whether students have made progress in achieving the objective of the lesson. Educators pass out small pieces of paper with one or two questions that would indicate how well students understood the lesson. As students leave the classroom, they hand the exit slip to the educator. This information can help educators plan for the next day's instruction. Exit slips do not always have to be in a written form. An educator can ask students a question that they answer orally before they transition from the lesson. For example:

> "In science today, we have been studying what happens during the water cycle. We learned a few new words that help us understand what happens in a water cycle. Before you leave science class today, I would like you to tell me one thing that someone might do if they were caught in *precipitation*. As you leave class, meet me at the door and say, 'One thing that someone might do if they were caught in precipitation is. . . .'"

PART THREE: INSTRUCTIONAL APPLICATIONS

Educators can use many of the aforementioned classroom-based assessments as instructional approaches as well; word mapping, word sorts, and example/non-example tasks are some ways to help students' improve their language-based skills. In fact, these types of informal assessments are most effective when they have *also* been used in instruction. Moreover, some of the strategies we outline next can also be used as informal assessments. The important point to remember about any of the language-based activities discussed in this chapter is that they require explicit and systematic instruction. This recommendation aligns with others that we have made throughout the book. The following instructional applications for building language and comprehension are most effective when taught with a gradual release of responsibility (Pearson & Gallagher, 1983) and with an emphasis on collaborative learning in which students have opportunities for discussion with peers (Fisher & Frey, 2008).

Teaching Structured Academic Conversations

Emergent bilinguals must have ample opportunities to practice academic language with educator support. According to Zweirs and Hamerla (2018), one way to engage in this practice in the classroom is through academic conversations, which are "sustained and purposeful conversations about school topics" (p. 1). Academic conversations can be the avenue through which educators lead students to use academic language and vocabulary across content areas. Students can be given supports, such as sentence frames, that give them the academic language with which to talk about the content. A cross-content example might look like _____ and _____ are alike/different because . . . , or *I wonder what would happen if* _____ *and* _____, or *Based on* _____, *I think that* _____. In addition to using sentence frames, emergent bilinguals must know how to sustain the conversation. In part, the ability to sustain a conversation comes from how an educator sets up the interaction. As Zwiers and Hamerla (2018) suggest, there must be a foundation on which to build. Some conversation prompts will yield more conversation than others. Consider these two examples: "Turn and talk to your partner and answer this question: Did the main character show kindness?" and "Use examples from the story to defend this position: The main character was a good leader in a time of difficulty." The first example may elicit a yes or no response, whereas the second question could instigate an academic conversation that uses complex language, such as "One reason for this is that _____. We think that _____."

Another approach that encourages vocabulary growth and the use of academic language is Instructional Conversations (IC) and Literature Logs (Saunders & Goldenberg, 1999). In ICs, educators facilitate a small group discussion regarding stories students have read or key concepts that students are learning about. Educators facilitate this conversation by establishing a clear academic goal, by ensuring that rates of talk among the students is higher than the educator, by supporting conversation through asking questions, by reviewing statements made by students, and by informally assessing understanding through the conversation. A key element in an IC is collaborating toward an end goal, where a final product or evidence of the conversation is created among the students and educator in the group. The literature logs provide the space for students to write about the stories and concepts they discussed in the Instructional Conversation.

Providing Comprehension Strategies Instruction

Although building vocabulary knowledge is a crucial factor in supporting comprehension, educators can use other strategies as well, such as:

- Expanding on prior knowledge.
- Providing an introduction to the text before reading.
- Asking questions for clarification throughout reading (August, McCardle, & Shanahan, 2014).
- Offering a lesson preview of a text in students' home language (Goldenberg, 2013).

Moreover, students should be taught to use their own strategies for reading (Breiseth, 2016), such as:

- Rereading text.
- Visualizing what is read.
- Reading ahead.
- Taking a picture walk.
- Using graphic organizers.

Educators should use an explicit approach in teaching students how to use their own strategies to monitor comprehension. For example, they can model using a think-aloud: "I'm thinking that this story will likely be about a girl who got lost while she was walking through the mountains. I think that because I see this picture of a girl with a backpack, and she looks tired and lost." When teaching students how to use graphic organizers, educators should demonstrate the process through modeling, focusing on achieving the standard through using the graphic organizer, and not simply teaching the students how a graphic organizer works. Instead of saying "Today, I will show you how to use a web graphic," an educator might say, "Today in social studies, we are discussing how to learn about different points of view on issues. To do this, we will read part of this book and use this graphic organizer to help us see various points of view."

Another strategy for improving comprehension is a well-researched approach called *collaborative strategic reading* (CSR; Klingner & Vaughn, 1998), which entails four strategies: preview, click or clunk, get the gist, and wrap up. First, students preview the text, either by looking at the headings, subheadings, and/or illustrations. This step can also be done in a student's home language if that resource is available. Then, students "click or clunk," which means that they state when some part of the reading makes sense (click) or when some part of the text does not make sense (clunk). After assistance from the teacher to make sense of the "clunk," the students then engage in the third step, get the gist. To get the gist, students summarize the reading to determine its essence. In the fourth step, students wrap up the reading by asking a who, what, where, when, or why question.

Creating a Word-Conscious Classroom

Graves and Watts-Taffe (2008) set forth six principles for fostering word consciousness in a classroom. Based on these principles, on an appreciation for culturally and linguistically sustaining practices (Paris & Alim, 2014; Valdés, 2017), and on an understanding that instruction in students' home language is beneficial (Goldenberg, 2013), we offer the following suggestions for promoting word consciousness to sustain multilingualism.

- Create a multilingual word-rich environment.
- Recognize and promote the skillful use of words in writing and speaking, pointing out bilingual or multilingual uses of words in texts.
- Promote wordplay among languages, such as code meshing and translanguaging in oral conversations.
- Foster word consciousness through writing, such as code meshing and translanguaging in writing.
- Involve students in original investigations, using their language of choice for meaning-making. Promote the use of bilingual dictionaries and resources in investigations.
- Teach students about words, including cognates and morphemes that are shared among languages.

SUMMARY

In this chapter, we discussed the complex nature of comprehending text in the content areas and the involvement of several language-based skills—academic language, word consciousness, and morphological awareness—all of which fall under the umbrella of vocabulary and language. We affirmed the viewpoint that vocabulary knowledge *is* content knowledge, and that without a focus on teaching and assessing vocabulary, educators may lose an opportunity to make comprehension possible for emergent bilinguals. When educators balance formal assessments with a variety of informal classroom-based assessments, they gain a better picture of how emergent bilinguals make meaning in literacy and in the content areas. We concluded with strategies for the classroom that use systematic and authentic approaches to comprehension and vocabulary development.

CHAPTER 7

Assessing Writing

Jamilah is a third-grade student at Riverview Elementary, who was born in Somalia and came to the United States when she was 5 years old. She enrolled in kindergarten at Riverview halfway through the school year. Her family (including aunts, uncles, and cousins who moved to the United States several years before Jamilah and her parents arrived) primarily speak Somali at home, although some of the younger children mostly speak English, especially when they are playing together.

Jamilah is generally doing well in school and is happy and eager to learn. She is a wonderful storyteller and likes to share anecdotes about her family and friends and the activities they do together on weekends and holidays. She has many good ideas that she can articulate well to her teacher and peers, and she is excited to write them down. She also loves to learn new English words that express her ideas just so. Yet, one area that seems somewhat difficult for her is translating all these words and ideas into print. She is concerned about writing "correctly" and is (sometimes overly) attentive to capitalization, punctuation, and spelling. Her writing is laborious and slow, and she frequently looks up words or asks how to spell them.

Jamilah's teacher, Mr. Parson, is concerned that Jamilah will become frustrated, because her difficulties with spelling and handwriting slow the writing process. He worries that Jamilah will eventually lose her motivation to write. Although Riverview has adopted a strong system for screening and monitoring progress in reading, writing remains an area where Mr. Parson and his colleagues feel they need more assessment and instructional knowledge and resources. Mr. Parson would like to find a way to support Jamilah's development of fluent transcription skills, while at the same time fostering her love of storytelling (and hopefully, story writing).

Just as students bring cultural, linguistic, and affective resources to the task of learning to read, they also bring these resources to the task of learning to write. In this case, Jamilah has cultural assets that include funds of knowledge developed within her family and community that she draws on to create stories; she has linguistic assets, such as her knowledge that word choice is important for conveying ideas; and she has motivational assets that undergird her willingness to engage and persist in writing, even while some aspects of the task might be difficult. A challenge for Mr. Parson is to foster the further development of Jamilah's assets while supporting her needs, so that her writing develops in ways that advance her overall language and literacy growth. Fortunately, understanding writing development can help educators like Mr. Parson break this complex task into its interrelated parts, and to think about how to leverage students' strengths and address their needs in systematic ways that effectively support learning to write.

Proficient writing is key to children's success in school. Writing is an essential element of literacy development—indeed, there are strong connections between learning to write and learning to read, with development in one area supporting development in the other (Graham & Hebert, 2011). Writing is critical in order for students to communicate what they are learning in school, not only because grading is partly based on completing assignments and tests for accountability purposes but also because the act of engaging in writing serves to increase critical thinking skills (Shanahan, 2004). Writing is also important for long-term postsecondary education and vocational success (Graham & Perin, 2007). Beyond its impact on success in school and later life, writing can be a tool that students use to develop and convey their personal, social, and cultural identities (Ferdman, 1990; Fitzgerald & Amendum, 2007).

Unfortunately, many students do not attain proficient writing levels in school; in fact, national assessment data have indicated that 72%–73% of fourth, eighth, and 12th graders perform below proficient in writing (National Center for Educational Statistics, 2012; Salahu-Din, Persky, & Miller, 2007). As a group, ELs perform at lower levels than non-ELs, with 90% of non-ELs performing at or above basic levels, compared to 58% of ELs performing at or above basic levels (NAEP, 2007). Although national assessment data do not provide the entire picture of the writing development of children in schools, these statistics are alarming given the central role that writing plays in students' success in school and later life, as well as its potential to provide a positive and enriching way for students to express themselves and engage in learning.

In this chapter, we first describe foundational perspectives on writing development that have direct implications for writing assessment and instruction. Then we briefly discuss formal writing assessments that are used in schools, followed by a more in-depth discussion of classroom-based assessments that can be used to guide instruction. We describe important contextual factors that educators should consider in assessing emergent bilingual students' writing and end with instructional applications.

FOUNDATIONAL IDEAS

Theories We Call Upon

Researchers have proposed a "simple view of writing" (Berninger & Amtmann, 2003) that is helpful for thinking about how to assess and provide instruction that supports writing development in children in general, and may also be helpful for thinking about how to assess and support the instruction of emergent bilinguals. According to this simple view (depicted in Figure 7.1), writing is made up of three components: *transcription, text generation,* and *self-regulation.* A student's engagement in any of these components is constrained by *cognitive resources,* such as attention and memory (McCutchen, 2006). Lack of fluency in one component (e.g., transcription) constrains the other components, because each component requires cognitive resources, and they must work in concert for successful text production. In Jamilah's case, her lack of fluent transcription skills could limit her text generation, not because she doesn't have good ideas to write about (she does!), but because she must devote a lot of attention and working memory to form letters and spell the words she wants to write, leaving fewer cognitive resources to devote to idea generation, word choice, and composing interesting sentences.

The development of the transcription and text generation components of writing occurs at multiple levels of language, including letter–sound, word, sentence, and discourse levels (Whitaker, Berninger, Johnston, & Swanson, 1994). At the letter–sound and word levels, beginning writers develop an awareness of the alphabetic principle and graphophonemic relationships, and begin to transcribe letters, sounds, and words (Ehri, Gibbs, & Underwood, 1988). As beginning writers gain an awareness of and use writing conventions, they begin to separate words with spaces and thoughts with punctuation (Tolchinsky, 2006), and thus generate and transcribe text at the sentence level. As they gain knowledge of content and writing genres, they begin to

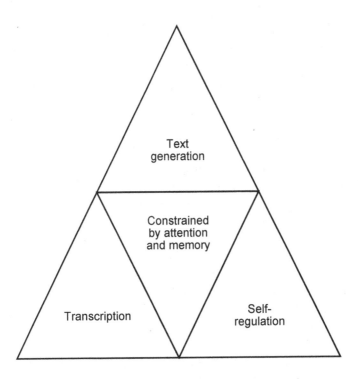

FIGURE 7.1. A "simple view" of writing (e.g., Berninger & Amtmann, 2003).

produce longer units of writing at the *discourse* level (McCutchen, 2006). Next we further describe the components of writing, along with specific considerations for emergent bilinguals in these areas.

Components of Writing

What Is Transcription?

Transcription is the encoding of sounds, words, sentences, and longer passages into print, and involves both spelling and handwriting. Spelling requires **phonological coding** (that includes the analysis and synthesis of phonemes in words; Berninger & Swanson, 1994) and **orthographic coding** (that involves representing a word in memory and accessing the spelling of the word either as a whole, as clusters of letters, or as single letters at a time; Berninger & Fuller, 1992). Spelling presents a challenge for many beginning writers (Graham, Harris, & Chorzempa, 2002) and can place significant constraints on the development of other writing processes. Thus, accounting for spelling is an important component of assessment of students' writing.

Spelling can be particularly difficult in English, which does not have a completely **transparent orthography.** In other words, English spelling patterns are not always consistent in the way they appear and sound, because there is not a one-to-one relationship between each phoneme (sound) and grapheme (letter). English orthography is not completely *opaque*, because many spelling patterns are fairly consistent (such as most consonant sounds and simple rimes in CVC words), but many other spelling patterns are more variable. For example, the words *though, through, tough, trough,* and *bough* all contain the spelling pattern *ough*, which looks the same in each word but is pronounced in five different ways (it rhymes with *go, too, buff, off,* or *cow*, all of which also have completely different spelling patterns)! Students whose home language has a transparent orthography, such as Spanish, might find learning to spell in English particularly confusing, since learning the spelling of one word might not necessarily transfer to spelling another word that sounds similar.

Handwriting involves integrating phonological and orthographic coding with the **motor system** that allows for the physical formation of letters and words (Berninger, 2009). Beginning writers must allocate significant working memory resources to this **orthomotor integration,** limiting higher-order writing processes. Therefore, accounting for fluent handwriting skills is also an important component of early writing assessment. For emergent bilinguals, handwriting might pose additional challenges if their home language writing system is not alphabetic For example, some systems, such as English and other Western languages, are alphabetic, with individual symbols (letters) representing phonemes; some systems, such as Chinese characters, are **logographic,** with individual symbols representing morphemes; and yet other systems, such as Japanese, are **syllabic,** with individual symbols representing syllables. Thus, learning to write in English might also mean learning to write by using a whole new symbolic system.

Considerable evidence supports the importance of transcription skills with respect to writing quality and quantity. These relationships have been documented early in writing development; letter-writing fluency has been shown to relate to kindergarten spelling (Al Otaiba et al., 2010), and spelling and letter-writing fluency have been shown to relate to kindergarten writing achievement (Kim et al., 2011). These connections persist over time; researchers have found that spelling is a strong predictor of writing quality from first grade to as late as seventh grade (Abbott, Berninger, & Fayol, 2010). Moreover, intervention studies have shown improvements in students' writing quality and quantity in response to interventions targeting handwriting and spelling (see McMaster, Kunkel, Shin, Jung, & Lembke, 2018, for a review).

The importance of transcription skills are reflected in the core standards, including reading standards that address phonemic awareness and phonics skills described in Chapter 5, given that decoding and encoding using phonemic awareness and phonics skills are "two sides of a coin" (Ehri, 2000, p. 19), as well as in English language arts and writing standards.

COMMON CORE: TRANSCRIPTION SKILLS, GRADES 1–3

- ◆ Print all upper- and lowercase letters.
- ◆ Use end punctuation for sentences.
- ◆ Use conventional spelling for words with common spelling patterns and for frequently occurring irregular words.
- ◆ Spell untaught words phonetically, drawing on phonemic awareness and spelling conventions.
- ◆ Use conventional spelling patterns and generalizations (e.g., word families, position-based spellings, syllable patterns, ending rules, meaningful word parts) in writing words.
- ◆ Use spelling patterns and generalizations (e.g., word families, position-based spellings, syllable patterns, ending rules, meaningful word parts) in writing words.

Text Generation

Text generation is the process of "turning ideas into words, sentences, and larger units of discourse" (McCutchen, 2006, p. 123), and is distinct from the transcription of ideas into actual print (Berninger & Swanson, 1994). Text generation draws on linguistic sources, including semantic knowledge (including meanings of words or vocabulary; e.g., Coker, 2006; Olinghouse & Leaird, 2009); syntactic knowledge (understanding of syntax or grammatical sentence structure); and knowledge about various topics, text structures, and genres (McCutchen, 2006).

Emergent bilinguals might experience particular difficulties with text generation for a variety of reasons, including fewer English vocabulary words in their repertoire or having background knowledge that diverges from what is expected in class to complete an assigned topic. In addition, text generation can be challenging for emergent bilinguals if their home language grammar (or syntax) is different from English syntax. For instance, a child whose home language is Spanish might write *My brother has five years* instead of *My brother is five years old*. Maintaining the idea *and* the correct syntax at the same time could be especially taxing on working memory. Text generation skills are also largely dependent on knowing text structure and genre.

COMMON CORE TEXT GENERATION SKILLS, WORD AND SENTENCE LEVELS

- Use common, proper, and possessive nouns.
- Use singular and plural nouns with matching verbs in basic sentences (e.g., *He hops; We hop*).
- Use frequently occurring conjunctions (e.g., *and, but, or, so, because*).
- Produce and expand on complete simple and compound declarative, interrogative, imperative, and exclamatory sentences in response to prompts.
- Use collective nouns (e.g., group) and irregular plural nouns (e.g., *feet, children, teeth, mice*).
- Form and use regular and irregular verbs.
- Form and use the past tense of frequently occurring irregular verbs (e.g., *sat, hid, told*).
- Produce, expand on, and rearrange complete simple and compound sentences (e.g., *The boy watched the movie; The action movie was watched by the little boy*).
- Explain the function of nouns, pronouns, verbs, adjectives, and adverbs in general and their functions in particular sentences.
- Form and use regular and irregular plural nouns (e.g., *children*) and abstract nouns (e.g., *childhood*).
- Form and use the simple verb tenses (e.g., *I walked; I walk; I will walk*).
- Ensure subject–verb and pronoun–antecedent agreement.
- Produce simple, compound, and complex sentences.

Like transcription, text generation has been demonstrated to be uniquely related to overall writing quality and quantity. Skilled writers are able to generate language more *efficiently* than less-skilled writers, and this efficiency is a key predictor of writing quality (Dellerman, Coirier, & Marchand, 1996). This finding holds true for children just beginning to develop writing skills: Juel, Griffith, and Gough (1986) reported that the number of ideas generated uniquely predicted first and second graders' writing quality. Efficiency with language leads to greater language production and thus longer texts, and text length has been found to provide a strong index of text production fluency as well as quality (e.g., Berninger & Swanson, 1994).

Similar to intervention studies examining transcription skills, intervention studies examining text generation have shown improvements in students' writing quality

COMMON CORE TEXT GENERATION SKILLS, DISCOURSE LEVEL

- Create informative/explanatory texts about a topic.
- Describe and write a narrative event or sequence of events in an organized way; provide a reaction to what happened.
- Recall information from experience, and use information from different sources to answer questions.
- Write opinion pieces with support for a point of view.
- Write routinely over extended periods of time, and set aside time for research, reflection, and revision for a range of tasks, purposes, and audiences.

and quantity (McMaster et al., 2018). And, similar to transcription skills, the core standards with respect to text generation reflect the importance of text generation at the word, sentence, and discourse levels.

What Is Self-Regulation?

Self-regulation relates to a student's ability to manage his or her own behaviors and affective responses to a task, rather than relying on external prompts or intervention. When applied to writing in the classroom, self-regulation relates to the student's ability to manage the overall writing process, from setting goals for writing (usually related to a purpose presented by the teacher), to planning and organizing writing, persisting in the writing task, revising and evaluating, and reinforcing when writing goals are met. Because writing is such a complex process and involves multiple components, a student's self-regulation skills are important to consider in assessment and instruction (we return to this point later in the chapter).

What Are the Cognitive Demands of Writing?

As we mentioned earlier, the development of each component of writing requires cognitive resources, such as attention and memory (Berninger, 2009; McCutchen, 2006). Students who experience difficulty with one component of writing (like Jamilah does with the handwriting and spelling skills involved in transcription) have limited cognitive resources available for other components (such as word selection and sentence construction involved in text generation, or the planning, organizing, and revising aspects of self-regulation). For example, attentional and memory resources can constrain the writer's ability to avoid grammatical errors and maintain linguistic connections within and between sentences and in larger units of text. When students are immersed in getting their thoughts down, it might be difficult to spell words accurately (transcription) or maintain the same tense (in text generation), for instance. These difficulties can result in written text that is overly simple at best and very difficult for readers to decipher or understand at worst, and does not do justice to the knowledge or ideas that the writer is trying to convey.

The cognitive demands of writing are likely magnified for many emergent bilinguals for several reasons: they must grapple with the complex and multidimensional task of translating ideas into text (words, sentences, passages); with encoding and transcribing that text into print; and with regulating the entire process. As they translate text from one language into the other, they must also navigate the similarities and differences between their home language and English, which include differences in the transparency of the orthographies of the two languages, differences in the writing systems, differences in syntactic rules, and so on.

Text generation likely also places additional demands on emergent bilinguals' cognitive resources, because they may need to mentally translate ideas and words from their home language into English before they can transcribe them into print. In turn, the effort needed to engage in these text generation and transcription tasks can diminish the mental resources needed for self-regulation tasks, such as planning and revising (e.g., Chenoweth & Hayes, 2001; Silva, 1993; Smith, 2018), leading to written products that are more simplistic than those of their monolingual English-speaking peers. These demands become greater through the grade levels as students encounter increasing expectations to use complex vocabulary and syntax in their writing, as well as to write using a variety of complex text structures, different genres, and academic content (Bulté & Housen, 2014; Campbell, Espin, & McMaster, 2013; Cumming, 2016; Harrison et al., 2016; Smith, 2018). As noted in Chapter 1, it is for this reason that emergent bilinguals who enter school in the upper grades may have difficulty keeping up with the quick flow of advanced content knowledge and the expectations that they incorporate academic concepts into their generation of text.

At the same time, the cognitive flexibility afforded by bilingualism can serve as an asset in students' writing, just as it does in other aspects of literacy (as described in Chapter 4). For example, in spelling, emergent bilingual students may transfer their knowledge of their home language orthography to attempt to spell English words. In generating text, these students may show particular strengths as they draw on assets, such as linguistic resources (e.g., using cognates in choosing words); cultural assets (e.g., using their insider knowledge to write about culturally specific experiences or perspectives); and motivational assets (e.g., capitalizing on a desire to share a personal story, explore an identity, or express an opinion). In addition, access to multiple languages provides emergent bilinguals with a greater range of linguistic resources to use in their writing, which can enhance the quality of writing. For example, in a multicultural take on Mother Goose rhymes, Elya (2016) meshes words from Spanish to create enriched bilingual sentences, such as "Sí, sir, sí, sir, three bags llenas" as a line in *Baa, baa, black sheep.* Such texts could be used as **mentor texts,** which are texts that serve as models of the text structure or genre that emergent bilinguals are being asked to follow and that demonstrate how they can incorporate their home language into their English writing in ways that enhance the text (Lee & Hansfield, 2018).

Because each component of writing is integral to the overall quantity and quality of students' writing (e.g., Berninger, 2009; Graham, McKeown, Kiuhara, & Harris, 2012; McCutchen, 2006), writing assessment that taps into each of these areas is needed to gather information to improve students' overall writing development. In addition, writing assessment is needed at multiple levels of language, including letter–sound, word, sentence, and passage levels (Whitaker et al., 1994). Assessment of each component should begin at each level of language early on to identify and address potential writing difficulties. Many students, including emergent bilinguals, are not identified as experiencing difficulty with writing until they reach the later grades, when it becomes much harder to ameliorate writing challenges with instruction and intervention (Artiles et al., 2005; Klingner et al., 2006; Smith et al., 2018). Long-term writing difficulties can have an enduring impact on motivation and self-efficacy, both of which are key ingredients for successful writing (Bruning & Kauffman, 2016; Graham, Berninger, & Fan, 2007). Fortunately, such negative outcomes can be prevented with effective early identification and instruction, both of which require strong assessment systems.

PART ONE: THE FORMAL ASSESSMENT OF WRITING AT SCHOOL

In contrast to systems for evaluating reading, systems for assessing writing are far less formalized and are used less consistently in schools. For example, many state achievement tests do not include a writing component for all grades, and often do not assess writing until the later grades. A handful of published, norm-referenced standardized tests are available for identifying and diagnosing writing difficulties; however, as in reading and other academic areas, these tests have not necessarily been normed based on samples of students who represent the diverse language backgrounds of emergent bilinguals in today's schools (García, McKoon, & August, 2006).

Particular problems that all educators face in assessing writing, and that may present specific challenges for educators working with emergent bilinguals, include (1) writing assessments are often scored in holistic and subjective ways, compromising reliability and increasing the possibility of systematic bias; (2) there is not always a strong match between what is assessed on published writing assessments and how writing is taught in schools (Salvia et al., 2017); and (3) many assessments assume that students have the background knowledge to produce a writing sample that represents their writing skills; students without the relevant cultural or experiential knowledge thus might not adequately convey skills that they actually have. For example, many writing tests require students to respond to written or pictorial prompts. Consider the following writing-prompt sample from a state writing test: "Think of your favorite place to play when you were younger. Describe this place and explain why it was your favorite." An emergent bilingual student who is a refugee from a war-torn country might not have experienced a "favorite place to play" in his or her early childhood and might have difficulty coming up with a response to this prompt. Because of these issues, educators should use caution in administering, interpreting, and using results from published, formal assessments in writing with emergent bilinguals.

PART TWO: CLASSROOM-BASED ASSESSMENTS THAT GUIDE INSTRUCTION

Fortunately, assessments that have evidence of reliability and validity for instructional decision making (primarily for screening and progress monitoring) also have shown some promise for use with ELs. In the next sections, we describe assessments that align with components of the simple view of writing (transcription, text generation, and self-regulation) at the word, sentence, and passage levels of language.

Screening and Monitoring Progress in Writing

Screening and monitoring student progress in writing can assist educators in identifying students who might experience difficulty with writing and in determining students' overall growth, which in turn can aid educators in determining appropriate instruction. In this section, we identify assessment approaches that can be used to screen and monitor students' writing progress and make instructional decisions using CBM, which we discussed in Chapter 5 (Deno, 1985).

Just as CBM has proved to be a well-researched and validated approach to screening, monitoring student progress, and making data-based decisions in reading, there is also evidence that CBM can be used for screening and monitoring student writing progress. Specifically, CBM in writing has been demonstrated to have evidence of reliability, validity, and sensitivity to growth for diverse samples of elementary students (McMaster & Espin, 2007; McMaster, Ritchey, & Lembke, 2011; Ritchey et al., 2016) and to show promise for ELs (Campbell et al., 2013; Keller-Margulis, Payan, Jaspers, & Brewton, 2016; Smith, 2018). We discuss five CBM approaches (letter writing, sound spelling, word dictation, picture-word prompts, and story prompts) that can be used to screen and monitor student writing progress at the letter–sound, word, sentence, and passage levels (see also Table 7.1 for a summary).

Letter Writing and Sound Spelling

Letter writing (Ritchey, 2006) assesses students' ability to write individual upper- and lowercase letters from dictation. Each letter is dictated aloud (*not* in alphabetical order, to avoid having the student write the letters from rote memory), and the student is prompted to write both the upper- and lowercase version of the letter. Responses are scored on the basis of legibility; reversals are scored as correct unless the reversal is another valid letter (e.g., *b/d, p/q*).

Sound spelling requires children to spell individual letters after being presented with a sound (e.g., write the letter that makes the /t/ sound). The student can write either the upper- or lowercase version of the letter. In a manner similar to letter writing, responses are scored based on legibility; reversals are scored as correct unless the reversal is another valid letter (e.g., *b/d, p/q*). In this way, basic encoding can be assessed at a stage when students have emerging, but perhaps incomplete, word-spelling skills. Complete administration and scoring directions for both letter writing and sound spelling are provided in Coker and Ritchey (2015).

TABLE 7.1. Screening and Progress Monitoring in Writing at Different Levels of Language

Level of language	Simple view of writing components	
	Transcription	Text generation
Letter–sound	Letter writing or sound spelling	
Word	Word dictation	
Sentence	Picture-word prompt	Picture-word prompt
Passage		Story prompt

Word Dictation

The word dictation assessment is designed to capture transcription skills at the word level and is appropriate for students who are just beginning to write words (Hampton & Lembke, 2016; Lembke, Carlisle, & Poch, 2015; Lembke, Deno, & Hall, 2003). Word dictation is individually administered for 3 minutes. The examiner dictates words, using spelling patterns found in many core reading and writing curricula, including the CCSS (National Governors Association, Center for Best Practices & Council of Chief State School Officers, 2010) with one repeat, and students write down each word (see Figure 7.2). Scores include words written (WW), words spelled correctly (WSC), correct letter sequences (CLS; any two adjacent letters that are correctly placed according to the correct spelling of the word, which allows for partial credit that accounts for the student's developing orthographic knowledge), and correct minus incorrect letter sequences (CILS). Complete scoring directions can be found at *http://arc.missouri.edu/dbi_early.aspx.*

Figure 7.3 shows the scored responses to the word-dictation assessment of an emergent bilingual (Spanish-speaking) second-grade student named Eduardo. Note that Eduardo stopped after the word *cloud* because his 3 minutes were up, and only his errors are listed in Figure 7.3; other words were spelled correctly. CLS are indicated by upward carets (∧), and incorrect letter sequences are indicated by downward carets (∨). For example, for the word *list,* Eduardo gets an upward caret before the *l* because the first letter is correct. From *l* to *e* is incorrect, and from *e* to *s* is incorrect, so there are downward carets around the *e.* From *s* to *t* is correct, and the *t* is the correct last letter, earning upward carets around *t.*

A close inspection of Eduardo's spelling assessment provides a lot of information that is potentially useful for instruction. At first glance, it might appear that Eduardo doesn't understand English spelling well, because he incorrectly spelled 15 out of 27 words. However, his spelling also reveals many strengths as well as areas where he

1. hat	16. zone
2. drop	17. frame
3. list	18. goal
4. bed	19. flop
5. plus	20. nest
6. sock	21. tube
7. game	22. sleep
8. dig	23. flash
9. clap	24. prize
10. just	25. loop
11. mine	26. wake
12. score	27. cloud
13. gear	28. blend
14. swim	29. globe
15. ramp	30. raid

FIGURE 7.2. Sample word dictation list.

Word dictation list	Student's errors	Score	Interpretation
list	∧lvevs∧t∧	CLS = 3 ILS = 2	Vowel sounds /ĭ/ and /ĕ/ are not present in Spanish and are difficult for a non-native speaker to differentiate.
plus	∧p∧lvavs∧	CLS = 3 ILS = 2	The /ŭ/ vowel sound is similar to the vowel /ă/ in Spanish.
just	vyvavs∧t∧	CLS = 2 ILS = 3	Y can be pronounced with a /j/ sound in Spanish; ŭ is similar to the vowel a in Spanish.
mine	∧mvav∧nv	CLS = 3 ILS = 2	In Spanish, ai would be pronounced similar to the long i in English.
score	∧s∧c∧o∧rv	CLS = 4 ILS = 1	Eduardo is using sound–spelling strategies to this point and will need instructional support with the silent-e rule in English.
gear	∧gv∧hv∧vr∧	CLS = 2 ILS = 4	The Spanish vowel i makes what would be the long-e sound in English.
swim	∧svuv∧m∧	CLS = 3 ILS = 2	Eduardo's spelling is easily decodable based on Spanish vowel-sound spellings.
zone	vsvo∧nv	CLS = 1 ILS = 3	Spanish does not have a /z/ sound—it is pronounced as /s/; Eduardo will need support with the silent-e rule in English.
frame	∧f∧rv∧vmv	CLS = 2 ILS = 3	Eduardo has identified a portion of the diphthongized vowel a (ayee) and represented it with the long-e sound (Spanish vowel i); he will need support with the silent-e rule.
goal	∧g∧ov	CLS = 2 ILS = 1	Eduardo represents the ō with o alone, typical in both Spanish and English words.
tube	(no attempt)	(na)	Eduardo will need support with the silent-e rule in English.
flash	∧f∧h∧∧sv	CLS = 4 ILS·= 1	There is no sh digraph in Spanish spelling.
prize	∧p∧rvav∧vsve∧	CLS = 3 ILS = 4	In Spanish ai is pronounced like the long i sound in English; no /z/ sound in Spanish.
loop	∧h∧ovp∧	CLS = 3 ILS = 1	Vowel teams are not used to create a single sound in Spanish.
cloud	∧c∧lvavu∧d∧	CLS = 4 ILS = 2	Eduardo's spelling is easily decodable based on Spanish vowel-sound spellings.

FIGURE 7.3. Eduardo's scored errors in response to the word dictation prompt. Adapted from Smith (2018).

needs specific guidance. For example, he spelled most of the CVC, CCVC, and CVCC words correctly (e.g., *hat, drop, sock, clap*), demonstrating facility with many common sounds and simple English word-family patterns. (This was likely supported by some transfer between the sounds in English and Spanish). In fact, even for words not spelled correctly, he wrote many of the first and last consonant sounds and consonant blends correctly. For words not spelled correctly, Eduardo often appeared to tap into his knowledge of Spanish orthography to attempt to spell the words, such as spelling *plus* as PLAS, with the Spanish vowel *a* being closest to the sound of the English short *u*. In this way, Eduardo demonstrated good phonetic encoding in his alphabetic spelling. His patterns of errors generally reveal that he is not a "poor speller" who has general difficulties with transcription, because he does seem to have a developing understanding of English orthography and applies his knowledge of Spanish orthography to attempt English words that he does not know how to spell. Eduardo might benefit from explicit instruction both in specific vowel sounds that differ from Spanish and in English spelling patterns, such as the long-*e* rule.

Picture-Word Prompts

Picture-word prompts are designed to capture transcription and text generation at the sentence level, and are appropriate for students learning to connect words into sentences (Lembke et al., 2015; McMaster, Du, & Petursdottir, 2009). Each prompt consists of words and pictures of what the words represent. After having students practice, the examiner instructs them to write sentences using the prompts. After 3 minutes, the examiner instructs students to stop, and scores the writing samples for words written (WW), words spelled correctly (WSC), and correct word sequences (CWS), which are two adjacent words spelled correctly that were used correctly in the context of the sentence. Complete scoring directions can be found at *http://arc.mis-souri.edu/dbi_early.aspx* or at *www.progressmonitoring.org/pdf/ewscoring.pdf.*

Figure 7.4 shows a transcribed sample of an emergent bilingual student's scored response to a picture-word prompt, and Figure 7.5 provides an interpretation of the student's performance. The sample is scored for CWS, which are indicated by upward carets (∧), and incorrect word sequences, which are indicated by downward carets (∨). To be correct, the word has to be capitalized (if it's at the beginning of the sentence) and spelled correctly, be grammatically correct in the context of the sentence, and punctuated correctly (if it's at the end of the sentence). For example, the sentence *you can draw people* has downward carets (∨) at the beginning, because *you* is not capitalized, and at the end, because there is no period; but there are upward carets (∧) from *you* to *can, can* to *draw,* and *draw* to *people,* because these words are spelled and used correctly in the context of the sentence. The remaining sentences are missing capital letters, punctuation, and verbs that help the sentences make sense. This student would likely benefit from instruction about how to construct simple sentences, including teaching him that every sentence should start with a capital and end with a period, include a subject and a verb, and make sense. The student might need further explicit instruction about what subjects and verbs are and support in building his vocabulary of English nouns and verbs that he can draw from.

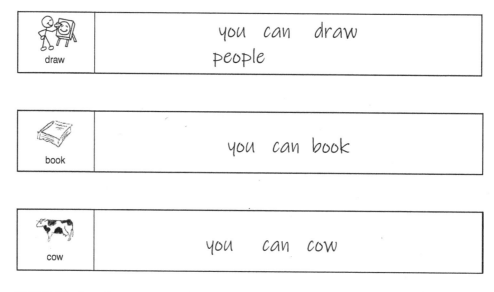

FIGURE 7.4. Sample picture-word form with student response. Adapted from Smith (2018).

Story Prompts

Story prompts capture transcription and text generation at the passage level and can be administered individually or to groups of students in all elementary grades (e.g., Lembke et al., 2003; Lembke et al., 2015; McMaster et al., 2009; McMaster & Campbell, 2008). Story prompts are designed to reflect the experiences that students attending U.S. schools will be able to relate to, and have simple vocabulary and sentence structures (e.g., "*I was on my way home from school when . . .*"). Each prompt is printed at the top of a page, followed by lines on which students write their responses. The examiner provides 30 seconds for students to think about what they will write, and then 3 minutes for them to respond to the prompt. Students' samples are scored

Prompt	Student's scored response	Interpretation
draw	∨you∧can∧draw∧people∨	This student appears to have some concept of putting words together to make a sentence and, when given the verb *draw,* can make a complete sentence with a subject and verb. However, it is not clear whether the student understands the meaning of the words (semantic knowledge) or that every sentence needs a verb, or what verbs might make sense (syntactic knowledge). He is also relying on a pattern (You can . . .) and is writing very simple sentences. Finally, he does not appear to be applying conventions of capitalizing and punctuating sentences.
book	∨you∧can∨book∨	
cow	∨you∧can∨cow∨	

FIGURE 7.5. A student's scored picture-word response with interpretation.

for WW, WSC, and CWS. Scoring directions can be found at *http://arc.missouri.edu/dbi_early.aspx* or at *www.progressmonitoring.org*.

Learning Needs Assessments in Writing

Although CBM tasks can be useful as overall indicators of students' writing proficiency and for monitoring responsiveness to instruction, additional assessments likely will be needed to provide further insight into a student's specific writing strengths and needs. To gain such insights, it is useful to collect information about the student's *writing process* (what happens during writing), and about the student's *writing products* (the tangible results of the writing process). Tables 7.2 and 7.3 (adapted from McMaster & Lembke, 2016) feature examples of observations and assessments of the writing process and writing product in the areas of transcription, text generation, and self-regulation. This information can help determine emergent bilinguals' relative strengths and needs, which can inform the focus and content of instruction.

Spelling inventories are another tool for examining students' knowledge of different spelling patterns to determine the stage of their spelling development, which can help identify the focus of spelling instruction. For example, *Words Their Way with English Learners* (Helman, Bear, Templeton, Invernizzi, & Johnston, 2012) provides spelling inventories that help estimate students' stages of spelling and reading

TABLE 7.2. Observing the Writing Process in Transcription, Text Generation, and Self-Regulation

Transcription	Text generation	Self-regulation
*Does the student . . .	Does the student . . .	Does the student . . .
• hold the pencil or pen comfortably? • write without excessive erasing or scribbling? • form letters independently without referring to a model? • produce letters and words fluently without painstaking effort? • sustain writing for an extended time? • spell words without stopping frequently to ask for help or to look up word spellings?*	• generate ideas appropriate to the assignment? • produce text fluently without excessive starting and stopping, erasures, crossing out, scribbling, or wadding up paper? • revise his or her writing?	• find an appropriate time and place to write? • show that she or he understands the task (e.g., by restating in his/her own words, asking for clarification)? • use a planning strategy before starting to write (e.g., make a concept map or outline)? • gather and organize information needed to complete the task? • self-monitor, evaluate, and revise during writing? • seek help when needed? • set goals and self-reward when they are met?

*Although asking for help and looking up spellings are functional skills that should be encouraged at specific points in the writing process (such as during revising), it is important that students do not become overreliant on these strategies, such that they slow the writing process.

TABLE 7.3. Assessing the Writing Product in Transcription, Text Generation, and Self-Regulation

Transcription	Text generation	Self-regulation
Handwriting	*Does the student . . .*	*Does the student . . .*
Does the student write all letters . . .	• use correct punctuation and capitalization?	• have completed planning documents (e.g., outlines, word webs)?
• in upper- and lowercase legibly?	• use correct parts of speech (nouns, verbs, adjectives, determiners, prepositions)?	• produce multiple drafts with clear revisions from one to the next, including adding, dropping, changing, or rearranging parts of the writing?
• in the correct direction?		
• using smooth strokes?	• produce simple and compound sentences?	
• in a regular size (not too large or too small)?	• produce the expected amount of text compared to peers?	
• with proper slant?		• show evidence of correcting punctuation, capitalization, spelling, etc.?
• with correct spacing between letters and words?	• use varied vocabulary?	
• evenly on lines?	• produce text in the appropriate genre (e.g., story, sequence [first-then-last], cause–effect, etc.)?	• have completed goal-setting and tracking documents (e.g., graph of progress)?
Spelling		
Does the student correctly write words using . . .	• structure the text appropriately (e.g., paragraphs, titles, headings)?	
• simple consonants and vowels?		
• pairs of consonants?		
• silent letters (e.g., *climb*)?		
• long vowel sounds ?		
• multisyllabic words?		
• prefixes and suffixes?		

development, which can then be aligned with instruction matched to specific areas of need.

Writing rubrics are designed to distinguish between beginning and more proficient writers on the basis of composition elements, such as idea generation, organization, voice, word choice, sentence fluency, conventions, and presentation. One widely used resource for writing rubrics is the 6 + 1 Trait® Rubrics (*https://educationnorthwest. org/traits/traits-rubrics*), which includes rubrics for students in grades K–2 and 3–12. Coker and Ritchey (2015) also provide rubrics for opinion, narrative, and informational/expository writing for beginning writers (grades K–2) that are aligned with CCSS (National Governors Association, Center for Best Practices & Council of Chief State School Officers, 2010). In Figure 7.6, we apply an example of a writing rubric to the following student writing sample.

> Mr Parson and 2 students wen
> after school to get buz.
> O no, they mist the bus
> Mr Parson yell to the bus
> driver and Oto yell too.
> But he no here the yell.
> She cri because she miss the bus.

Element	3—Excellent	2—Good	1—Weak	0—Absent
Event sequence	Multiple related events are included and each is described clearly, OR one event is described in detail.	Multiple related events are included and one is described in detail, OR only one event is described with insufficient detail.	Multiple related events are included and each one is not described clearly, OR one event is not described well.	
Character details	Actions, thoughts, and feelings of characters are described in clear detail.	Actions, thoughts, and feelings of characters include somewhat clear descriptions.	Actions, thoughts, and feelings of characters are mentioned but not described in detail.	
Temporal words	At least three temporal words (e.g., *first, next, last*) are used appropriately.	At least two temporal words (e.g., *first, next, last*) are used appropriately,	At least one temporal word (e.g., *first, next, last, before, after*) is used appropriately.	
Sense of closure	More than one sentence is used to provide a sense of closure.	At least one sentence is used to provide a sense of closures.	A clause or phrase is used to provide a sense of closure.	

FIGURE 7.6. Rubric for narrative text (adapted from Coker & Ritchey, 2015, p. 198) applied to Jamilah's sample.

The benefit of having a written product is that it provides additional information about a student's strengths and needs. For example, the student was able to write a descriptive paragraph that clearly related to a picture; that had a clear beginning, middle, and end; and that used some reasonably well-chosen words. It also reveals information about the student's handwriting (e.g., reversal of *s*); orthographic knowledge (including inconsistent use of word endings, such as *miss* instead of *missed* and *cri* vs. *cried*, and use of homophones, such as *here* vs. *hear* and *mist* vs. *missed*); inconsistent use of articles (*bus* vs. *the bus*); inconsistent use of capitals and punctuation (e.g., correctly capitalized names but no quotation marks); and inconsistent sentence structure and syntax (e.g., an attempt to write compound sentences and possibly confusing word order in the home language to express ideas in English, such as in " . . . *he no here the yell*" vs. " . . . *he didn't hear them yell*." All of this information could be used to inform instruction in both the transcription and text-generation components of writing.

Additional Assessment Practices That Support Writing for Emergent Bilinguals

Beyond conducting assessments on word, sentence, and passage levels of language and on the transcription, text generation, and self-regulation components of writing, educators should consider additional factors when assessing emergent bilingual students' writing for the purpose of informing instruction. These additional factors include those related to the contexts in which writing development takes place (Ball, 2006). Understanding the contexts in which students are learning to write can provide meaningful assessment information that can be used for making instructional decisions. Educators might ask, "What are the contexts in which my students are learning to write, and to what extent (and in what ways) do these contexts support or hinder that learning? To what extent (and in what ways) do these contexts align (or not align) with each other?" Figure 7.7 is a template (filled in by Mr. Parson about Jamilah's contextual factors; a blank template is given in Appendix F) that educators can use to consider contextual factors that might influence students' writing and thus how assessments might be created, administered, and interpreted.

Applying these considerations to Jamilah's case, Mr. Parson might think about the following:

- **School characteristics.** Jamilah attends an urban elementary school with many other children who have similar language and cultural backgrounds, some of whose families have been in the United States for decades, and others whose families are relative newcomers. There is a strong emphasis on learning communities within the building, with lots of opportunities for collaboration among peers. These school characteristics might support Jamilah's writing development, because her experiences in school likely reinforce the cultural and motivational assets she brings to writing.

- **Learning environments.** In addition to having a collaborative, community-focused school environment, Jamilah has many rich opportunities to enhance her knowledge repertoire outside the classroom. It might be helpful to find out more about what types of writing resources she has at home and about what aspects of writing are valued in her family and community, so as to make connections between her experiences at home and at school. Also, children sometimes attend class on Saturdays or at other times to learn their home languages or engage in other types of literacy learning; it would be helpful to find out if Jamilah participates in these activities.

- **Instructional activities.** Mr. Parson gives his students many opportunities to generate and share ideas as communities of writers. However, he has not provided enough systematic, explicit instruction in specific writing skills. More explicit instruction might be particularly necessary in understanding why Jamilah is struggling with the transcription component of writing and might shed light on how to augment instruction to further align it with her needs as well as her strengths.

- **Student characteristics.** Knowing about Jamilah's assets can help Mr. Parson think about how to capitalize on writing strengths as a way to get a good assessment of her needs. For example, using Jamilah's motivation to be a good writer as a reason for monitoring progress and for providing instruction in transcription skills can be used to encourage her to try her best, even when the writing tasks are difficult.

Contextual factor	How does this context support writing development?	How could this context be improved to support writing development?	Implications for assessment and instruction
School characteristics (e.g., urban, suburban, rural; student population; socioeconomic status; building culture)	*Riverview has a strong community culture that encourages children in collaborating and sharing their work with their classmates and with other members of the school community.*	*We could capitalize on the existing community culture to build more intentional writing communities that emphasize collaborative writing opportunities and projects.*	*In addition to assessing Jamilah's independent work, find ways to assess her processes and products as part of collaborative work.*
Learning environments in and outside of school (e.g., What are the varied contexts in which students have opportunities to write? How might writing activities that take place outside of school be used to support writing in school?)	*Outside of school, Jamilah has a wealth of opportunities to build on her funds of knowledge and draw from in her writing. In school, there are many opportunities to write on a wide range of topics.*	*Continue to encourage Jamilah in generating text that draws from her funds of knowledge and home language, and use these assets to expand her writing repertoire.*	*Find out more about writing practices in Jamilah's home, and consider ways to reinforce those practices in school and vice versa.*
Instructional activities (e.g., How is writing taught? How are the various purposes for writing conveyed?)	*We use a writer's workshop to share ideas as a writing community, but there's not a lot of explicit instruction in specific writing skills.*	*Provide more explicit instruction that will address Jamilah's transcription needs.*	*Be sure to use assessments that tap Jamilah's developing transcription skills as well as her development in text generation. This will involve multiple measures (e.g., progress monitoring, rubrics to analyze writing samples).*
Students' own knowledge and affective assets (motivational, interests, self-concept, self-interests; see Chapter 3)	*Jamilah really enjoys sharing information about her family and community experiences. She also seems to really enjoy elaborating on these experiences to make up stories. She enjoys telling and writing stories and seems genuinely interested in improving her writing.*	*Capitalize on Jamilah's knowledge, experiences, imagination, and interests to keep her motivated to engage in some of the more technical writing skills that will ultimately help her improve as a writer.*	*Show Jamilah the connection between her developing writing skills and how they will help her improve as a writer overall. Use her progress monitoring data as a way to support her in setting goals and charting progress over time.*

FIGURE 7.7. Contextual factors that educators might consider as part of writing assessments.

163

PART THREE: INSTRUCTIONAL APPLICATIONS

In our discussion about the various forms of assessment data, we have provided some suggestions about how assessment information might inform instruction. In this section, we offer some additional recommendations about how to apply students' writing assessment data to instruction.

Providing Explicit and Systematic Instruction in Writing

In general, students who experience difficulty with writing are more likely to benefit from explicit and systematic instruction in which connections to reading are made very clear (Berninger, Nielson, Abbott, Wijsman, & Raskind, 2008). Explicit, systematic instruction is carefully sequenced; consists of clear steps; and includes modeling (using examples and non-examples), guided practice with scaffolding and specific feedback, and sufficient independent practice. It can also include procedure charts, writing folders with directions, bilingual dictionaries, and other hands-on and visual materials that make the writing process clear.

Syntheses of research on writing instruction indicate that instructional approaches with the strongest effects include the explicit teaching of transcription skills (e.g., handwriting and spelling; Datchuk & Kubina, 2012; Graham, McKeown, et al., 2012; McMaster et al., 2018); the explicit teaching of writing processes, strategies, and text structure; and using creativity and imagery in writing (Graham, Bollinger, et al., 2012); and self-regulated strategy development (Baker, Chard, Ketterlin-Geller, Apichatabutra, & Doabler, 2009; Graham, McKeown, et al., 2012). Graham, McKeown, et al. (2012) also found that when instruction incorporates prewriting activities, peer-assisted learning, goal setting, assessing writing, word processing, and extra writing time, student outcomes are improved.

Viewing all of these findings as a whole, researchers (Graham, Bollinger, et al., 2012) recommend that comprehensive writing instruction should include the following elements: (1) providing students with time to write every day, (2) teaching students to use the writing process for a variety of purposes, (3) teaching students how to develop fluency in transcription and sentence construction skills, and (4) creating an engaged community of writers. These recommendations fit very well with others that are specific to students with diverse language backgrounds. For example, Ball (2006) emphasizes the importance of explicit instruction with modeling, scaffolding, feedback, and guided and independent practice; of communicating high expectations to all learners, of creating classroom learning communities, of ensuring that students have ample time and classroom space for writing, and of emphasizing the strong connection between reading and writing.

Focusing on Specific Components of Writing

We have described learning needs assessment tools that can help educators gather information on students' writing processes and products. Once students' specific strengths and areas of need have been identified, it is time to match their needs with specific forms of instruction. In the next sections, we offer brief summaries of these activities for each of the three components of writing.

Transcription

Depending on specific needs, transcription instruction can emphasize either handwriting or spelling, or both. Effective handwriting instruction typically includes some combination of visual cues and verbal modeling, with adequate time for students to trace and copy example letters and then write them independently. It is important to limit the number of letters to be practiced in a given session (e.g., three letters at a time). Frequently used, easier letters should be taught first (e.g., *t, a, s*), before letters that are less frequent (e.g., *q, z*), and letters that have easily confused or reversible letters (e.g., *b, d, p, q*) should be taught separately.

Effective spelling interventions typically highlight phonemic awareness (see Chapter 5), focusing on word building, word sorting, word hunting, and word study of spelling patterns that are frequently encountered in text or used in student writing. Educators should learn about emergent bilinguals' home language and writing systems, including whether there is a written language that uses an alphabetic or other writing system and specific information about that writing system's orthography and how much it overlaps with English. This information can be used to explicitly support students in recognizing similarities and differences between the two writing systems and encourage them to use what they know from their home language as they attempt to spell English words, but also explicitly highlights differences that will need to be learned and practiced. The example of Eduardo earlier in this chapter illustrates how a student can use linguistic aspects to support spelling, but might also have specific learning needs related to understanding English orthography.

Text Generation

As we described earlier, text generation includes thinking of ideas to write about (which requires creativity and/or content knowledge, depending on the genre) and the words to express those ideas, and using knowledge of sentence and text structure to organize ideas into a coherent form. Generating texts also requires an understanding of the various purposes for writing and the audience for whom the writing is intended. For emergent bilinguals, it may be especially important to emphasize a variety of purposes that both encourage self-expression and exploration of culture and identity, but also highlight the range of purposes and audiences involved in school-based writing activities (Ball, 2006). It will also likely be necessary to provide explicit instruction in basic sentence-writing skills that will support students in writing longer pieces of discourse.

Sentence Construction. Students often need explicit instruction in how to construct simple (and later more complex) sentences. To do so, it is helpful to teach the five "rules" for writing sentences (Schumaker & Sheldon, 2005) as follows: Every complete sentence (1) starts with a capital letter, (2) ends with a punctuation mark, (3) has a subject, (4) has a verb, and (5) should make sense (keeping in mind that, depending on a student's English proficiency, this rule might be difficult and additional support might be needed). Each rule can be taught explicitly with modeling, demonstration, guided practice with scaffolding and feedback, and independent practice.

Sentence Combining. When students can identify the components of sentences and formulate their own simple sentences, they can begin to generate sentences that are more complex. Students who struggle with writing will likely need explicit instruction in grammatical strategies they can use, such as combining simple sentences into compound sentences. Learning to use such strategies can help to improve the quantity and quality of students' writing (Saddler, Behforooz, & Asaro, 2008; Saddler & Graham, 2005). Sentence-combining instruction should start by combining sentences using words like *and, but,* and *because.* Once students master simple combining, they can learn to embed adjectives and adverbs, and later adjectival and adverbial phrases to create more complex sentences. Emergent bilinguals may need additional instruction in the *meanings* of various words and word types and their functions in sentences, as well as instruction related to English syntax (e.g., word order that might be different from the word order in a student's native language). Scaffolds such as sentence frames, in which sample sentences with blank spaces serve as models to beginners, may be useful initially, but should be withdrawn fairly quickly so that students do not become reliant on them.

Text Structure Instruction. Students also benefit from learning to identify important elements of different text structures in reading (e.g., story grammar for narrative texts, clue words, such as *first, next,* and *last* for sequence; *same* and *different* for compare–contrast; *because* for cause–effect) that they can use in their writing. Furthermore, because writing about a text that students have read can lead to better writing *and* reading comprehension outcomes, teaching text structure in the context of texts that students are reading provides a great opportunity to emphasize reading–writing connections. Having students create story maps or concept maps that contain information from texts they are reading is one way to integrate reading and writing skills. Similarly, having students write summaries or responses to questions about what they have read by using key words that align with specific text structures (e.g., a summary of what comes first, next, and last in a particular sequence of steps) can support understanding of text structures through both reading and writing. Students might also benefit from using sentence frames or sentence starters as scaffolds for constructing text and from using mentor texts.

Building Fluency. Both writing and reading outcomes improve when students write on a regular basis, so it is critical to provide many occasions for them to practice writing in ways that integrate text generation and transcription of that text into print. The aim, of course, is to improve both the quantity *and* quality of writing, so building fluency should occur in the context of increasing the production of *quality* writing. Fluency-building activities also can help build stamina, which is important when sustained writing is required. They can be particularly effective with a goal-setting component (Parker, Dickey, Burns, & McMaster, 2012). For example, start by providing the student(s) with a writing prompt. Provide a short time (no more than 1 minute) to plan, and then ask the student(s) to begin writing. After 3 minutes, tell the student(s) to stop writing, and count the number of words written. Have the student(s) graph this number. Then, repeat this activity with another prompt, encouraging the student(s) to write more words the second time. Count and graph the number of words written the second time, and celebrate improvement.

Self-Regulated Strategy Development

A critical element of writing instruction involves teaching the writing process, which typically entails generating ideas about a particular topic; planning and organizing the writing; writing a draft; and then revising the work. Many students benefit from strategy instruction that teaches systematic ways in which to remember and execute specific writing processes. For students who struggle with writing, remembering and executing strategies can be a cognitively demanding task in itself, and so finding ways to support this process so that students can focus on writing is important.

One well-researched way to support students' effective strategy use is self-regulated strategy development (SRSD), in which students are taught to use strategies that help them remember important text generation processes and to regulate their use of these writing processes. SRSD incorporates explicit instruction, modeling, mnemonics, and scaffolding for students until they reach mastery and can use the strategies with few or no supports (Baker et al., 2009). SRSD was developed by Graham and Harris (1996), and has been shown to improve students' writing quality and quantity across a wide range of grade levels.

There are six basic stages of SRSD instruction, illustrated in Figure 7.8. Throughout this process, students learn self-regulation procedures including goal setting, self-monitoring, self-reinforcement, and self-instruction. A number of different strategies

Stage 1: *Develop background knowledge.*	Preteach skills needed for using the strategy (e.g., how to revise a story).
Stage 2: *Discuss the strategy.*	Discuss the benefits of the strategy and how and when to use it.
Stage 3: *Model the strategy.*	Model how and when to use the strategy.
Stage 4: *Memorize the strategy.*	Teach students to use mnemonics and self-instructions to recall the strategy.
Stage 5: *Scaffold use of the strategy.*	Scaffold students' use of the strategy through collaborative writing and guided practice.
Stage 6: *Apply the strategy.*	Support students as they apply the strategy independently to various writing tasks and evaluate their own performance.

FIGURE 7.8. Six stages of self-regulated strategy development.

(e.g., planning writing in different genres, selecting vocabulary words, and learning the components of different text structures, such as opinion essays and revising work) are taught by using the SRSD approach (see Harris, Graham, Mason, & Friedlander, 2008).

Connecting Writing and Reading

Learning to read and write involves many similar processes; therefore, supporting development in one area should support development in the other. However, emergent bilingual students will need explicit and systematic instruction in both areas. Reading and writing do not need to be taught separately and, indeed, it often makes sense to combine instruction in both areas. For example, phonics and spelling instruction can be integrated, as spelling words reinforces letter–sound correspondences needed to sound out and read them, and vice versa. When students generate text, whether at the sentence, paragraph, or passage level (e.g., as part of sentence or text structure instruction), having them read their own writing aloud can promote reading fluency and comprehension. Similarly, encouraging students to write in response to texts they read can also promote fluency and comprehension while also improving writing skills.

SUMMARY

In this chapter, we highlighted the importance of writing to students' overall literacy development and the key components of writing (transcription, text generation, and self-regulation) that should be the focus of assessment and instruction. We discussed the cognitive demands of writing in general, and the particular demands as well as assets that may influence emergent bilingual students' writing development. Although writing is often less emphasized as part of assessment and instruction in schools, we strongly encourage educators to view writing development as a critical part of literacy assessment and instruction. Key takeaways include the fact that instructionally relevant writing assessments do exist, particularly for progress monitoring and assessment needs, at the letter–sound, word, sentence, and passage levels. Writing should be assessed in terms of both process and product, and contextual factors should be considered as well. Finally, given the strong connection between reading and writing, these aspects of literacy should not be assessed or taught in isolation. Rather, assessment and instruction in both reading and writing can reinforce emergent bilingual students' development in both areas, leading to improved reading and writing outcomes.

CHAPTER 8

Creating Responsive Systems for Connecting Assessment and Instruction

It is late January, and the fourth-grade teachers (Mr. Hassan, Ms. Ellsworth, and Ms. Fien), the literacy specialist (Mr. Reed), the EL specialists (Ms. Farhan and Mr. Rigby), the reading interventionist (Ms. Guest), the special education teacher (Ms. Kelly), and the principal (Dr. Shire) are gathered for their monthly literacy data team meeting. In these meetings, the group reviews the fourth graders' literacy data from the district's new assessment system. This information includes benchmarking data, which are collected from all fourth graders in fall, winter, and spring of the school year; progress monitoring data, which are collected weekly for students receiving Tier 2 or 3 intervention; and additional learning needs assessment data that teachers have for specific students whom they wish to discuss in depth during the data team meeting.

As the educators gather in the school conference room, Ms. Farhan passes around a plate of Aano Baraawe. "It's basically like Somali fudge!" she explains as Ms. Fien closes her eyes and savors the treat. "My daughter and I made a big batch last night, and I promised her I'd share it with you all."

"It's perfect with my afternoon tea!" says Dr. Shire. The group settles in, and Dr. Shire briefly asks everyone about their week so far, and then it's time to get down to business. Mr. Reed turns on his computer and displays the winter reading data on the large LCD screen on the wall.

"Let's get a class-by-class overview, starting with Mr. Hassan's class, and then we'll talk about specific concerns in more depth," says Dr. Shire.

Mr. Reed filters the data to show Mr. Hassan's class. "Wow!" says Ms. Ellsworth. "Looks like almost all of your class met the winter benchmark!"

"Yeah," says Mr. Hassan, "We've been working really hard, since my fall data didn't look so great. I've really been honing in on my kids' morphological awareness and vocabulary learning and tying that in with writing, and thanks to the strategies that Ms. Farhan and Mr. Reed suggested last time, the kids are really taking off. In fact, they are super excited about words now—they can't get enough! And Mr. Rigby and Ms. Guest have done an amazing job of reinforcing the strategies and making connections to their small-group instruction with the kids we identified for supplemental intervention. I think we'll see good growth for most of those students when we look at their progress monitoring data. I do want to come back to discussing Aaden later—he's the one child who has shown little progress. Ms. Guest and I aren't quite sure where to go next with him."

The group then reviews the other two classes' winter data, and then returns to the handful of students that each teacher identified as needing more in-depth discussion. For each student, the teacher presents the weekly progress data, along with relevant learning needs assessment information. A few of the students are having similar difficulties with word endings. "I'm never sure whether and how much to correct that!" says Ms. Guest.

"I have some suggestions for ways you can incorporate more explicit instruction," says Ms. Kelly.

"And let's not forget about seeing how they're using their home languages to try to figure out those pieces," says Ms. Farhan. Ms. Farhan and Ms. Kelly offer to attend the next fourth-grade team meeting to discuss some strategies in more depth, and the teachers eagerly accept.

At the end of the meeting, Dr. Shire thanks everyone for their time and efforts. "We're all working really hard as a team to support the literacy development of our students, and our assessment data show that our work is really paying off! I hope you all feel good about the progress our students are making, and that you are encouraged by the next steps we have planned for those who need additional supports."

This example of a monthly data team meeting illustrates how staff members, working together using the procedures they have developed and implemented many times, efficiently identify students who may need extra support to be successful and make concrete plans for providing them with additional learning opportunities. The school featured in this vignette has established a framework for literacy improvement based on the MTSS concept, which we discussed earlier in the book. In this chapter we focus on the importance of MTSS, what work is required to implement them, and how they can support emergent bilingual students.

In each chapter so far, we have zeroed in on a key strand of language and literacy assessment with emergent bilinguals, highlighting theories and foundational concepts that undergird that topic. We have shared information on both the formal, standardized assessments that are used in each strand and the informal, classroom-based formative assessments that guide daily instruction. In each chapter we have also described follow-up instructional practices that can be implemented to support growth in the language or literacy area.

• In Chapter 1, we honed in on demographic data about emergent bilingual students in the United States, what types of programs they participate in, and why current assessment practices are inadequate to support their growth. Key ideas that readers should take away are an understanding of literacy development and how it might look different for emergent bilingual students, the complex process of learning an additional language, and the symbiotic relationship between language and literacy learning. We provided a set of guiding principles for conceptualizing assessment with emergent bilinguals.

- In Chapter 2, we provided an overview of the different types of formative and summative, norm- and criterion-referenced, and formal and informal assessments that are used for decision making in schools. We discussed assessments for screening, progress monitoring, and identifying students' learning needs. We also described tiered systems for using the data in ways that are responsive to student learning needs.

- In Chapter 3, we examined the cultural, linguistic, and affective resources that students bring to school and how educators can learn more about them. The reader learned how cultural responsiveness is connected to assessment and the importance of using an asset-based framework to obtain a holistic view of what students know and can do.

- In Chapter 4, we examined the assessments of oral language growth, including the standardized measures used across the United States to measure yearly progress for EL students. Descriptors highlighted the levels of language development, so that readers have an idea of the steps that lead to English language proficiency. We delved into the many ways to better understand students' language skills through receptive and expressive oral language activities and through their reading and writing behaviors. We suggested teaching practices that support language development.

- In Chapter 5, we explored assessments of beginning reading, in particular for phonemic awareness, phonics, and fluency. We delved into how emergent bilinguals' home languages might influence the early stages of their reading development. The reader learned how teachers can become well informed about the features of a student's home language, and how that knowledge can help them support specific reading objectives.

- In Chapter 6, we described how educators assess comprehension and knowledge of academic language, both of which are crucial skills for literacy and content-area success in school. We shared a variety of formal and classroom-based informal assessments that educators can use to better understand their students' advancing language and comprehension skills and to propel their students' growth forward. The reader learned that systematic and authentic assessment approaches provide a richer picture of emergent bilinguals' understanding of complex language and texts.

- In Chapter 7, we discussed the integral position that writing has in meaningful literacy development. We outlined the key components of writing—transcription, text generation, and self-regulation—and how they are measured in standardized ways and also embedded in instructionally relevant writing assessments and instruction.

The reader learned how to assess writing and reading together, and how to notice and build on the multilingual assets that emergent bilinguals bring to the classroom.

The seven chapters leading to this point in the book all contribute to the reader's understanding of key aspects of language and literacy development with emergent bilinguals and how these various components are assessed in formal and informal ways. Figure 8.1 illustrates the breadth of information that leads to putting an *assessment to instruction* system in place. One critical topic still needs to be addressed, however, and that is how to establish responsive and ongoing assessment practices systematically in a school setting. That topic is the focus of this chapter.

In order to establish a system that optimizes the use of formal and informal assessments for emergent bilinguals and influences the instruction students receive in the classroom, a systematic framework that involves all school personnel needs to be conscientiously enacted. As introduced in Chapter 2, this framework is known as MTSS. Here we first present the foundational ideas related to MTSS frameworks: what the subcomponents are, what the research says about effective systemwide approaches to literacy improvement, and how these approaches can become culturally and

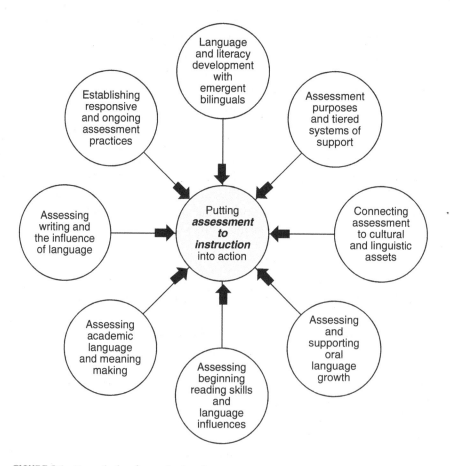

FIGURE 8.1. Knowledge from the book to put *assessment to instruction* into action.

linguistically responsive. Once we've laid the foundation, we outline the structures that effectively connect assessment and instruction in MTSS: collecting relevant data, analyzing and sharing results with stakeholders, and creating opportunities for staff to plan and test instructional innovations based on student learning data. Since each member of the school community has a role to play in putting MTSS into practice, in another section key aspects of these roles and responsibilities are outlined. The chapter also includes a set of three realistic scenarios in which we highlight how assessment results can lead to emergent bilingual students getting the instruction they need at the right moment. We conclude by sharing some final ideals for educators to keep in mind, as they ensure that their assessment practices are systematic, responsive, and tailored to the assets emergent bilinguals possess and set high expectations for their success.

FOUNDATIONAL IDEAS

In Chapter 2 we described a systemwide approach to academic improvement known as MTSS, and in Figure 2.1 we illustrated the three tiers of instructional support that are enacted through an MTSS framework: Tier 1 (core instruction), Tier 2 (supplementary intervention), and Tier 3 (individualized/intensive intervention). We highlighted a variety of assessments that generate data for making decisions about what support is needed for each student to thrive in school. In this section, we reconnect to the ideas presented earlier, taking a deeper look at the rationale behind MTSS, deconstructing the components necessary for its success, and sharing efforts that have been made to help MTSS become more culturally and linguistically responsive.

MTSS as a Systemwide Approach to Literacy Improvement

The driving rationale behind an MTSS approach is that systemic structures must be in place to help all students be successful at school, and that these structures and practices must involve all members of the school community, including educators, administration, specialists, students, and families (Forman & Crystal, 2015; Jimerson, Burns, & VanDerHeyden, 2016; Johnson, Mellard, Fuchs, & McKnight, 2006). Core elements for success in MTSS include:

- A clear vision and ability to prioritize, including the use of a comprehensive implementation plan.
- Schoolwide coordination and organizational support.
- Effective leadership.
- Identification and reliable use of research-based instructional practices appropriate to identified needs.
- Professional learning opportunities for educators involved in instruction and intervention to assure effective implementation.
- Access to relevant screening, progress monitoring, and learning needs data that are used for instructional decision making and program planning.
- Delivery of tiered services based on students' levels of need. (Forman &

Crystal, 2015; Harn, Basaraba, Chard, & Fritz, 2015; Jimerson et al., 2016; Johnson et al., 2006)

The key components or pillars of an effective MTSS framework can be concisely described as (1) quality core instruction, (2) data-driven decision making, (3) tiered interventions, and (4) professional learning (Path to Reading Excellence in School Sites [PRESS], 2019), accompanied by a commitment to culturally and linguistically relevant practices (Brown & Doolittle, 2008) that is embedded in the framework. However, committed leadership and clear communication among all stakeholders (PRESS, 2018) is essential in order for MTSS to be successful. These four key components are described in the following sections.

Quality Core Instruction

Most of students' days are spent in their home classrooms where they should experience instruction that matches their literacy developmental needs and expands upon their strengths and experiences using evidence-based, systematic, and explicit instruction that has a solid research foundation (Gibbons, Brown, & Niebling, 2019; Morrow & Gambrell, 2019). As we've reiterated throughout this book, emergent bilinguals should receive tailored instruction that supports their language development, that provides access to comprehensible content, and that builds on their linguistic and cultural assets (Helman, 2016). Quality core instruction also implies that students have adequate time for literacy learning activities—a recommended 90 minutes per day—and that if students need extra help on core literacy expectations, they receive supplemental instruction within the classroom to clarify, review, practice, or look at material in a new way (Hattie, 2008; Johnson et al., 2006). A solid core instructional program for each student is the foundation for a working MTSS system, because if students do not receive effective instruction in their home classrooms, there will never be enough resources schoolwide to intervene at the Tier 2 level to meet all of their academic needs (Burns & Gibbons, 2012; Gibbons et al., 2019).

Data-Driven Decision Making

In Chapter 2, we described the levels of assessments that should be collected through well-conceived MTSS. They include reliable and valid universal screeners, progress monitoring tools, and learning needs assessments (see Figure 2.1). In addition to *collecting* these data, it is critical for educators working on school improvement to *analyze* the data, so that human and material resources can be allocated to best ensure that instruction and intervention will further student progress (Burns & Gibbons, 2012). There are a number of processes that support the analysis of data in schools.

- Target scores are clearly defined.
- Data-collection procedures are efficient, and data are accessible to all educators and administrators who need it.

- The school plan outlines systematic processes for using the data.
- Time is allocated for collaborative decision making.
- There is an existing procedure within the organization for analyzing data and assigning resources.
- Collective decisions are made with input from key stakeholders based on students' responsiveness to instruction or intervention.
  (Harn et al., 2015; Johnson et al., 2006; PRESS, 2018)

Tiered Interventions

An effective MTSS for literacy achievement features instruction at multiple tiers, depending on how students are performing in the identified academic area. Many MTSS experts believe that, with high-quality core instruction, approximately 80% of students should be successful in meeting academic expectations within their home classrooms with the use of differentiation and teacher-provided support. An additional 15–20% of students are likely to need supplementary instruction at the Tier 2 level, given either within or outside of the classroom by an interventionist who may or may not be the classroom teacher. Students receiving Tier 2 interventions need focused instruction based on the most-basic literacy development area that they have yet to master (e.g., phonemic awareness, phonics, fluency, or reading comprehension; Burns, Maki, Karich, Hall, McComas, & Helman, 2016), with an emphasis on oral language and vocabulary development for emergent bilinguals (Vadasy & Sanders, 2010, 2011). Approximately 5% of students may not show adequate growth after receiving instruction at the Tier 1 or Tier 2 levels, and will require more intense and individualized instruction at the Tier 3 level (Burns & Gibbons, 2012; Fuchs, Fuchs, & Compton, 2012).

Leadership teams composed of key school personnel, working with classroom teachers and with parental input, should plan for the kinds of tiered support that students at the school most need. These supports may include working with a reading interventionist or literacy specialist, having grade-level teams collaborate for a shared differentiation block of time, or finding other ways to provide intervention through coteaching or collaboration strategies (e.g., Honigsfeld & Dove, 2016). Tiered interventions must be delivered in a consistent and high-quality manner. If many of the students are emergent bilinguals, interventions at both the Tier 2 and Tier 3 levels ought to address academic goals with adequate embedded language support (Vadasy & Sanders, 2010, 2011). Students should be treated equitably, which means that they should profit from the best research-based interventions, beginning when they are first diagnosed as needing them, and that the supports are accessible given their current linguistic resources. Emergent bilingual students who do not respond positively to Tier 2 interventions need to be considered at case meetings with key literacy personnel, EL specialists, and other people who are knowledgeable about the linguistic and cultural aspects of the student's background. Whenever possible, data from assessments in the student's home language should be explored before making any high-stakes educational decisions.

Professional Learning

There are a number of reasons why ongoing and job-embedded professional learning is needed to successfully implement an MTSS framework. First of all, educators need to know about and be able to put into practice the highest quality instruction and intervention at all tiers of the system and in all areas of language and literacy development. This includes a working knowledge of second-language development and the scaffolds required to support students who are becoming literate in a new language (Lucas & Villegas, 2013). Second, educators must administer and analyze many of the informal classroom-based assessments that will inform the next steps in instruction and intervention for students. In addition, educators need to know how to collaborate with other stakeholders in identifying student learning needs, have the sanctioned time to do so, and have opportunities to contribute their professional ideas, while also learning from others how to propose context-based teaching solutions to improve the instruction students receive (Helman & Pekel, in press).

Having a high-quality professional learning plan allows groups of educators to compare student assessment data to grade-level standards and benchmarks through structures such as professional learning communities (PLCs), in which assessment-to-instruction conversations are explicit and focused (Helman & Rosheim, 2016). Ideally, as part of an MTSS-focused PLC structure, educators meet on a monthly basis to analyze the most recent screening, progress monitoring, or learning needs assessment data. The team determines whether there is a classwide problem (i.e., Are more than 50% of students scoring below the benchmark?); which students need a Tier 2 intervention, and if so, what the Tier 2 intervention should be; and whether there are students who are not responding to the Tier 2 intervention, and thus need a different intervention (Burns & Gibbons, 2012). On alternate PLC meeting dates, groups of educators bring artifacts of student work from classroom assignments and informal assessments, assess whether students are approaching the standards, and share teaching practices that are promoting student success. This site-focused professional learning ensures that educators can make immediate connections to their classroom practice.

Professional learning has the most impact when it is job embedded and long term (Joyce & Showers, 2002). One well-established approach to making this happen is through coaching structures in which teachers, educational assistants, or interventionists meet with literacy coaches who provide feedback on instruction, model research-based teaching practices, or collaboratively plan lessons (Elish-Piper & L'Allier, 2010). We discuss the importance of partnerships between literacy coaches and instructional personnel later in this chapter.

Enhancing MTSS for Cultural and Linguistic Responsiveness

Many of the standard practices that are put forward in MTSS plans are highly beneficial for emergent bilinguals as well as monolingual English-speaking students. For example, emergent bilingual students will profit from being a part of school systems that screen all students in relation to grade-level benchmarks to identify those students who may "fall through the cracks." MTSS structures also deliver tiered interventions tailored to each student's needs. Professional learning opportunities related to literacy instruction that support educators in all schools are especially critical for educators who work in the more-complex area of teaching students to read and write in a new language.

The National Center on Response to Intervention produced an informational report on the topic of appropriately using assessments to improve the outcomes of EL students (Esparza Brown & Sanford, 2011). The report highlights the need for educators to understand the process of acquiring an additional language and to learn about their students' home languages to better understand the specific linguistic challenges their students face. It emphasizes that current screening and progress monitoring assessments that have been validated with monolingual English-speaking students are also helpful in planning instruction for EL students (Esparza Brown & Sanford, 2011). The authors also note that data on students' language and literacy skills in their home languages provide important information about *whether* additional supports are needed and, *if so,* which ones are most appropriate (Esparza Brown & Sanford, 2011). As we have described throughout this book, it is critical to take into account students' language and literacy progress in both the home language and in English when planning instruction and intervention.

ENHANCING TIER 1 INSTRUCTION

♦ Use culturally and linguistically responsive teaching approaches and classroom structures that have been shown to work with students from diverse backgrounds.

♦ Use explicit and systematic language development practices.

♦ Support, extend, and transfer home language skills.

♦ Use small-group instruction.

♦ Augment assessment data with informal classroom data of student learning.

At the Tier 2 level in an MTSS framework, emergent bilinguals should receive interventions that address their area of reading need, with methods that have been shown to have promising results (Klingner & Edwards, 2006). In a recent policy document issued by America's Promise Alliance, Aspen Education & Society Program, and Council of Chief State School Officers (2018), a number of recommendations that support educational equity within systematic reform efforts were put forward. Among them are ways to communicate an equity vision and measurable targets, such as the California Department of Education's *California English Language Roadmap* and the Wisconsin Department of Public Education's training for staff members on implicit bias (America's Promise Alliance et al., 2018).

The Wisconsin Department of Public Instruction serves as a model for one state's concerted efforts to integrate equity into MTSS frameworks. Equity is placed at the center of the state MTSS framework, and it is achieved through a universal level of supports that include high-quality instruction, the strategic use of data, and collaboration (Wisconsin RTI Center, 2017). Surrounding and encompassing the universal core of the model are evidence-based practices, family and community engagement, positive culture, strong shared leadership, and systematic implementation (Wisconsin RTI Center, 2017).

QUESTIONS TO CONSIDER FOR MAKING MTSS MORE CULTURALLY AND LINGUISTICALLY RESPONSIVE

- How can the school staff become more informed about the process of learning to read and write in a new language?
- How can the school staff become more informed about characteristics of the home languages students possess?
- To what degree do students receive a core curriculum of literacy instruction that is evidence based and has been shown to work with students from diverse cultural and linguistic backgrounds?
- Is there evidence that the assessments in use have been validated with culturally and linguistically diverse students?
- How are students from different demographic and linguistic backgrounds faring at the Tier 1, 2, and 3 levels of the MTSS program?
- What evidence is there that the interventions in use have been validated with culturally and linguistically diverse students?
- Who is advocating for culturally and linguistically diverse students on campus, and how can their voices be prioritized and better understood?
- How can the school staff and leadership more effectively ensure equitable outcomes for all students?
- How can the voices of families, community members, and diverse students be included in MTSS planning?

PART ONE: STRUCTURES THAT ENABLE MTSS

In this section, we revisit many of the ideas presented in Chapter 2 and earlier in this chapter that enable the success of MTSS at a school site. Although some of the structures we discuss may exist at the district or state levels (e.g., district or state directives), we concentrate on the school level, because typically the school is the place over which educators, administrators, families, communities, and students have the most control and are most affected by MTSS plans. If school sites are constrained by outside forces, we encourage leadership teams and others to innovate in their own setting and also advocate for improved policies at the level that guides policy. Here, we describe several ways that educators and school leaders can establish processes and procedures within MTSS that support the key goals of quality core instruction, data-driven decision making, delivery of tiered interventions, and job-embedded professional learning.

Systems for Collecting Relevant Data

The first step in creating an MTSS that is driven by data about student learning is to collect the right types of data throughout the school year. In Chapter 2, we outlined the kinds of assessments and their purposes within an RTI/MTSS structure. Universal screeners are used initially and at designated points throughout the year to identify students who are not yet meeting grade-level benchmarks and will likely profit from supplementary literacy instruction. For students who are receiving supplementary interventions, brief learning needs assessments should be conducted to identify the explicit additional instruction they require. Once students are receiving a supplementary intervention, progress monitoring assessments should inform on a weekly basis the extent to which the extra help is leading to student growth and/or what other types of support may be needed (see Figure 2.1). In Chapter 4, we described the use of standardized English language proficiency assessments (ELPAs) to both identify EL students and then to monitor their language growth on a yearly basis. In addition to using formalized structures for collecting data on students' language and literacy growth, classroom teachers and specialists will need to regularly collect informal classroom-based assessment data. These data guide every aspect of language and literacy instruction: from the vocabulary and language structures they should learn next, to the area of reading development they should focus on, to the next steps in writing development that will best support their progress.

Principals and their leadership teams on site should help streamline the collection of these relevant data by fortifying the structures that enable data collection and giving educators the support they need to gather the data. Some ideas for improving data collection include:

- Create a yearlong schedule that outlines when universal screening measures, ELPAs, and other standardized tests will be administered.
- Ensure that universal screening measures are valid and reliable, and that educators administer them correctly and consistently.
- Clearly define target scores for universal screening measures.
- Develop procedures for collecting screening, progress monitoring, and learning needs data throughout the grade levels.
- Use both general outcome measures and skill-specific measures to monitor the long-range and immediate progress of students receiving interventions.
- If necessary, compare emergent bilinguals' language and literacy data with those of a "true peer," that is, a student peer who has a similar schooling background and language proficiency (Brown & Doolittle, 2008).
- Clearly communicate the procedures for data collection and handling to all staff.
- Find ways to combine human resources to facilitate the efficient collection of language and literacy data on site.
- Use data from multiple assessment measures when making program placement and other academic decisions.

When data collection is handled efficiently and the results give high-quality information that leads to student learning, educators will be more likely to appreciate the time spent collecting it. In the next section, we discuss ways that data can work to improve programs through structured stakeholder conversations.

Structuring Data Conversations with Stakeholders

Data don't mean very much if they don't influence instructional decisions and school-wide goals in a meaningful way. The key to putting data to work is holding conversations in a variety of settings so that all stakeholders understand the purpose of the MTSS framework and can evaluate its success in helping students succeed in literacy. The following examples illustrate some of the ways that key stakeholders can view data, analyze them, and propose the next steps for schoolwide improvement based on what the data uncover.

Instructional Staff and School Leaders

As noted previously, two of the main pillars of MTSS are data-driven decision making and professional learning. When educators participate in conversations about data at school, both of these components are enhanced: (1) academic planning is not based on philosophy or intuition, but rather on evidence of student learning, and (2) participants in data conversations learn how to identify students who need help in becoming successful in their literacy learning and, in collaboration with colleagues, share instructional solutions to support them. At minimum, data meetings for school leaders and instructional staff should take place as soon as results from the universal screening assessments are available. These meetings can take place as part of a larger staff meeting, at which schoolwide data and trends are presented first, and then teams of educators from each grade level examine their section of data in greater depth. Or, data meetings can be scheduled in a half-day slot three times a year.

During data meetings, educators review the universal screening data first at the grade level, then at the classroom level, and finally at the individual student level. Learning trends are identified by demographic groups; if some groups of students are not meeting benchmark levels as expected, an action plan is created to better serve them. Action steps may involve a change in curriculum, a plan for differentiation, or the scheduling of a professional learning session to support educators' use of a novel evidence-based practice. Data meetings are also a time in which student learning progress can be reviewed on an individual basis to double check that students are on track to meet benchmark goals; at this time, supplementary resources are allocated on the basis of the systematic plan outlined in the MTSS framework (Burns & Gibbons, 2012).

Grade-Level Teams

Less formal than the comprehensive data-analysis meeting just described, but equally as important, are grade-level team meetings attended by teachers from the same grade level (or grade band for small schools). These meetings are ideal forums in which colleagues share students' work in relation to grade-level standards to ensure that all students profit from the collective pedagogical knowledge and experience of educators. During these meetings, teachers review the classroom products or assessment results of their students and classify them according to whether they are below, approaching, meeting, or exceeding the benchmarks. Then, the group discusses a plan for differentiating instruction that will assist all students in making progress. For example, using the following literacy expectation for grades 3–4—that students will determine the main idea of a text and explain how it is supported by key details—the team can review students' written attempts to meet the standard and devise a collective rubric to evaluate whether they were successful or not. For students who were not successful, the team can brainstorm teaching practices that have worked to propel students forward in this area. At the end of the meeting, team members agree to collect additional data on the success of this approach for their next conversation.

Related data conversations that also involve grade-level teams are vertical team meetings, in which one grade level (e.g., second grade) meets with the next grade level up (e.g., third grade) to discuss data on student language and literacy progress. Educators from both grade levels profit from discussing the work of students at the grade levels before and after them so that high expectations can be upheld and successful teaching practices can be shared.

Educator–Student Conferences

Students have the most at stake in their educational success, yet they are often not included in data conversations about their progress. One way to have these conversations in supportive and age-appropriate ways is to schedule short educator–student conferences on a regular basis. These one-on-one conversations can take place in a manner similar to a personalized reading or writing conference during which educators share the ways in which students are progressing, and students can share their

STRUCTURING EDUCATOR–STUDENT CONFERENCES

- ◆ Introduce the conference as a time and place to share information about the student's learning.
- ◆ Introduce the topic: "Today we will be talking about [content area or assessment result]." If applicable, have artifacts of student work in the area being discussed.
- ◆ Invite the student to share what he or she feels is going well in relation to the area being discussed.
- ◆ Invite the student to share what is hard or causing difficulty in the area being discussed.
- ◆ Invite the student to share what he or she would like to do better in this area.
- ◆ Share data from the student's work in the area being discussed. Tell the student what the data mean (e.g., not yet meeting, approaching, or meeting the standard).
- ◆ Show an example of what "meeting the standard" looks like in the area being discussed.
- ◆ Set specific goals for student learning to bridge the gap between current performance and desired performance.
    - ❖ What will the educator do to support success?
    - ❖ What will the student do to support success?
- ◆ Make a plan for meeting again to discuss progress.

success stories, learning challenges, and feelings about the content area, and set goals to guide their future efforts. Receiving feedback on one's current performance in relation to models of what proficient performance looks like is one of the most effective instructional strategies in educators' toolboxes (Hattie, 2008).

Conversations with Families

Culturally and linguistically responsive MTSS frameworks give careful thought about how to form bidirectional relationships with parents and other family members who care deeply about their children's academic success. A bidirectional relationship entails not only sharing information with families, it also entails learning about students' family life and incorporating family input into the school program. Family involvement is crucial; but, as has been noted elsewhere in this book, developing a trusting reciprocal relationships takes time. Sharing scores on students' language proficiency exams or a state- or district-mandated literacy assessments in a one-shot conference at school will likely feel unsatisfying at best to both parties.

Honest conversations about students' achievement data as measured against national standards can be difficult to have. Family members may feel worried that their children are not progressing well, or they may not understand the information they are given because educational jargon is used. On the other hand, educators may shy away from sharing data that show that students are not yet achieving benchmark standards, because they instead communicate simply that students are working hard (despite still being behind). In a longitudinal study of seven immigrant students' progress through elementary school, researchers found that the majority of the families whose children experienced roadblocks to academic success did not come away from parent–teacher conferences with accurate information about their children's progress (Helman et al., 2016).

To help set the stage for meaningful conversations about data with family members, Delgado Gaitán (2004) suggests that educators:

- Develop a relationship with family members outside of the conference time so that conversations feel less threatening.
- Ensure that interpreters are available during conferences.
- Provide all documentation in English and in the family's home language.
- Offer child care during conference times.
- Practice ahead of time and use common terms, rather than professional jargon, to describe the information.
- Listen to what family members say about their child's learning and how it compares to that of other children in the family.
- Check in frequently to make sure that family members understand what is being shared.
- Use multiple forms of oral and written communication throughout the year to stay in touch.
- Encourage family members to bring up questions at any time throughout the year.

Collaboration Structures on Site

In order for collaborative conversations about data and instruction to become a regular part of the MTSS structure on site, various systems must be in place. We outline some of the most common arrangements in the next sections.

Common Planning Time

School leaders are often able to construct the school schedule in ways that allow staff members who can profit most from meeting on a regular basis (e.g., grade-level teams or common content-area teachers) to have their planning block at the same time. Having a common planning time reduces the need for educators to meet before or after school, which are often not ideal times to think deeply. When a common planning time cannot be worked into the daily schedule, efforts can be made to include shared planning as a part of regular staff meetings or during PLCs.

Professional Learning Communities

A key part of effective MTSS is professional learning, and PLCs are a primary vehicle for sharing and taking in new professional knowledge. PLCs can be used to analyze student achievement data, to become familiar with new evidence-based literacy instruction practices, to share what is working in each other's classrooms, to learn from the EL specialist or special education teacher, and so much more. PLCs provide an opportunity for a range of educators to meet together to share resources and problem solve. Bringing together the perspectives and educational background experiences of many professionals enhances the practice of everyone involved and creates a sense of responsibility for all students, a team spirit that everyone is working together to help the school improve.

Coaching

Hearing about evidence-based language and literacy instruction at a professional development workshop or reading about it in a book could be a first step toward implementation. To help that learning take root and become part of an educator's repertoire usually requires much more than that, however. One form of job-embedded professional learning that allows educators to try out new practices, get feedback, observe a more experienced colleague use the practice, and/or participate in a collaborative conversation about its use is coaching support. Coaching is often provided by a literacy coach on site or in the district; however, if a literacy coach is not available, peer coaching can also take place with some structural support for shared planning and observation time.

Common Intervention Time

As educators look for creative ways to differentiate instruction for students and provide Tier 2 interventions for students who need extra support, one solution that has arisen is the use of a common intervention time. In this scheduling innovation, for a set period of time each day (or 4 days a week) students move to a different place on campus where they will work on literacy goals at their current level of need. For example, students who might profit from a fluency intervention receive that intervention in another setting under the guidance of a highly trained professional. Students who are meeting reading benchmarks at their grade level get supplemental instruction, perhaps in a larger group, in an area that will help them advance as well. During common intervention time, all instructional staff, and sometimes even noninstructional staff and volunteers, participate in leading instructional activities that allow students to receive instruction at their level of literacy development.

Coteaching

Many forms of coteaching are available (cf. Honigsfeld & Dove, 2016) for educators who are interested in pursuing this model of collaboration. The basic premise is that two educators work in partnership to teach, observe, scaffold, and/or diagnose student learning during a lesson. The roles that each educator takes on vary, depending on the purpose of the lesson and the goals for coteaching. A frequent form of coteaching involves an EL specialist or a special educator working alongside a classroom teacher to conduct a classroom lesson. The specialist may provide support for emergent bilinguals or others, or she may collect observation data on what students do or say during the lesson to discuss with the teacher later, or she may use her specialized knowledge to present content in a way that is accessible to specific learners. Coteaching gives students extra support during the lesson and can be the basis for collegial conversations for both teachers as they work together to learn about and improve instruction for all their students.

Push-In Models for Specialist Support

When educational specialists such as EL teachers, special educators, educational assistants, and interventionists introduce small-group instruction into the general education classroom, colleagues have an additional way to learn from one another. The specialist is able to make connections between what is going on in the classroom setting and small-group work, and the classroom teacher learns about the supplemental support the students receive, and then can share background knowledge about the students' performance during home-classroom time. Both educators are likely to develop questions about particular students' strengths and challenges in the other setting. Together, these conversations help educators to gain more holistic understandings of their students and to acquire new teaching practices as well.

Peer Tutoring within or across Classrooms

Collaboration does not need to happen only with the adults in the classroom. There are a number of ways for students to become teachers throughout the day as well. From cross-classroom reading buddies to within-classroom interventions, such as

PALS (Fuchs et al., 1997), students can become empowered to work with their peers to support reading and writing and both members of the partnership learn in the process. Peer tutoring is not only an effective way to give students opportunities for additional reading or writing time, it is also a powerful way to develop leadership skills and show responsibility. It is also a great way to motivate students to become invested in the growth of their learning partner.

PART TWO: ROLES OF INDIVIDUALS IN SUSTAINING A COHESIVE ASSESSMENT-TO-INSTRUCTION SYSTEM

The "system" in a multi-tiered system of support signifies that practices must be institutionalized, not carried out independently at will or in isolation. For this problem-solving and school-improvement system to work, each member of the school community must contribute to and work collectively for common goals (Eagle, Dowd-Eagle, Snyder, & Holtzman, 2015; Johnson et al., 2006). In this section, we describe the important roles that individuals play to ensure that there is a connection between what is assessed and what is taught, a key aspect of an effective MTSS framework.

The Teacher's Role

The K–5 classroom teacher plays perhaps the most important role in the assessment-to-instruction system. As the primary instructor of language and literacy, the classroom teacher provides quality core literacy instruction to all students in the general education classroom, which includes providing linguistic supports for emergent bilinguals. The classroom teacher is also responsible for administering a majority of the assessments that are given, such as universal screeners, learning needs assessments, IRIs, a range of formative assessments, and other daily checks for understanding.

The International Literacy Association (2018) outlines this standard for classroom teachers in the area of literacy assessment and evaluation: "Understand, select, and use appropriate assessments to gather evidence on students' language acquisition and literacy development for instructional and accountability purposes."

Once assessments have been administered, classroom teachers are an integral part of the follow-up data conversations and collaborative planning. The classroom teacher can call upon any of the stakeholders (e.g., literacy specialist, EL specialist, or special educator) for their expertise in language and literacy scaffolding and differentiation. More important, the classroom teacher is responsible for a classroom environment where students' linguistic and cultural resources are sustained and celebrated throughout the general education curriculum.

The Literacy (Reading) Specialist's Role

The primary role of the literacy specialist (or the reading specialist) is to provide literacy instruction to students, especially those who are experiencing difficulty (International Literacy Association, 2018). Literacy specialists should have a foundational understanding of how to administer and evaluate literacy interventions and progress monitoring assessments and how to communicate with other educators about assessment results. They are well versed in the theories of language and literacy development and how they improve literacy education for students. Literacy specialists also collaborate with EL specialists to analyze data and plan appropriate instructional next steps for emergent bilingual students who face roadblocks to their progress in reading.

Literacy/reading specialists are also knowledgeable about culturally and linguistically relevant practices and essential concepts of diversity and equity, and use their knowledge to inform language and literacy assessment practices. The International Literacy Association (2018) summarizes the competencies of reading/literacy specialists in the area of literacy assessment and evaluation: "Understand, select, and use valid, reliable, fair, and appropriate assessment tools to screen, diagnose, and measure student literacy achievement; inform instruction and evaluate interventions; assist teachers in their understanding and use of assessment results; advocate for appropriate literacy practices to relevant stakeholders."

The EL Specialist's Role

EL specialists (also called EL teachers, ESL teachers, or ELD teachers) are knowledgeable about language acquisition and development. They teach targeted language instruction and administer informal and formal assessments for emergent bilinguals in speaking, listening, reading, and writing.

An EL specialist is likely to be well versed in the characteristics of levels of English language proficiency (as described in Chapter 4), and can provide instructional supports and scaffolds based on those levels. He or she is sufficiently knowledgeable about the standards and assessments related to English language proficiency (e.g., WIDA, ELPA) and how to use them in instruction.

When a group of educators convene to discuss language and literacy instruction and assessments, an EL specialist may help them in analyzing data from a perspective of language development and the unique needs of specific emergent bilingual students. They may be able to notice cross-linguistic opportunities and challenges, such as shared cognates or phonology across languages. In addition, EL specialists are valuable resources when reviewing language and literacy curriculum and assessments to determine language demands.

Many EL specialists have had coursework in asset-based pedagogies, such as culturally and linguistically relevant and sustaining practices. Thus, they will likely be familiar with how to use asset-based pedagogies in instruction and assessment, and may be able to identify when instruction and assessment may not be capitalizing on students' linguistic and cultural resources, and may help customize instructional resources to meet the needs of diverse students.

EL specialists are likely to be disposed toward advocating for emergent bilinguals, because they are aware of the opportunities and challenges that bilingual speakers may face in school and society (Lucas & Villegas, 2013). Finally, many of them have developed relationships with emergent bilinguals' families and communities and can be called upon to help strengthen these partnerships.

The Special Educator's Role

The special educator brings to the table specialized knowledge related to assessment, individualized instruction, collaborative problem solving, and due-process systems. Many of the instructional approaches that special educators are familiar with have been demonstrated to not only benefit students with disabilities, but also a wide range of learners who experience difficulty with various aspects of literacy. Thus, a special educator may have a lot to offer, regardless of whether or not an emergent bilingual student is being considered for referral to special education.

The special educator will be knowledgeable about the assessments used for identifying and diagnosing specific academic or behavioral difficulties and disabilities, including how to administer, score, and interpret data from standardized achievement and diagnostic tests. The special educator should also have the expertise needed to establish a student's current performance level, setting specific learning goals and objectives, monitoring progress toward those goals, and using progress monitoring data to make instructional decisions.

With respect to individualized instruction, the special educator should be knowledgeable about and skilled in modifying or adapting instructional materials to support a student's success in accessing the general education curriculum. He or she should also be well versed in intensifying or individualizing instruction using specialized instructional strategies, including the use of highly explicit instruction, cognitive and metacognitive strategies, computer-adaptive instruction and other technologies, and other research-validated techniques. In addition, the special educator will likely be skilled in addressing behavior issues that sometimes co-occur with academic difficulties that the students experience.

Regarding collaborative problem solving, many special educators have had extensive coursework, as well as experience, related to working with teams of multidisciplinary professionals, administrators, family members, and students, and will likely be able to effectively communicate assessment results to a range of stakeholders, as well as seek input from a variety of perspectives and connect assessment findings to instructional solutions. The special educator might be able to support other educators and families in making connections with helpful resources within the educational system as well as in the broader community. For example, the special educator might be aware of parent advocacy groups for students with special needs or of organizations dedicated to supporting individuals with specific disabilities (such as learning disabilities or autism spectrum disorders).

Finally, the special educator can be consulted about due process, in the event that a concern arises that a student's literacy difficulties go beyond a language-learning issue, and that special education services might be warranted. She or he will know the necessary steps, time frames, and student and parental rights regarding the referral, evaluation, eligibility determination, and instructional programming process. The special educator will also know how to design and implement an individualized education plan (IEP), and will work in close collaboration with other educators (e.g., general educator, EL specialist, other service providers such as speech–language pathologists) who play direct roles in carrying out that plan.

The Literacy Coach's Role

As defined by the International Literacy Association (2018), a literacy coach works primarily with teachers to facilitate schoolwide improvement of student literacy outcomes. Some of the important functions of the literacy coach are to provide job-embedded professional learning for staff members, for example, through coaching, planning and facilitating PLCs, sharing and modeling research-based teaching practices, and helping to select or develop assessments and teaching materials (International Literacy Association, 2018). Literacy coaches meet with principals on a regular basis to analyze progress toward literacy achievement goals and set concrete next steps in the school action plan (Helman & Pekel, in press).

Six standards outlined in the *Standards for the Preparation of Literacy Professionals 2017* (International Literacy Association, 2018) relate to the areas of foundational knowledge in language and literacy, curriculum and instruction, assessment and evaluation, diversity and equity, learners and the literacy environment, and professional learning and leadership. These standards make it clear that the literacy coach must have a strong knowledge base about learning and teaching in the language arts, know how to align instruction to the standards, be able to oversee assessment and intervention practices, advocate for cultural and linguistic equity for students, facilitate and coach teachers in creating responsive and engaging literacy-learning environments, and guide adult learning opportunities. Based on the comprehensiveness of this role description, the on-site literacy coach is without a doubt the key player in addressing the design and implementation of the literacy strand of a school's MTSS. It is crucially important, however, that the literacy coach be able to help many stakeholders contribute to the literacy instruction and intervention systems that are created and feel ownership in them.

The Principal's Role

Without the active involvement of principals, site-based MTSS frameworks will not become established and flourish. Principals lead the school planning process, oversee the appropriate use of assessments, foster an atmosphere of equity for students from linguistically diverse communities, structure regular opportunities for the staff to meet to review student-learning data and set the next steps for instruction, and involve families and communities in understanding and contributing to their children's education (International Literacy Association, 2018). Principals work in partnership with leadership teams on site that typically include literacy coaches, EL specialists, special educators, grade-level teacher representatives, and others to ensure that assessment results are reviewed, that gaps in instructional support are noted, and that resources are put into place to address identified instructional needs (Helman & Pekel, in press).

Although principals may not have the same level of specialized knowledge that an EL specialist has about language development, or that a literacy specialist has about literacy learning and instruction, or that a special educator has about learning difficulties, they must have sufficient knowledge in these areas to construct a school vision and manage the work of professionals in a variety of roles. In order to be successful in this undertaking, principals need an understanding of:

- Literacy and English language development standards.
- The importance of multiple forms of assessment and their appropriate uses and limitations.
- How assessment and instruction fit together in MTSS.
- How to advocate for students and families of diverse cultural and linguistic backgrounds.
- The social nature of language and literacy learning and the importance of student engagement in the classroom.
- Ways to structure ongoing professional collaboration focused on student learning and evidence-based teaching practices.
(International Literacy Association, 2018)

The Family's Role

Families provide children with care, security, oversight, and an initial enthusiasm for engaging with the outside world. Families bestow their language, their religious and cultural practices, and their values and experiences on their children, and offer them a way to see who they are in the world. As described in Chapter 3, family members pass along the funds of knowledge of previous generations, thereby giving their children a sense of identity and belonging in a complex world. Because families know the most about their children, they possess a wealth of information that will help educators better understand the language, literacy, socioemotional, and academic strengths and growth trajectories of their students. In other words, families are a resource for educators to create stronger relationships and improve instruction with their children. When educators take the time to visit homes, hold conferences, ask for input from families, and spend time in local communities, many opportunities arise for gathering some of this important background information.

Family involvement should be bidirectional, not a one-way stream of information from educator to parent. It is certainly important for parents to hear about how their children are performing at school, and what their latest score on the language proficiency exam is. It is also critical that parents have opportunities to share what they know, advocate for what they believe their children need, and ask questions about their children's instructional and intervention experiences at school. In a longitudinal study of seven immigrant students and their families, researchers found that, although a variety of obstacles held parents back from regular engagement with educators, they continued to do many things to support their children's success at school (Helman et al., 2016). Educator practices that encouraged a deeper relationship between home and school and valued the cultural and linguistic resources that students brought with them had powerful effects on students' connection to the classroom and to preventing disenfranchisement (Helman et al., 2016; Ingram, Wolfe, & Lieberman, 2007).

In a study of how educators and parents interpreted score reports from the annual language proficiency assessments students are given, researchers found that parents were most focused on identifying their child's current proficiency level. Because of the gap between when the assessment is given and when schools receive the results, parents did not have much of a chance to discuss the results with teachers (Kim et al., 2016). The report suggested that, to be more meaningful for parents, the score reports should simplify technical language, be accessible in the family's home language, include information on the student's year-to-year language growth, provide the reports in a more timely manner, and help parents understand the educational decisions that are made on the basis of the information (Kim et al., 2016). As has been highlighted throughout this book, family members are essential stakeholders in helping educators build bridges between school learning and out-of-school knowledge.

COLLABORATING WITH FAMILIES

- Establish families' preferred mode of communication, and communicate with them on a frequent basis.
- Communicate child's needs and strengths.
- Translate assessment information and use interpreters on a regular basis.
- Know that cultural differences can influence families' understanding of assessment information.
- Schedule meetings that facilitate families' attendance (taking transportation, work schedules, child care, and so on into account).
- Explain the purpose of assessments and the consequences of their use.
- Use nontechnical, plain language to interpret assessment data.
- Be solution-oriented; be sure not to communicate blame in some way.
- As appropriate, include students in meetings and prepare them to be actively engaged in discussing assessment outcomes.

From Salvia, Ysseldyke, and Witmer (2017).

PART THREE: FROM ASSESSMENT TO SUPPORT: GIVING EMERGENT BILINGUALS THE RIGHT INSTRUCTION AT THE RIGHT TIME

Bringing together information from multiple chapters in this section we present two examples of educators working together to use different types of assessment data to respond in proactive ways that support emergent bilingual students. In the first example, we reconnect with the case of Jamilah from Chapter 7. We describe the plan that the educators working with Jamilah created to provide her with the support and the "just right" instruction she needed to progress in her writing development. In a second example, we zoom in on a school with a significant discrepancy in achievement between emergent bilinguals and monolingual English-speaking students. The educators and the leadership team identified a number of positive actions to include in their literacy MTSS plan and took concrete steps to implement their ideas in responsive and inclusive ways.

Responding to a Student Who Needs Explicit Support

In Chapter 7, we introduced Jamilah, who loves storytelling and is motivated to write, but has difficulty with spelling. Mr. Parson has gathered some writing assessment data, including three scored word dictation samples and a completed checklist of her spelling strengths and needs; her school-bus writing sample and rubric along with a checklist of her text generation strengths and needs; and his notes on the school environment, the home and classroom learning environment, and her cultural, linguistic, and motivational assets. He presents this information during the third-grade data-team meeting. He and his colleagues determine the following priorities for Jamilah.

1. Continue to develop her story-writing interest and skills by setting aside some "free writing" time, in which she will brainstorm ideas and write rough drafts, without worrying about spelling or sentence structure. Encourage code meshing, in which she can embed Somali words, either when she cannot think of an appropriate English word or when use of the Somali word particularly enhances the idea she is trying to convey. She will later return to these rough drafts to revise them, following explicit spelling and sentence structure instruction.

2. Provide explicit spelling instruction and practice for 10 minutes per day, 2–3 days per week, using spelling patterns specified in the third-grade core curriculum and standards, as well as additional words that Jamilah wants to use in her writing. This explicit instruction and practice will include word building and word sorting for the spelling patterns and word study for her "spell to write" words.

3. Alternate spelling instruction with 2–3 days of explicit instruction and practice related to sentence construction (with support from the EL specialist, given her difficulties with English syntax). For practice, include sentences that Jamilah generated in her free writing to edit for appropriate subject–verb agreement and word order.

4. Monitor Jamilah's spelling progress weekly with word dictation and reexamine her data at the next data-team meeting. Use the spelling and text generation checklists and rubric to gauge areas of progress and of continued needs, and to facilitate discussion in a follow-up meeting about next steps.

Making Schoolwide Changes

Educators and the leadership team at Riverview Elementary have been committed to the literacy success of all students at their school for many years. They began by creating an MTSS plan 3 years ago that would help them use assessment data three times a year to identify which students seemed to be on track in their literacy learning and which students might need extra support to meet grade-level benchmarks. The staff felt committed to the principles of MTSS and the use of data to offer instruction and intervention tailored to the needs of students.

Data have helped the leadership team and, in turn, the instructional staff, at the school to understand which students are thriving in their classrooms and which students are not profiting as much from their instructional program. Two years ago, results of the fall screening assessment showed that approximately 40% of students at the school were meeting benchmark goals in literacy, yet the other 60% were not. A deeper look into the data showed that students who had been classified as EL based on their language proficiency exam scores were meeting grade-level benchmarks at a much lower rate (20%). Because more emergent bilingual students have enrolled in the school each year, the number of students not meeting grade-level benchmarks would continue to increase if nothing was done to support students' success.

Dr. Shire, the principal, along with Mr. Reed, the literacy specialist, and Ms. Farhan, one of the EL specialists, met to discuss the fall's universal screening data and to plan for the whole-staff data meeting. They knew that the data would be eye opening to the staff and that they would feel compelled to make an immediate and concerted effort to address the issue. They also understood that, in order to address the pressing need for literacy instruction and intervention that was better tailored to the school's emergent bilingual students, they would need the input of the school's literacy professionals and the EL staff. They knew that the improvement plan would need to be multiyear in scope and would require an "all-hands-on-deck" approach. During the whole-staff data meeting, disaggregated literacy results were presented and discussed. Then, the literacy specialist and EL teams suggested a number of "first steps" to add to the MTSS plan. Based on the staff meeting discussion, the following priorities and first steps were identified.

1. Increase educator knowledge about learning to read and write in a new language. The two EL specialists proposed a readable professional article for the staff that would be the focus of the next PLC meetings. One or the other of the EL specialists would attend each small-group PLC to facilitate the discussion and answer questions that surfaced from the article.

2. Learn more about the strengths and concerns of family members from the Somali community, the largest group of emergent bilinguals at the school. Ms. Farhan volunteered to facilitate a focus group for the school leadership team in which family members shared their perceptions of what the school does well and what it could improve upon and what strategies they feel best support their children's learning at home. At a later time, the leadership team will share the ideas that emerge with the whole staff.

3. Begin a discussion in grade-level team meetings about how educators embed language development in their literacy lessons. The staff agreed to take note of some of the ways they intentionally clarify language, teach vocabulary, check for student understanding, and build sentence structures during their teaching. At the next grade-level meeting, they will share their instructional approaches and learn from others. This will lead to self-reflection about the needed next steps and the creation of a grade-level-based action plan for increasing language support in literacy lessons.

The leadership team at the school understood that the steps they proposed were simply the beginning of a long-term process for making their MTSS plan more culturally and linguistically responsive. They felt strongly, however, that these steps would inform the journey, and that the formal and informal assessment data they collected along the way would point them in the right direction.

SUMMARY

This chapter has served as a blueprint of material presented in the book, guiding the reader to take information from each previous chapter and put it together into a cohesive plan. We described in detail the essential components of MTSS and how data analysis and professional learning are integrally woven into the plan's success. Many people play key roles in the success of MTSS at a school, including principals, literacy coaches, EL specialists, special educators, teachers, interventionists, students, and parents. We described the contributions that each of these people makes and the collaborative discussions and actions that work in synchrony to establish responsive and ongoing assessment and instruction practices systematically on site. We concluded with one example of how a team worked together to meet the needs of an individual student who needed writing support and another example of adaptations made at the whole-school level to begin to address the literacy success of emergent bilinguals.

THEMES FROM THROUGHOUT THE BOOK

- ◆ Get to know students' multilingual resources.
- ◆ Focus on students' assets.
- ◆ Look at assessment and instruction through a language development lens.
- ◆ Match assessments to their specified purposes.
- ◆ Use multiple measures to make instructional decisions.
- ◆ Use data-based, systematic, and collaborative approaches to decision making.

MOVING FORWARD

As we come to the end of this book, we want to take a moment to wish readers well on their future journeys and to encourage them to put what they have learned from this book into practice with students and colleagues. While we have sought to be practical and classroom focused throughout, we also have attempted to share our *ideals* for what language and literacy assessment with emergent bilinguals should involve. In Chapter 1 we shared a list of guiding principles for understanding assessment with emergent bilingual students, including the importance of assessments being asset focused, eliciting students' bilingual resources, and not categorizing students or assigning them a fixed "ability." These principles highlighted the importance of using a balanced assessment framework that provides useful information for all stakeholders and consists of multiple measures, making it possible for students to demonstrate what they know and can do. As we conclude, we offer our own set of IDEALS for potential next steps the reader might take to extend the professional learning that has begun.

IDEALS

Innovate: Move beyond the approaches you've tried before. Use and add to the suggestions provided in this book.

Develop understanding and empathy: Put yourself in the shoes of emergent bilingual students and their families. What practices would you find helpful and supportive?

Equity-focused: Keep equity at the heart of your assessment and instruction practices. What can you do to ensure that all students have opportunities to flourish in the classroom?

Advocate for bilingualism and family empowerment. Support students who operate in bilingual and multilingual worlds by working toward sustaining their language and culture.

Learn: Start a professional learning community to try out some ideas from the book in collaboration with colleagues.

Study: Use action research approaches to study your implementation of culturally and linguistically responsive assessment for learning.

Appendix
Assessment Resources

Planning Form for Strategies to Support Language Development

Support strategies	Entering	Beginning	Developing	Developing	Expanding	Moderately developed	Bridging	Reaching	Advanced
A language-learning community									
Clear and explicit language instruction									
Connect to what students know									
Active engagement									

Sound Isolation Task Template

Check the assessment area:

☐ Beginning sound

☐ Final sound

☐ Medial sound

Materials: Picture cards or objects

Directions: Before you begin, make sure the student knows all of the names of the pictures or objects. You can say, "Let's review these pictures first. Can you tell me the names of these things? [If the student doesn't know the name of a picture card or object, practice it before the assessment]. "Now, I am going to show you a picture. Can you tell me the beginning sound? Here is an example. This is a picture of a *pear*. The beginning sound in the word *pear* is /p/. "

Word	Sound said by student
1.	
2.	
3.	
4.	
5.	
6.	
7.	
8.	
9.	
10.	

APPENDIX C

Segmenting and Blending Template

SEGMENTING AND BLENDING TASKS

Check the assessment area:

☐ Segmenting sounds

☐ Blending sounds

Materials: Word lists (two-, three-, or four-phoneme words)

Directions for segmenting: "I am going to say a word. Then I want you to break up that word into each sound. Just like this: the word *lap* has three sounds /l/ /a/ /p/."

Directions for blending: "I am going to say three sounds. Then I want you to blend these sounds together to make a word. Just like this: /b/ /i/ /g/. Together those sounds make the word *big*."

	Word	Sound said by student
1.		
2.		
3.		
4.		
5.		
6.		
7.		
8.		
9.		
10.		

Phonemic Awareness Skill Tracker

Student's name: _____

Task	Date	Date	Date	Date	Date	Date	Date	Date
Sound isolation: initial								
Sound isolation: medial								
Sound isolation: final								
Blending								
Segmenting								
Manipulation: initial								
Manipulation: medial								
Manipulation: final								

Phonics Skill Tracker

Student's name: _____

Task	Date	Date	Date	Date	Date	Date	Date	Date
Letter sounds								
CVC words								
Digraphs with short vowels								
Consonant blends								
Silent-*e* words								
Vowel-team words								
Complex consonant-cluster words								
r-controlled words								
Multisyllabic words								

Contextual Factors That Educators Might Consider as Part of Writing Assessment

Contextual factor	How does this context support writing development?	How could this context be improved to support writing development?	Implications for assessment and instruction
School characteristics (e.g., urban, suburban, rural; student population; socioeconomic status; building culture)			
Learning environments in and outside of school (e.g., What are the varied contexts in which students have opportunities to write? How might writing activities that take place outside of school be used to support writing in school?)			
Instructional activities (e.g., How is writing taught? How are the various purposes for writing conveyed?)			
Students' own knowledge and affective assets (motivational, interests, self-concept, self-interests; see Chapter 3)			

Glossary

Academic language: the oral and written language that is used to communicate in academic settings.

Additive approach: providing a range of instructional programs that support students' English acquisition or literate bilingualism in school.

Advanced readers: a developmental level of reading characterized by readers who can read at the level of efficient adult readers.

Affective filter (Krashen, 1982): how comfortable a student feels learning a new language in a specific environment. When the affective filter is high, students feel anxiety and nervousness about risk taking in speaking and learning the new language; when the affective filter is low, students feel less anxiety and more comfortable speaking and learning the new language.

Alliteration: repetition of identical initial consonant sounds in adjacent or closely associated words or syllables within a group of words.

Alphabetic principle: the principle that letters represent particular sounds in predictable ways in the English writing system.

Alternate-form reliability: a form of test reliability calculated as the correlation between scores for the same students on two different forms of the same test.

Asset-based pedagogies: instructional approaches that use students' assets (such as their language and culture) in teaching, learning, and assessing.

Basic interpersonal communicative skills (**BICS**; Cummins, 1979): the everyday language skills used to communicate for social purposes.

Beginning readers: a developmental level of reading characterized by readers who have typically developed sight recognition of a number of frequently used words, and reread familiar memorized texts, although not yet with full one-to-one tracking.

Bias: as it relates to assessment, error that is not random, but rather systematically inflates or deflates scores of students from specific populations.

Cognates: words that have a common origin and thus a similar structure and meaning across languages. Example: *television* (English) and *televisión* (Spanish).

Common underlying proficiency (**CUP**; Cummins, 1991): one's shared knowledge and skill proficiencies across languages.

Concepts about print: understanding aspects of the writing system (e.g., left-to-right directionality).

Concurrent validity: the extent to which an assessment correlates with another similar assessment given around the same time.

Criterion-referenced assessment: an assessment that provides information about student performance in relation to some criterion, such as a benchmark or grade-level standard.

Culturally-sustaining pedagogies (Paris & Alim, 2014): teaching and learning practices that perpetuate, foster, and maintain students' multilingualism and multiculturalism.

Curriculum-based measurement (**CBM**; Deno, 1985): see general outcome measurement.

Emergent readers: students who explore print and texts and are beginning to learn about the written language system but are yet to develop sound–symbol correspondences and phonetic decoding skills. They mimic the reading and writing behaviors of more experienced others.

English as a second language (ESL); English language development (ELD) educators: specialist teachers hired to work with students who are learning English.

Explicit instruction: instruction in which the educator clearly states learning goals, models the task at hand, and provides guided support.

Expressive language: what language learners are able to produce (in speaking and writing).

Fluency: the ability to decode and understand text at the same time (Samuels, 2006).

Formal assessment: assessments that typically involve administration of standardized tests for the purpose of assessing overall student achievement, either to compare students to normative peer groups or to identify an individual student's specific strengths and weaknesses in a particular subject area.

Formative assessment: assessments that are used to monitor student progress within a curriculum or instructional program to determine whether the instruction is effective and whether students are learning, and to identify students' specific strengths and needs.

Funds of knowledge (Moll, Amanti, Neff, & Gonzalez, 1992): students' acquired historical and social knowledge of home, culture, language, community, and environment.

General outcome measure: an assessment that entails measurement of a brief behavior (e.g., reading aloud for 1 minute) that correlates strongly with overall reading proficiency.

Home-language survey: a survey or questionnaire given by the school or school district that helps to identify languages spoken in a child's home. The home language survey is conducted when the student enters school for the first time and helps teachers determine if English language services may be warranted.

Informal assessment: typically nonstandardized assessments that help educators gauge whether students are learning specific content; it can include educator-made quizzes and tests, portfolio assignments and other work samples, and even observations and interviews.

Informal reading inventory (IRI): a type of learning needs assessment wherein educators listen to one student read while they record reading behaviors of decoding, fluency, vocabulary, and comprehension.

Intermediate readers: a developmental level of reading characterized by readers who have developed good fluency in materials at the upper-elementary level and, because of their speed in processing text, generally prefer reading silently.

Internal consistency: a form of test reliability, calculated as the correlation between scores on individual test items.

Language transfer (also known as cross-linguistic transfer): the notion that language learners apply knowledge of their home language while learning and speaking the new language.

Learning needs assessments: assessments used to identify students' specific strengths and needs in order to develop appropriate instructional plans or to make instructional changes when student progress monitoring data indicate this need.

Literate bilingualism: proficiency in oral language as well as in reading and writing both the language of school and of home.

Logographic: a type of writing system in which individual symbols represent morphemes.

Mentor text: texts that serve as models of the text structure or genre that students are being asked to follow.

Metalinguistic awareness: the ability to think *about* language in a general way, beyond the concreteness of words used in a specific language.

Miscue analysis: a systematic analysis of students' reading behaviors taken during and after a student reads a text (or part of a text) aloud.

Morpheme: the smallest unit of a word that carries meaning.

Morphological awareness: being aware that words are made up of parts (called *morphemes*) that have individual meaning.

Morphology: how words are put together and changed with meaningful parts, such as *kind–kinder–kindness*.

Motor system: the system that allows for the physical formation of letters and words.

Multi-tiered system(s) of support (MTSS): a schoolwide prevention and intervention framework for instruction and behavior that includes screening, progress monitoring, and increasingly intensive instructional supports.

Norm-referenced assessment: an assessment that provides information about student performance in relation to "typical" peers.

Orthographic coding: representing a word in memory and accessing the spelling of the word either as a whole, as clusters of letters, or as single letters at a time.

Orthomotor integration: integrating phonological and orthographic coding with the motor system that allows for the physical formation of letters and words.

Phonemic awareness: the ability to isolate, segment, blend, and manipulate individual phonemes (single sounds).

Phonics: a method of teaching the use of letter–sound correspondences to read words in an alphabetic writing system.

Phonological awareness: awareness of the sound structure of language (including rhyming, syllabication, and phonemic awareness).

Phonological coding: the analysis and synthesis of phonemes in words.

Phonology: the sounds of the language.

Pragmatics: how language is used in particular contexts.

Predictive validity: the extent to which an assessment correlates with another similar assessment given at a later time.

Progress monitoring: assessments that are used to track students' performance over time in order to evaluate the effectiveness of instruction and to determine the need for further intervention.

Psychometric: technical features of an assessment, such as reliability and validity, that indicate the extent to which information from an assessment is trustworthy and appropriate for a particular use.

Receptive language: what language learners understand (through listening and reading).

Reliability: the trustworthiness, consistency, or stability of a measure, indicated by a relative absence of random error in measurement (Salvia, Ysseldyke, & Bolt, 2017).

Response processes: the way students respond to test questions, as well as how their responses are scored.

Response to intervention (RTI): an approach in which children's responsiveness to research-based interventions implemented prior to the special education referral process is considered; see also multi-tiered system(s) of support (MTSS).

Running records: an informal reading assessment in which an educator records the reading behaviors of an individual student while the student reads aloud.

Screening tools: assessments that are used to identify students at risk and to determine the need for supplemental literacy intervention, such as those provided within multi-tiered systems of support.

Semantics: the meanings of words and concepts and the schemata that hold them together.

Standardized tests: tests that are administered and scored according to a specific, predetermined procedure.

Subtractive approach: tacitly or explicitly asking students to shroud their home language while at school, serving to erase the student's home language skills.

Summative assessment: an assessment that is used to evaluate whether and what a student has learned, often as the culmination of an instructional unit or end of an academic term.

Syllabic: a type of writing system in which individual characters represent syllables.

Syntax: the way in which meaningful phrases and sentences are put together.

Text structure: the way in which written text is organized and structured.

Tier 1: in multi-tiered systems of support, research-based core instruction delivered with fidelity to all students in the general education classroom.

Tier 2: in multi-tiered systems of support, research-based supplemental intervention delivered with fidelity to some students who require additional support.

Tier 3: in multi-tiered systems of support, research-based intervention that supplements or supplants core instruction, delivered to students with the most intensive instructional needs (often delivered prior to, or as part of, special education).

Transitional readers: a developmental level of reading characterized by readers who are in a progressing state; they are no longer fledglings, but are not yet completely proficient, either.

Translanguaging: enacting features of more than one language within the cohesive and interdependent language systems under their control (García, 2009).

Transparent orthography: an orthography (conventional spelling system of a language) in which there is a one-to-one phoneme–grapheme correspondence; in other words, spelling patterns are always consistent in the way they appear and sound.

Working memory: short-term memory that is related to processing language and comprehension.

Validity: the extent to which an assessment measures the content or construct of interest.

Variability: as it relates to progress monitoring data, erratic fluctuations in a student's progress.

Word consciousness: an awareness and curiosity of how words work in different contexts; an interest in learning new words.

References

Abedi, J. (2002). Standardized achievement tests and English language learners: Psychometric issues. *Educational Assessment, 8,* 231–257.

Abbott, R. D., Berninger, V. W., & Fayol, M. (2010). Longitudinal relationships of levels of language in writing and between writing and reading in grades 1 to 7. *Journal of Educational Psychology, 102*(2), 281–298.

Afflerbach, P. (2018). *Understanding and using reading assessment, K–12* (3rd ed.). Newark, DE: International Literacy Association.

Al Otaiba, S. A., Puranik, C. S., Rouby, D. A., Greulich, L., Sidler, J. F., & Lee, J. (2010). Predicting kindergarteners' end-of-year spelling ability based on their reading, alphabetic, vocabulary, and phonological awareness skills, as well as prior literacy experiences. *Learning Disability Quarterly, 33,* 171–183.

America's Promise Alliance, Aspen Education & Society Program, & the Council of Chief State School Officers. (2018). States leading for equity. Retrieved from *https://ccsso.org/resource-library/ states-leading-equity-promising-practices-advancing-equity-commitments.*

American Educational Research Association. (2014). *Standards for educational and psychological testing.* Washington, DC: Author.

Anderson, R. C., & Nagy, W. E. (1992). The vocabulary conundrum. *American Educator, 16*(4), 14–18, 44–47.

Anderson, R. C., & Pearson, P. D. (2002). A schema-theoretic view of basic processes in reading comprehension. In P. D. Pearson, R. Barr, M. L. Kamil, & P. B. Mosenthal (Eds.), *Handbook of reading research* (Vol. 1, pp. 255–291). New York: Routledge.

Artiles, A. J., Rueda, R., Salazar, J. J., & Higareda, I. (2005). Within-group diversity in minority disproportionate representation: English language learners in urban school districts. *Exceptional Children, 71,* 283–300.

Au, K. H. (1998). Social constructivism and the school literacy learning of students of diverse backgrounds. *Journal of Literacy Research, 30*(2), 297–319.

Au, K. P. (1980). Participation structures in a reading lesson with Hawaiian children: Analysis of a culturally appropriate instructional event. *Anthropology and Education Quarterly, 11*(2), 91–115.

August, D., McCardle, P., & Shanahan, T. (2014). Developing literacy in English language learners: Findings from a review of the experimental research. *School Psychology Review, 43*(4), 490–498.

August, D., & Shanahan, T. (2006). *Developing literacy in second-language learners: Report of the National Literacy Panel on Language-Minority Children and Youth.* Mahwah, NJ: Erlbaum.

Baker, S. K., Chard, D. J., Ketterlin-Geller, L. R., Apichatabutra, C., & Doabler, C. (2009). Teaching writing to at-risk students: The quality of evidence for self-regulated strategy development. *Exceptional Children, 75*(3), 303–318.

Ball, A. F. (2006). Teaching writing in culturally diverse classrooms. In C. A. MacArthur, S. Graham, & J. Fitzgerald (Eds.), *Handbook of writing research* (pp. 293–310). New York: Guilford Press.

Bandura, A. (1977). Self-efficacy: Toward a unifying theory of behavioral change. *Psychological Review, 84,* 191–215.

Bear, D. R., Invernizzi, M., Templeton, S., & Johnston, F. (2020). *Words their way: Word study for phonics, vocabulary, and spelling instruction* (7th ed.). Boston: Pearson.

Beaver, J. M., & Carter, M. A. (2006). *The Developmental Reading Assessment—Second edition (DRA2).* Upper Saddle River, NJ: Pearson.

Beck, I., McKeown, M., & Kucan, L. (2002). *Bringing words to life.* New York: Guilford Press.

Beck, I. L., McKeown, M. G., & Omanson, R. C. (1987). The effects and uses of diverse vocabulary instructional techniques. In M. G. McKeown & M. E. Curtis (Eds.), *The nature of vocabulary acquisition* (pp. 147–163). Hillsdale, NJ: Erlbaum.

Berninger, V. W. (2009). Highlights of programmatic, interdisciplinary research on writing. *Learning Disabilities Research and Practice, 24*(2), 69–80.

Berninger, V. W., & Amtmann, D. (2003). Preventing written expression disabilities through early and continuing assessment and intervention for handwriting and/or spelling problems: Research into practice. In H. L. Swanson, K. R. Harris, & S. Graham (Eds.), *Handbook of learning disabilities* (pp. 345–363). New York: Guilford Press.

Berninger, V. W., & Fuller, F. F. (1992). Gender differences in orthographic, verbal, and compositional fluency: Implications for assessing writing disabilities in primary grade children. *Journal of School Psychology, 30,* 363–382.

Berninger, V., Nielsen, K., Abbott, R., Wijsman, E., & Raskind, W. (2008). Writing problems in developmental dyslexia: Under-recognized and under-treated. *Journal of School Psychology, 46*(1), 1–21.

Berninger, V. W., & Swanson, H. L. (1994). Modifying Hayes and Flower's model of skilled writing to explain beginning and developing writing. In E. C. Butterfield (Ed.), *Children's writing: Toward a process theory of the development of skilled writing* (pp. 57–81). Greenwich, CT: JAI Press.

Bialystok, E. (2007). Acquisition of literacy in bilingual children: A framework for research. *Language Learning, 57,* 45–77.

Bialystok, E., Craik, F. I., & Luk, G. (2012). Bilingualism: Consequences for mind and brain. *Trends in Cognitive Sciences, 16*(4), 240–250.

Bishop, R. S. (1990). Mirrors, windows, and sliding glass doors. *Perspectives, 1*(3), ix–xi.

Borrello, V. (2016). Comments on the U.S. Department of Health and Human Services and U.S. Department of Education Draft Policy Statement on Family Engagement from the Early Years to the Early Grades. Retrieved from *https://cdn.ymaws.com/nafsce.org/resource/resmgr/Policy/NAFSCE-Comment-on-USDE-HHS-F.pdf.*

Branum-Martin, L., Tao, S., & Garnaat, S. (2014). Bilingual phonological awareness: Reexamining the evidence for relations within and across languages. *Journal of Educational Psychology, 1*(107), 111–125.

Breiseth, L. (2016). Reading comprehension strategies for English language learners. Retrieved from *www.ascd.org/ascd-express/vol5/51breiseth.aspx.*

Briceño, A., & Klein, A. (2018). Running records and first grade English learners: An analysis of language related errors. *Reading Psychology, 43*(9), 335–361.

Brown, J., & Doolittle, J. (2008). A cultural, linguistic, and ecological framework for response to intervention with English language learners. *Teaching Exceptional Children, 40,* 66–72.

Brown, L. T., Mohr, K. A., Wilcox, B. R., & Barrett, T. S. (2018). The effects of dyad reading and text difficulty on third-graders' reading achievement. *Journal of Educational Research, 111*(5), 541–553.

Brown, R. (1973). *A first language: The early stages.* London: George Allen & Unwin.

Bruning, R. H., & Kauffman, D. F. (2016). Self-efficacy beliefs and motivation in writing development. In C. A. MacArthur, S. Graham, & J. Fitzgerald (Eds.), *Handbook of writing research* (2nd ed., pp. 160–173). New York: Guilford Press.

Bulté, B., & Housen, A. (2014). Conceptualizing and measuring short-term changes in L2 writing complexity. *Journal of Second Language Writing, 26,* 42–65.

Burns, M. K., & Gibbons, K. (2012). *Implementing response-to-intervention in elementary and secondary schools.* New York: Routledge.

Burns, M. K., Maki, E. E., Karich, A. C., Hall, M., McComas, J. J., & Helman, L. (2016). Problem-analysis at Tier 2: Using data to find the category of the problem. In S. Jimerson, M. K. Burns, & A. M. VanDerHeyden (Eds.), *Handbook of Response to Intervention: The science and practice of multi-tiered systems of support* (2nd ed., pp. 293–307). New York: Springer.

Campbell, H., Espin, C. A., & McMaster, K. L. (2013). The technical adequacy of CBM writing measures with English language learners. *Reading and Writing: An Interdisciplinary Journal, 26*(3), 431–452.

Catts, H. W., Hogan, T. P., & Fey, M. E. (2003). Subgrouping poor readers on the basis of individual differences in reading-related abilities. *Journal of Learning Disabilities, 36*(2), 151–164.

Center for Applied Linguistics & the University of Houston. (2002). *Diagnostic Assessment of Reading Comprehension (DARC).* Washington, DC: Author.

Chapman, J. W., & Tunmer, W. E. (1995). Development of young children's reading self-concepts: An examination of emerging subcomponents and their relationship with reading achievement. *Journal of Educational Psychology, 87*(1), 154–167.

Cohen, D. K., & Ball, D. L. (1999). Instruction, capacity, and improvement (Consortium for Policy Research in Education [CPRE] Research Report Series, RR-43, University of Pennsylvania, Graduate School of Education). Retrieved from *www.cpre.org/sites/default/files/researchreport/783_ rr43.pdf.*

Coker, D. L. (2006). Impact of first-grade factors on the growth and outcomes of urban schoolchildren's primary-grade writing. *Journal of Educational Psychology, 98,* 471–488.

Coker, D. L., & Ritchey, K. D. (2015). *Teaching beginning writers.* New York: Guilford Press.

Collier, V. (1987). Age and rate of acquisition of second language for academic purposes. *TESOL Quarterly, 21*(4), 617–641.

Conradi, K., Jang, B. G., & McKenna, M. C. (2014). Motivation terminology in reading research: A conceptual review. *Educational Psychology Review, 26*(1), 127–164.

Cowie, B., Jones, A., & Otrel-Cass, K. (2011). Re-engaging students in science: Issues of assessment, funds of knowledge and sites for learning. *International Journal of Science and Mathematics Education, 9*(2), 347–366.

Crosson, A. C., & Lesaux, N. K. (2010). Revisiting assumptions about the relationship of fluent reading to comprehension: Spanish-speakers' text-reading fluency in English. *Reading and Writing, 23*(5), 475–494.

Cumming, A. (2016). Writing development and instruction for English language learners. In C. A. MacArthur, S. Graham, & J. Fitzgerald (Eds.), *Handbook of writing research* (2nd ed., pp. 364–376). New York: Guilford Press.

Cummins, J. (1979). Cognitive/academic language proficiency, linguistic interdependence, the optimum age question and some other matters. *Working Papers on Bilingualism, 19,* 121–129.

Cummins, J. (1981). The role of primary language development in promoting educational success for language minority students. In California State Department of Education (Ed.), *Schooling and language minority students: A theoretical framework* (pp. 3–49). Los Angeles: California State University, National Evaluation, Dissemination and Assessment Center.

Cummins, J. (1991). Language development and academic learning. In L. Malavé & G. Duquette (Eds.), *Language, culture and cognition* (pp. 161–175). Clevedon, UK: Multilingual Matters.

Cunningham, P. M., & Hall, D. P. (2008). *Month by month phonics for first grade.* Greensboro, NC: Carson-Dellosa.

Datchuk, S., & Kubina, R. (2012). A review of teaching sentence-level writing skills to students with writing difficulties and learning disabilities. *Remedial and Special Education, 34*(3), 180–192.

de Jong, E. J., & Harper, C. A. (2005). Preparing mainstream educators for English-language learners: Is being a good educator good enough? *Educator Education Quarterly, 32*(2), 101–124.

Delgado Gaitán, C. (2004). *Involving Latino families in schools: Raising student achievement through home–school partnerships.* Thousand Oaks, CA: Corwin Press.

Dellerman, P., Coirier, P., & Marchand, E. (1996). Planning and expertise in argumentative composition. In G. Rijlaarsdam, H. van den Bergh, & M. Couzijn (Eds.), *Theories, models, and methodology in writing research* (pp. 182–195). Amsterdam: Amsterdam University Press.

Deno, S. L. (1985). Curriculum-based measurement: The emerging alternative. *Exceptional Children, 52,* 219–232.

Dunn, L. M., & Dunn, D. M. (2007). *Peabody Picture Vocabulary Test* (4th ed.). Minneapolis, MN: NCS Pearson.

Durgunoglu, A. Y., Nagy, W. E., & Hancin-Bhatt, B. J. (1993). Cross-language transfer of phonological awareness. *Journal of Educational Psychology, 85*(3), 453–465.

Dworin, J. E. (2006). The family stories project: Using funds of knowledge for writing. *The Reading Teacher, 59*(6), 510–520.

Eagle, J. W., Dowd-Eagle, S. E., Snyder, A., & Holtzman, E. G. (2015). Implementing a multi-tiered system of support (MTSS): Collaboration between school psychologists and administrators to promote systems-level change. *Journal of Educational and Psychological Consultation, 25,* 160–177.

Ehri, L. C. (1995). Phases of development in reading words. *Journal of Research in Reading, 18,* 116–125.

Ehri, L. (2000). Learning to read and learning to spell: Two sides of a coin. *Topics in Language Disorders, 20,* 19–36.

Ehri, L. C., Gibbs, A. L., & Underwood, T. L. (1988). Influence of errors on learning the spellings of English words. *Contemporary Educational Psychology, 13*(3), 236–253.

Elish-Piper, L., & L'Allier, S. (2010). Examining the relationship between literacy coaching and student reading gains in grades K–3. *The Elementary School Journal, 112,* 83–106.

Elya, S. M. (2016). *La Madre Goose: Nursery rhymes for los niños.* New York: Penguin Random House.

Epstein J. L., & Sheldon, S. B. (2006). Moving forward: Ideas for research on school, family, and community partnerships. In C. F. Conrad & R. Serlin (Eds.), *SAGE handbook for research in education: Engaging ideas and enriching inquiry.* Thousand Oaks, CA: SAGE.

Escamilla, K., Hopewell, S., Butvilofsky, S., Sparrow, W., Soltero-González, L., Ruiz-Figueroa, O., et al. (2013). *Biliteracy from the start: Literacy squared in action.* Philadelphia: Caslon.

Esparza Brown, J., & Sanford, A. (2011). *RTI for English language learners: Appropriately using screening and progress monitoring tools to improve instructional outcomes.* Washington, DC: U.S. Department of Education, Office of Special Education Programs, National Center on Response to Intervention.

Every Student Succeeds Act, Public Law No. 114-95, § 1177 (2015).

Ferdman, B. (1990). Literacy and cultural identity. *Harvard Educational Review, 60*(2), 181–205.

Fisher, D., & Frey, N. (2008). *Better learning through structured teaching: A framework for the gradual release of responsibility.* Alexandria, VA: ASCD.

Fitzgerald, J., & Amendum, S. (2007). What is sound writing instruction for multilingual learners. In S. Graham, C. A. MacArthur, & J. Fitzgerald (Eds.), *Best practices in writing instruction* (pp. 289–307). New York: Guilford Press.

Flanders, N. (1970). *Analyzing teacher behavior.* Reading, MA: Addison-Wesley.

Fletcher, J. M., Stuebing, K. K., Morris, R. D., & Lyon, G. R. (2013). Classification and definition of learning disabilities: A hybrid model. In H. L. Swanson, K. R. Harris, & S. Graham (Eds.), *Handbook of learning disabilities* (pp. 33–50). New York: Guilford Press.

Forman, S. G., & Crystal, C. D. (2015). Systems Consultation for Multitiered Systems of Supports (MTSS): Implementation issues. *Journal of Educational and Psychological Consultation, 25*(2/3), 276–285.

Fountas, I. C., & Pinnell, G. S. (2011). *Benchmark Assessment System: Years K–2, Levels A–N.* Portsmouth, NH: Heinemann.

Fuchs, D., Fuchs, L. S., & Compton, D. L. (2012). Smart RTI: A next-generation approach to multi-level prevention. *Exceptional Children, 78,* 263–279.

Fuchs, D., Fuchs, L. S., Mathes, P. G., & Simmons, D. C. (1997). Peer-assisted learning strategies: Making classrooms more responsive to diversity. *American Educational Research Journal, 34,* 174–206.

Fuchs, L. S., & Fuchs, D. (1992). Identifying a measure for monitoring student reading progress. *School Psychology Review, 21,* 45–58.

Fuchs, L. S., Fuchs, D., & Speece, D. (2002). Treatment validity as a unifying construct for identifying learning disabilities. *Learning Disabilities Research and Practice, 25,* 33–45.

García, G. E., McKoon, G., & August, D. (2006). Language and literacy assessment of language-minority students. In D. August & T. Shanahan (Eds.), *Developing literacy in second-language learners* (pp. 583–598). Mahwah, NJ: Erlbaum.

García, O. (2009). *Bilingual education in the 21st century: A global perspective.* West Sussex, UK: Wiley-Blackwell.

García, O., Bartlett, L., & Kleifgen, J. (2007). From biliteracy to pluriliteracies. In P. Auer & L. Wei (Eds.), *Handbook of applied linguistics* (Vol. 5, pp. 207–228). Berlin: Mouton/de Gruyter.

García, O., Johnson, S. I., & Seltzer, K. (2017). *The translanguaging classroom: Leveraging student bilingualism for learning.* Philadelphia: Caslon.

García, O., & Kleifgen, J. (2010). *Educating emergent bilinguals: Policies, programs, and practices for English language learners.* New York: Teachers College Press.

García, O., & Kleifgen, J. A. (2018). *Educating emergent bilinguals: Policies, programs, and practices for English learners* (2nd ed.). New York: Teachers College Press.

Gay, G. (2010). *Culturally responsive teaching: Theory, research, and practice* (2nd ed.). New York: Teachers College Press.

Gay, G. (2013). Teaching to and through cultural diversity. *Curriculum Inquiry, 43,* 48–70.

Gee, J. P. (2015). *Social linguistics and literacies: Ideology in discourses* (5th ed.). New York: Routledge.

Genesee, F., Geva, E., Dressler, C., & Kamil, M. L. (2006). Synthesis: Cross-linguistic relationships. In D. August & T. Shanahan (Eds.), *Developing literacy in second-language learning: Report of the National Literacy Panel on Language Minority Children and Youth* (pp. 153–174). Mahwah, NJ: Erlbaum.

Genesee, F., Lindholm-Leary, K., Saunders, W., & Christian, D. (2005). English language learners in U.S. schools: An overview of research findings. *Journal of Education for Students Placed at Risk, 10*(4), 363–385.

Goldenberg, C. (2011). Reading instruction for English language learners. In M. L. Kamil, P. D.

Pearson, E. Birr Moje, & P. P. Afflerbach (Eds.), *Handbook of reading research* (Vol. 4, pp. 684–710). New York: Routledge.

Goldenberg, C. (2013). Unlocking the research on English learners: What we know—and don't yet know—about effective instruction. *American Educator, 37*(2), 4–11.

Gonzalez, N., Moll, L. C., Tenery, M. F., Rivera, A., Rendon, P., Gonzales, R., et al. (1995). Funds of knowledge for teaching in Latino households. *Urban Education, 29*(4), 443–470.

Goodman, Y., Watson, D., & Burke, C. (2005). *Reading miscue inventory: From evaluation to instruction* (2nd ed.). Katonah, NY: Owen.

Gottlieb, M. (2012). *Common language assessment for English learners.* Bloomington, IN: Solution Tree.

Gottlieb, M. (2016). *Assessing English language learners: Bridges to educational equity: Connecting academic language proficiency to student achievement.* Thousand Oaks, CA: Corwin Press.

Gough, P. B., & Tunmer, W. E. (1986). Decoding, reading, and reading disability. *Remedial and Special Education, 7*(1), 6–10.

Graham, S., Berninger, V., & Fan, W. (2007). The structural relationship between writing attitude and writing achievement in first and third grade students. *Contemporary Educational Psychology, 32*(3), 516–536.

Graham, S., Bollinger, A., Booth Olson, C., D'Aoust, C., MacArthur, C., McCutchen, D., et al. (2012). *Teaching elementary school students to be effective writers: A practice guide* (NCEE 2012-4058). Retrieved from *http://ies.ed.gov/ncee/wwc/publications_reviews.aspx#pubsearch.*

Graham, S., & Harris, K. R. (1996). Self-regulation and strategy instruction for students who find writing and learning challenging. In M. Levy & S. Ransdell (Eds.), *The science of writing: Theories, methods, individual differences, and applications* (pp. 347–360). Mahwah, NJ: Erlbaum.

Graham, S., Harris, K. R., & Chorzempa, B. F. (2002). Contribution of spelling instruction to the spelling, writing, and reading of poor spellers. *Journal of Educational Psychology, 94*(4), 669–686.

Graham, S., & Hebert, M. (2011). Writing to read: A meta-analysis of the impact of writing and writing instruction on reading. *Harvard Educational Review, 81*(4), 710–744.

Graham, S., McKeown, D., Kiuhara, S., & Harris, K. R. (2012). A meta-analysis of writing instruction for students in the elementary grades. *Journal of Educational Psychology, 104*(4), 879–896.

Graham, S., & Perin, D. (2007). *Writing next: Effective strategies to improve writing of adolescents in middle and high schools—A report to Carnegie Corporation of New York.* Washington, DC: Alliance for Excellent Education.

Graves, M. F., & Watts-Taffe, S. M. (2002). The place of word consciousness in a research-based vocabulary program. In A. E. Farstrup & S. J. Samuels (Eds.), *What research has to say about reading instruction* (3rd ed., pp. 140–165). Newark, DE: International Reading Association.

Graves, M. F., & Watts-Taffe, S. (2008). For the love of words: Fostering word consciousness in young readers. *The Reading Teacher, 62*(3), 185–193.

Guthrie, J. T. (2004). Teaching for literacy engagement. *Journal of Literacy Research, 36*(1), 1–30.

Guthrie, J. T., Hoa, A. L. W., Wigfield, A., Tonks, S. M., Humenick, N. M., & Littles, E. (2007). Reading motivation and reading comprehension growth in the later elementary years. *Contemporary Educational Psychology, 32*(3), 282–313.

Guthrie, J. T., & Wigfield, A. (2000). Engagement and motivation in reading. In M. L. Kamil, P. B. Mosenthal, P. D. Pearson, & R. Barr (Eds.), *Reading research handbook* (Vol. 3, pp. 403–424). Mahwah, NJ: Erlbaum.

Guthrie, J. T., Wigfield, A., Barbosa, P., Perencevich, K. C., Taboada, A., Davis, M. H., et al. (2004). Increasing reading comprehension and engagement through concept-oriented reading instruction. *Journal of Educational Psychology, 96*(3), 403.

Hampton D. D., & Lembke E. S. (2016). Examining the technical adequacy of progress monitoring using early writing curriculum-based measures. *Reading and Writing Quarterly, 32,* 336–352.

Harn, B., Basaraba, D., Chard, D., & Fritz, R. (2015). The impact of schoolwide prevention efforts: Lessons learned from implementing independent academic and behavior support systems. *Learning Disabilities: A Contemporary Journal, 13*(1), 3–20.

Harris K. R., Graham S., Mason L. H., & Friedlander B. (2008). *Powerful writing strategies for all students*. Baltimore: Brookes.

Harrison, G. L., Goegan, L. D., Jalbert, R., McManus, K., Sinclair, K., & Spurling, J. (2016). Predictors of spelling and writing skills in first- and second-language learners. *Reading and Writing, 29*(1), 69–89.

Hasbrouck, J., & Tindal, G. (2017). *An update to compiled ORF norms* (Technical Report No. 1702). Eugene: Behavioral Research and Teaching, University of Oregon.

Hattie, J. (2008). *Visible learning: A synthesis of over 800 meta-analyses relating to achievement*. New York: Routledge.

Helman, L. A. (2004). Building on the sound system of Spanish: Insights from the alphabetic spellings of English-language learners. *The Reading Teacher, 57*(5), 452–460.

Helman, L. (2012). *Literacy instruction in multilingual classrooms: Engaging English learners in elementary schools*. New York: Teachers College Press.

Helman, L. (Ed.). (2016). *Literacy development with English learners: Research-based instruction in grades K–6*. New York: Guilford Press.

Helman, L., Bear, D. R., Templeton, S., Invernizzi, M., & Johnston, F. (2012). *Words their way with English learners: Word study for phonics, vocabulary and spelling*, (2nd ed.). Boston: Pearson.

Helman, L., & Pekel, K. (in press). Leadership of literacy: The principal's key role. In A. Swan Dagen & R. M. Bean (Eds.), *Best practices of literacy leaders* (2nd ed.). New York: Guilford Press.

Helman, L., Rogers, C., Frederick, A., & Struck, M. (2016). *Inclusive literacy teaching: Differentiating approaches in multilingual elementary classrooms*. New York: Teachers College Press.

Hoff, E. (2013). *Language development* (5th ed.). Belmont, CA: Wadsworth.

Honigsfeld, A., & Dove, M. G. (2016). Collaborative practices to support implementation of the Common Core State Standards with K–5 English language learners. In L. Helman (Ed.), *Literacy development with English learners: Research-based instruction in grades K–6* (pp. 282–308). New York: Guilford Press.

Hoover, W. A., & Gough, P. B. (1990). The simple view of reading. *Reading and Writing, 2*, 127–160.

Hopewell, S., & Escamilla, K. (2014). Struggling reader or emerging biliterate student?: Reevaluating the criteria for labeling emerging bilingual students as low achieving. *Journal of Literacy Research, 46*(1), 68–89.

Ingram, M., Wolfe, R., & Lieberman, J. (2007). The role of parents in high-achieving schools serving low-income, at-risk populations. *Education and Urban Society, 39*(4), 479–497.

International Literacy Association. (2017). *Characteristics of culturally sustaining and academically rigorous classrooms* (Literacy Leadership Brief). Newark, DE: Author.

International Literacy Association. (2018). *Standards for the Preparation of Literacy Professionals 2017*. Newark, DE: Author.

Jeynes, W. (2012). A meta-analysis of the efficacy of different types of parental involvement programs for urban students. *Urban Education, 47*(4), 706–742.

Jimerson, S., Burns, M. K., & VanDerHeyden. A. M. (Eds.). (2016). *Handbook of response to intervention: The science and practice of multi-tiered systems of support* (2nd ed.). New York: Springer.

Johnson, E. S., Jenkins, J. R., Petscher, Y., & Catts, H. W. (2009). How can we improve the accuracy of screening instruments? *Learning Disabilities Research and Practice, 24*, 174–185.

Johnson, E., Mellard, D. F., Fuchs, D., & McKnight, M. A. (2006). *Responsiveness to intervention (RTI): How to do it*. Lawrence, KS: National Research Center on Learning Disabilities.

Johnston, F., Invernizzi, M., Helman, L., Bear, D. R., & Templeton, S. (2015). *Words their way for prek and kindergarten*. Boston: Pearson.

Joyce, B., & Showers, B. (2002). *Student achievement through staff development* (3rd ed.). Alexandria, VA: Association for Supervision and Curriculum Development.

Juel, C., Griffith, P. L., & Gough, P. B. (1986). Acquisition of literacy: A longitudinal study of children in first and second grade. *Journal of Educational Psychology, 78*(4), 243.

Keller-Margulis, M., Payan, A., Jaspers, K. E., & Brewton, C. (2016). Validity and diagnostic accuracy of written expression curriculum-based measurement for students with diverse language backgrounds. *Reading and Writing Quarterly, 32*(2), 174–198.

Kim, A. A., Kondo, A., Blair, A., Mancilla, L., Chapman, M., & Wilmes, C. (2016). Interpretation and use of K–12 language proficiency assessment score reports: Perspectives of educators and parents (WCER Working Paper 2016-8). Retrieved from *www.wcer.wisc.edu/publications/working-papers*.

Kim, K., & Goodman, Y. (2011). Teaching strategies that revalue EL readers. In R. Meyer & K. Whitmore (Eds.), *Reclaiming reading* (pp. 99–110). New York: Routledge.

Kim, Y. S., Al Otaiba, S., Puranik, C., Folsom, J. S., Greulich, L., & Wagner, R. K. (2011). Componential skills of beginning writing: An exploratory study. *Learning and Individual Differences, 21*(5), 517–525.

Klingbeil, D. A., McComas, J. J., Burns, M. K., & Helman, L. (2015). Comparison of predictive validity and diagnostic accuracy of screening measures of reading skills. *Psychology in the Schools, 52*, 500–514.

Klingner, J. K., Artiles, A. J., & Barletta, L. M. (2006). English language learners who struggle with reading: Language acquisition or LD? *Journal of Learning Disabilities, 39*, 108–128.

Klingner, J. K., & Edwards, P. A. (2006). Cultural considerations with response to intervention models. *Reading Research Quarterly, 41*, 108–117.

Klingner, J. K., & Vaughn, S. (1998). Using collaborative strategic reading. *Teaching Exceptional Children, 30*(6), 32–37.

Krashen, S. (1982). *Principles and practice in second language acquisition.* Oxford, UK: Pergamon Press.

Kuhn, M. R., Schwanenflugel, P. J., & Meisinger, E. B. (2010). Aligning theory and assessment of reading fluency: Automaticity, prosody, and definitions of fluency. *Reading Research Quarterly, 45*(2), 230–251.

Ladson-Billings, G. (1995). Toward a theory of culturally relevant pedagogy. *American Educational Research Journal, 32*(3), 465–491.

Lee, A. Y., & Handsfield, L. J. (2018). Code-meshing and writing instruction in multilingual classrooms. *The Reading Teacher, 72*(2), 159–168.

Lembke, E., Carlisle, A., & Poch, A. (2015). *Curriculum-based measurement screening study 1* (Technical Report No.1 for the DBI-TLC Project). Minneapolis: University of Minnesota.

Lembke, E., Deno, S. L, & Hall, K. (2003). Identifying an indicator of growth in early writing proficiency for elementary school students. *Assessment for Effective Intervention, 28*, 23–35.

Lesaux, N. K., Crosson, A. C., Kieffer, M. J., & Pierce, M. (2010). Uneven profiles: Language minority learners' word reading, vocabulary, and reading comprehension skills. *Journal of Applied Developmental Psychology, 31*(6), 475–483.

Lesaux, N. K., & Harris, J. R. (2015). *Cultivating knowledge, building language: Literacy instruction for English learners in elementary school.* Portsmouth, NH: Heinemann.

Lesaux, N. K., & Marietta, S. H. (2012). *Making assessment matter: Using test results to differentiate reading instruction.* New York: Guilford Press.

Lesaux, N. K., & Siegel, L. S. (2003). The development of reading in children who speak English as a second language. *Developmental Psychology, 39*(6), 1005–1019.

Linan-Thompson, S., Cirino, P. T., & Vaughn, S. (2007). Determining English language learners' response to intervention: Questions and some answers. *Learning Disability Quarterly, 30*(3), 185–195.

Lucas, T., & Villegas, A. M. (2013). Preparing linguistically responsive educators: Laying the foundation in preservice educator education. *Theory into Practice, 52*(2), 98–109.

Lucas, T., Villegas, A. M., & Freedson-Gonzalez, M. (2008). Linguistically responsive educator education: Preparing classroom educators to teach English language learners. *Journal of Teacher Education, 59*(4), 361–373.

Lyon, G. R. (1995). Toward a definition of dyslexia. *Annals of Dyslexia, 45,* 3–27.

Mancilla-Martinez, J., Kieffer, M. J., Biancarosa, G., Christodoulou, J. A., & Snow, C. E. (2011). Investigating English reading comprehension growth in adolescent language minority learners: Some insights from the simple view. *Reading and Writing, 24*(3), 339–354.

Mancilla-Martinez, J., & Lesaux, N. K. (2011). The gap between Spanish speakers' word reading and word knowledge: A longitudinal study. *Child Development, 82*(5), 1544–1560.

McCabe, A., & Bliss, L. S. (2003). *Patterns of narrative discourse: A multi-cultural, life span approach.* Boston: Allyn & Bacon.

McCutchen, D. (2006). Cognitive factors in the development of children's writing. In C. MacArthur, S. Graham, & J. Fitzgerald (Eds.), *Handbook of writing research* (pp. 115–130). New York: Guilford Press.

McKenna, M. C., & Stahl, K. A. D. (2015). *Assessment for reading instruction.* New York: Guilford Press.

McLaughlin, B. (1985). *Second language acquisition in childhood: Vol. 2. School-age children* (2nd ed.). Hillsdale, NJ: Erlbaum.

McMaster, K. L., & Campbell, H. (2008). Technical features of new and existing measures of written expression: An examination within and across grade levels. *School Psychology Review, 37*(4), 550–566.

McMaster, K. L., Du, X., & Petursdottir, A. (2009). Technical features of curriculum-based measures for beginning writers. *Journal of Learning Disabilities, 42,* 41–60.

McMaster, K., & Espin, C. (2007). Technical features of curriculum-based measurement in writing: A literature review. *Journal of Special Education, 41,* 68–84.

McMaster, K. L., & Espin, C. A. (2017). Reading comprehension instruction and intervention: Promoting inference making. In D. Compton, R. Partial, & K. Cain (Eds.), *Theories of reading development* (pp. 463–488). Amsterdam: John Benjamins.

McMaster, K. L., Kunkel, A., Shin, J., Jung, P., & Lembke, E. (2018). Early writing intervention: A best evidence synthesis. *Journal of Learning Disabilities, 51*(4), 363–380.

McMaster, K., & Lembke, E. (2016). *Data-based instruction in beginning writing: A manual.* Minneapolis: University of Minnesota.

McMaster, K. L., Ritchey, K. D., & Lembke, E. (2011). Curriculum-based measurement of elementary students' writing: Recent developments and future directions. In T. E. Scruggs & M. A. Mastropieri (Eds.), *Assessment and intervention: Advances in learning and behavioral disabilities* (pp. 111–148). Bingley, UK: Emerald.

Moll, L. C. (1994). Literacy research in community and classrooms: A sociocultural approach. In M. R. R. Robert, B. Ruddell, & H. Singer (Eds.), *Theoretical models and processes of reading* (4th ed., pp. 179–207). Newark, DE: International Reading Association.

Moll, L. C. (2014). *L. S. Vygotsky and education.* New York: Routledge.

Moll, L. C., Amanti, C., Neff, D., & Gonzalez, N. (1992). Funds of knowledge for teaching: Using a qualitative approach to connect homes and classrooms. *Theory into Practice, 31*(2), 132–141.

Morrow, L. M., & Gambrell, L. G. (Eds.). (2019). *Best practices in literacy instruction* (6th ed.). New York: Guilford Press.

Nagy, W., & Townsend, D. (2012). Words as tools: Learning academic vocabulary as language acquisition. *Reading Research Quarterly, 47*(1), 91–108.

Nash, K., Panther, L., & Arce-Boardman, A. (2018). La historia de mi nombre: A culturally sustaining early literacy practice. *The Reading Teacher, 71*(5), 605–609.

National Assessment of Educational Progress. (2018). The Nation's Report Card: National student group scores and score gaps. Retrieved from *www.nationsreportcard.gov/reading_2017/#nation/ scores?*

National Center for Education Statistics. (2012). The Nation's Report Card: Writing 2011. Retrieved November 15, 2014, from *http://nces.ed.gov/pubsearch/pubsinfo.asp?pubid=2012470.*

National Governors Association Center for Best Practices & Council of Chief State School Officers. (2010). *Common Core State Standards.* Washington, DC: Authors.

New London Group. (1996). A pedagogy of multiliteracies: Designing social futures. *Harvard Educational Review, 66*(1), 60–93.

NGSS Lead States. (2013). *Next Generation Science Standards: For states, by states.* Washington, DC: National Academies Press.

Nieto, S. (2002). *Language, culture and teaching.* Mahwah, NJ: Erlbaum.

Northwest Evaluation Association (NWEA). (2013). Measures of academic progress. Retrieved June 14, 2019, from *www.nwea.org/content/uploads/2014/07/Comprehensive-Guide-to-MAP-K-12-Computer-Adaptive-Interim-Assessment.*

NWEA & Grunwald Associates. (2012). For every child, multiple measures: What parents and educators want from K–12 assessments. Retrieved from *www.nwea.org/resources/every-child-multiple-measures-parents-educators-want-k-12-assessments.*

Office of English Language Acquisition. (2018). National- and state-level high school graduation rates for English learners. Retrieved from *https://ncela.ed.gov/files/fast_facts/OELA_FF_HS_GradRates.pdf.*

Olinghouse, N. G., & Leaird, J. T. (2009). The relationship between measures of vocabulary and narrative writing quality in second- and fourth-grade students. *Reading and Writing: An Interdisciplinary Journal, 22,* 545–565.

Otto, B. W. (2017). *Language development in early childhood education* (5th ed.). New York: Pearson.

Paris, D., & Alim, H. S. (2014). What are we seeking to sustain through culturally sustaining pedagogy?: A loving critique forward. *Harvard Educational Review, 84*(1), 85–100.

Paris, D., & Alim, H. S. (Eds.). (2017). *Culturally sustaining pedagogies: Teaching and learning for justice in a changing world.* New York: Teachers College Press.

Parker, D. C., Dickey, B. N., Burns, M. K., & McMaster, K. L. (2012). An application of brief experimental analysis with early writing. *Journal of Behavioral Education, 21*(4), 329–349.

Partanen, E., Kujala, T., Näätänen, R., Liitola, A., Sambeth, A., & Huotilainen, M. (2013). Learning-induces neural plasticity of speech processing before birth. *Proceedings of the National Academy of Sciences of the USA, 110*(37), 15145–15150.

Path to Reading Excellence in School Sites (PRESS). (2019). *PRESS intervention manual.* Minneapolis: University of Minnesota.

Path to Reading Excellence in School Sites (PRESS). (2018). Multi-tiered systems of support implementation survey. Retrieved from *www.presscommunity.org.*

Pearson, P. D. (2015, October 15). Jeanne Chall Lecture: P. David Pearson [Harvard Education]. Retrieved from *www.youtube.com/watch?v=hH2qPllXprw.*

Pearson, P. D., & Gallagher, M. C. (1983). The instruction of reading comprehension. *Contemporary Educational Psychology, 8*(3), 317–344.

Pianta, R. C., Belsky, J., Houts, R., & Morrison, F. (2007). Opportunities to learn in America's elementary classrooms. *Science, 315,* 1795–1796.

Pitoniak, M. J., Young, J. W., Martiniello, M., King, T. C., Buteux, A., & Ginsburgh, M. (2009). Guidelines for the assessment of English-language learners. Retrieved from *www.ets.org/s/about/pdf/ell_guidelines.pdf.*

Proctor, C. P., Carlo, M., August, D., & Snow, C. (2005). Native Spanish-speaking children reading in English: Toward a model of comprehension. *Journal of Educational Psychology, 97,* 246–256.

Protacio, M. S., & Jang, B. G. (2016). ESL educators' perceptions about English learners' reading motivation. *Literacy Research: Theory, Method, and Practice, 65*(1), 166–181.

Richards-Tutor, C., Baker, D. L., Gersten, R., Baker, S. K., & Smith, J. M. (2016). The effectiveness of reading interventions for English learners: A research synthesis. *Exceptional Children, 82,* 144–169.

Ritchey, K. D. (2006). Learning to write: Progress-monitoring tools for beginning and at-risk writers. *Teaching Exceptional Children, 39,* 22–26.

Ritchey, K. D., McMaster, K. L., Al Otaiba, S., Puranik, C. S., Kim, Y.-S. G., Parker, D. C., et al. (2016). Indicators of fluent writing in beginning writers. In K. D. Cummings & Y. Petscher (Eds.), *The fluency construct: Curriculum-based measurement concepts and applications* (pp. 21–66). New York: Springer.

Rodríguez, D., Carrasquillo, A., & Lee, K. S. (2014). *The bilingual advantage: Promoting academic development, biliteracy, and native language in the classroom.* New York: Teachers College Press.

Saddler, B., Behforooz, B., & Asaro, K. (2008). The effects of sentence-combining instruction on the writing of fourth-grade students with writing difficulties. *Journal of Special Education, 42*(2), 79–90.

Saddler, B., & Graham, S. (2005). The effects of peer-assisted sentence-combining instruction on the writing performance of more and less skilled young writers. *Journal of Educational Psychology, 97*(1), 43–54.

Salahu-Din, D., Persky, H., & Miller, J. (2007). The Nation's Report Card: Writing 2007 (NCES 2008-468). Retrieved from *www.nationsreportcard.gov/writing_2007/w0015.aspx?subtab_id=Tab_2&tab_id=tab1#chart.*

Salvia, J., Ysseldyke, J., & Witmer, S. (2017). *Assessment in special and inclusive education* (13th ed.). Boston: Cengage Learning.

Samuels, S. J. (2006). Toward a model of reading fluency. In S. J. Samuels & A. E. Farstrup (Eds.), *What research has to say about fluency instruction* (pp. 24–46). Newark, DE: International Reading Association.

Sandberg, K. L., & Reschly, A. L. (2011). English learners: Challenges in assessment and the promise of curriculum-based measurement. *Remedial and Special Education, 32,* 144–154.

Saunders, W. M., Foorman, B. R., & Carlson, C. D. (2006). Is a separate block of time for oral English language development in programs for English learners needed? *The Elementary School Journal, 107*(2), 181–198.

Saunders, W. M., & Goldenberg, C. (1999). Effects of instructional conversations and literature logs on limited- and fluent-English-proficient students' story comprehension and thematic understanding. *The Elementary School Journal, 99*(4), 279–301.

Scarborough, H. S. (2001). Connecting early language and literacy to later reading (dis)abilities: Evidence, theory, and practice. In S. B. Neuman & D. K. Dickinson (Eds.), *Handbook of early literacy research* (pp. 97–110). New York: Guilford Press.

Schleppegrell, M. J. (2001). Linguistic features of the language of schooling. *Linguistics and Education, 12*(4), 431–459.

Schöber, C., Schütte, K., Köller, O., McElvany, N., & Gebauer, M. M. (2018). Reciprocal effects between self-efficacy and achievement in mathematics and reading. *Learning and Individual Differences, 63,* 1–11.

Schrodt, K., Fain, J. G., & Hasty, M. (2015). Exploring culturally relevant texts with kindergartners and their families. *The Reading Teacher, 68*(8), 589–598.

Schumaker, J. B., & Sheldon, J. B. (2005). *Fundamentals in the sentence writing strategy.* Lawrence, KS: Edge Enterprises.

Shanahan, T. (2004). Overcoming the dominance of communication: Writing to think and to learn.

In T. L. Jetton & J. A. Dole (Eds.), *Adolescent literacy research and practice* (pp. 59–73). New York: Guilford Press.

Shanahan, T., & Shanahan, C. (2008). Teaching disciplinary literacy to adolescents: Rethinking content-area literacy. *Harvard Educational Review, 78*(1), 40–59.

Silva, T. (1993). Toward an understanding of the distinct nature of L2 writing: The ESL research and its implications. *TESOL Quarterly, 27*(4), 657–677.

Silverman, R. D., & Hartranft, A. M. (2015). *Developing vocabulary and oral language in young children.* New York: Guilford Press.

Smith, R. A. (2018). *Monitoring motivation and academic growth in writing for young English language learners.* Unpublished dissertation, University of Missouri.

Snow, C. E., & Uccelli, P. (2009). The challenge of academic language. In D. R. Olson & N. Torrance (Eds.), *The Cambridge handbook of literacy* (pp. 112–133). New York: Cambridge University Press.

Stahl, K. A., & Bravo, M. A. (2010). Contemporary classroom vocabulary assessment for content areas. *The Reading Teacher, 63*(7), 566–578.

Stauffer, R. (1980). *The language experience approach to the teaching of reading* (2nd ed.). New York: Harper & Row.

Stecker, P. M., Fuchs, L. S., & Fuchs, D. (2005). Using curriculum-based measurement to improve student achievement: Review of research. *Psychology in the Schools, 42,* 795–819.

Stiggins, R. (2017). *The perfect assessment system.* Alexandria, VA: ASCD.

Sullivan, A. L. (2011). Disproportionality in special education identification and placement of English language learners. *Exceptional Children, 77,* 317–334.

Swan, M., & Smith, B. (Eds.). (2001). *Learner English: A teacher's guide to interference and other problems.* New York: Cambridge University Press.

Taylor, W. L. (1953). Cloze procedure: A new tool for measuring readability. *Journalism Quarterly, 30,* 415–433

Templeton, S., Bear, D. R., Invernizzi, M., Johnston, F., Townsend, D., Flanigan, K., et al. (2015). *Vocabulary their way* (2nd ed.). Boston: Pearson.

Templeton, S., & Gehsmann, K. M. (2014). *Teaching reading and writing: The developmental approach.* Boston: Pearson.

Therrien, W. J. (2004). Fluency and comprehension gains as a result of repeated reading: A meta-analysis. *Remedial and Special Education, 25,* 252–261.

Tolchinsky, L. (2006). The emergence of writing. In C. A. MacArthur, S. Graham, & J. Fitzgerald (Eds.), *Handbook of writing research* (pp. 83–95). New York: Guilford Press.

U.S. Department of Education, Office of English Language Acquisition, National Clearinghouse for English Language Acquisition. (2017, February). Profiles of English learners (ELs). Retrieved from *https://www2.ed.gov/about/offices/list/index.html.*

Vadasy, P. F., & Sanders, E. A. (2010). Efficacy of supplemental phonics-based instruction for low-skilled kindergarteners in the context of language minority status and classroom phonics instruction. *Journal of Educational Psychology, 102*(4), 786–803.

Vadasy, P. F., & Sanders, E. A. (2011). Efficacy of supplemental phonics-based instruction for low-skilled first graders: How language minority status and pretest characteristics moderate treatment response. *Scientific Studies of Reading, 15*(6), 471–497.

Valenzuela, A. (2010). *Subtractive schooling: US–Mexican youth and the politics of caring.* New York: State University of New York Press.

Valdés, G. (2017). Foreword. In O. García, S. I. Johnson, K. Seltzer, & G. Valdés (Eds.), *The translanguaging classroom: Leveraging student bilingualism for learning* (pp. v–vii). Philadelphia: Caslon.

Valdés, G., & Figueroa, R. A. (1994). *Bilingualism and testing: A special kind of bias.* Santa Barbara, CA: Praeger.

Vanderwood, M. L., & Nam, J. (2008). Best practices in assessing and improving English language learners' literacy performance. In A. Thomas & J. Grimes (Eds.), *Best practices in school psychology* (5th ed., pp. 1847–1855). Bethesda, MD: National Association of School Psychologists.

Vaughn, S., & Fuchs, L. S. (2003). Redefining learning disabilities as inadequate response to instruction: The promise and potential problems. *Learning Disabilities Research and Practice, 18,* 137–146.

Vygotsky, L. (1978). *Mind in society: The development of higher psychological processes.* Cambridge, MA: Harvard University Press.

Walley, A. C. (1993). The role of vocabulary development in children's spoken word recognition and segmentation ability. *Developmental Review, 13*(3), 286–350.

Wayman, M., Wallace, T., Wiley, H. I., Tichá, R., & Espin, C. A. (2007). Literature synthesis on curriculum-based measurement in reading. *Journal of Special Education, 41,* 85–120.

Wesche, M., & Paribakht, T. S. (1996). Assessing second language vocabulary knowledge: Depth versus breadth. *Canadian Modern Language Review, 53*(1), 13–40.

Whitaker, D., Berninger, V. W., Johnston, J., & Swanson, H. L. (1994). Intraindividual differences in levels of language in intermediate grade writers: Implications for the translating process. *Learning and Individual Differences, 6,* 107–130.

WIDA Consortium. (2018). *Annual technical report for ACCESS for ELLs 2.0.* Madison: Board of Regents of the University of Wisconsin System. Retrieved from *https://wida.wisc.edu/assess/choosing-assessment.*

WIDA Consortium. (2019). *WIDA performance definitions, speaking and writing, grades K–12.* Madison: Board of Regents of the University of Wisconsin System. Retrieved from *https://wida.wisc.edu/sites/default/files/resource/Performance-Definitions-Expressive-Domains.pdf.*

Wiig, E. H., Semel, E. M., & Secord, W. (2013). *Clinical evaluation of language fundamentals* (5th ed.). Minneapolis, MN: Pearson.

Williams, J. P., & Pao, L. S. (2013). Developing a new intervention to teach text structure at the elementary level. In H. L. Swanson, K. R. Harris, & S. Graham (Eds.), *Handbook of learning disabilities* (2nd ed., pp. 361–374). New York: Guilford Press.

Williams, K. T. (2001). *Group Reading Assessment and Diagnostic Evaluation (GRADE).* Circle Pines, MN: American Guidance Service.

Williams, K. T. (2007). *Expressive Vocabulary Test–2.* Minneapolis, MN: Pearson.

Wisconsin RTI Center. (2017). Wisconsin's framework for an equitable, multi-level system of supports. Retrieved from *www.wisconsinrticenter.org/district-implementation/overview-of-systems-change.*

Zwiers, J. (2013). *Building academic language: Essential practices for content classrooms, grades 5–12.* New York Wiley.

Zwiers, J., & Hamerla, S. (2018). *The K–3 Guide to academic conversations: Practices, scaffolds, and activities.* Thousand Oaks, CA: Corwin Press.

Index

Note. *f* or *t* after a page number indicates a figure or a table.

Fluency
  beginning readers and, 90–91, 95–96
  classroom-based instruction in, 120–121
  Common Core standards for, 95
  components of, 95, 95f
  defined, 12
  formal assessment for beginning readers, 99–103,
    102f, 103f
  as instruction focus, 166–167
  learning needs assessments for, 101–104, 102f, 103f
  screening and progress monitoring assessments
    for, 99–101
Fluency rubric, assessment uses of, 103–104, 103f
Funds of knowledge
  defined, 47
  home visits and, 57
  importance for assessments, 19, 47, 50
  importance for instruction, 48, 51, 58–59, 84–85,
    84f, 145–146
  scenario example, 51–52

G

General outcome measures, 32
Glossary, 203–207
"Guess the Covered Word" activity, 78

H

Handwriting
  learning needs assessments of, 160t
  orthomotor integration and, 148
Home language
  for administering assessments, 113
  and common underlying proficiency, 91–92
  linguistic features of, 91
Home learning, connecting with school learning,
    84–85, 84f
Home-language survey, 57–58
Hybrid language practices, 17–18, 18f
Hypotheses, making data-based, 41

I

I Say, You Say! task, 117–118
IDEALS acronym, 194
Informal reading inventories (IRIs), 33, 132–134
Instruction; *see also* Pedagogies
  assessment to support (*see* Assessment to support
    instruction)
  connecting with assessment (*see* Connecting
    assessment with instruction)
  quality core, MTSS and, 174–175

Instructional applications, for oral language
    development, 81–88
  clear, explicit instruction and, 83
  by connecting school and home learning, 84–85,
    84f
  examples of enhancements, 85–88, 86f
  language-learning community and, 81–82
  planning form for, 86, 87f, 88
  by promoting student engagement, 85
Instructional decision making
  framework for, 35–36, 37t, 38–42, 40f
  in Tier 1, 36, 37f, 38, 40f
  in Tier 2, 37f, 38, 40f
  in Tier 3, 37f, 38–42, 40f
Instructional programs
  subtractive *versus* additive approaches of, 5
  types of, 4–6
Interdependence hypothesis, multilingual students
    and, 16, 18f, 51, 62
Interest
  assessing, 55
    reflective questions for, 55f
  questions for identifying, 54f
Intermediate readers; *see* Advancing/intermediate
    readers
Interpersonal communicative skills; *see* Basic
    interpersonal communicative skills (BICs)
Interventions, tiered, MTSS and, 175

K

Knowledge
  sociocultural approach to acquisition of, 125–126
  student funds of; *see* Funds of Knowledge
  teacher, about students, 44
  word, continuum of, 130f

L

Language, symbiotic relationship with literacy,
    16–17
Language arts
  example/non-example assessment activity and,
    138f
  situations assessment activity and, 138
Language assessments
  federal policy and, 64–65
  informal, 69–70
    receptive oral, 69–74 (*see also* Receptive oral
      language)
  standardized, 65–67, 171
    federal regulations and, 65
    proficiency levels and, 68–69
Language background, student, 46f